Designing Video and Multimedia for Open and Flexible Learning

D0161995

In recent years there has been a resurgence in the use of video in teaching and training contexts, due to technological advances that enable good quality moving pictures through CD-Rom, DVD and broadband Internet. This book offers advice and assistance to a growing group of teachers and trainers, technical and support staff in the most effective deployment of video and multimedia in open and distance learning.

A bridge between research and practice, *Designing Video and Multimedia for Open and Flexible Learning* discusses:

- *what* to teach on video and *how* to teach it;
- when to choose and how to use other media for teaching;
- a framework of pedagogic design principles for video and multimedia;
- practical development advice for interactive multimedia.

With insights into the comprehensive process of designing, developing and managing distance learning materials, this book will appeal to readers with varying interests and responsibilities, including course development, educational video, audiovision and interactive multimedia design, as well as to students of general video and multimedia production.

Jack Koumi is a freelance consultant and trainer in the scripting and production of education media. He has conducted over 50 training projects in educational media in 20 countries. Previously, he worked for 22 years at the BBC Open University Production Centre, producing audio and video programmes in Science and Mathematics.

Designing Video and Multimedia for Open and Flexible Learning

Jack Koumi

Routledge
Taylor & Francis Group

LONDON AND NEW YORK

KH

First published 2006
by Routledge
2 Park Square, Milton Park, Abingdon, Oxon OX14 4RN

Simultaneously published in the USA and Canada
by Routledge
270 Madison Ave, New York, NY 10016

Routledge is an imprint of the Taylor & Francis Group, an informa business

© 2006 Jack Koumi

Typeset in Times by
HWA Text and Data Management, Tunbridge Wells
Printed and bound in Great Britain by
MPG Books Ltd, Bodmin

British Library Cataloguing in Publication Data
A catalogue record for this book is available from the British Library

Library of Congress Cataloging-in-Publication Data
A catalog record for this book has been requested

ISBN10: 0–415–38304–8 (hbk)
ISBN10: 0–415–38303–x (pbk)

ISBN13: 978–0–415–38304–2 (hbk)
ISBN13: 978–0–415–38303–5 (pbk)

10/19/06

Contents

Figures

Tables

Acknowledgements

Chapter 4 is an updated version of the paper by Koumi (1994a).

The sixty-nine illustrative drawings in Chapters 1 to 3, numbered Figure 1.1 to 3.2c, represent video clips. Thirty-nine of these clips were produced by the University of Sheffield's Learning Development and Media Unit, which has kindly granted permission to refer to them (acknowledged as 'LDMU' below). Kind permission to feature three other video clips has been granted by the Educational Broadcasting Services Trust. The corresponding figures are acknowledged as 'EBS' below.

The illustrations were drawn by Heather Koumi.

Series editor's foreword

The moving image, coupled with sound, is a powerful medium. It has the ability to grab the attention of a casual viewer and to engage learners. It has developed rapidly from the era of black and white silent moves, via video cassette to the high-quality productions that are available today. Its popularity amongst the general public is evident in the size of TV and cinema audiences and sales of DVDs.

Within a training environment instructional film has been in widespread use for over fifty years – particularly in the armed forces, industry and commerce. However, whilst many colleges and universities explored the use of CCTV in the 1960s the significant milestone in the use of the moving image and sound in higher education can be linked to a political rally in 1969 when the former UK Prime Minister Harold Wilson presented his vision of a 'University of the Air', a vision to be subsequently realised by Doris Lee in the form of the UK Open University. It was to be a university that would embrace the use of broadcast media and make higher education available to tens of thousands of students each year. In reality the broadcast component of an Open University degree was relatively modest but its impact was huge. It is noteworthy that the mega universities of the world, as well as other institutions, all include TV and video in the learning resources they offer their students – be it broadcast or made available by DVD or streaming video.

Whilst television is a powerful medium it is not cheap, as Greville Rumble has demonstrated, nor is learning from the medium automatic – as confirmed by Tony Bates. The successful production of educational television or video and its integration into a course of study requires an experienced academic and producer, skilled scriptwriter and technician, experienced cameraman and sounder recordist. Such teams are expensive and there are few individuals who possess this combination of experience and skill; Jack Koumi is one of these people. Prior to conducting the Educational TV course at the UK Open University for academics/producers from around the world he was a senior OU Producer responsible for numerous educational productions. His subsequent consultancy work around the world has given Jack a unique insight into the problems faced by institutions wishing to include TV and video materials into their teaching.

However, perhaps the major contribution Jack is making to the field is in his categorization of various media types that allows academics and producers to be fully aware of the potential of the medium and how the medium can be used to create different effects. For those of us involved in the production of teaching material, including the moving image, this book will be invaluable. The insights it provides will allow us to make maximum use of the potential of the medium and for our learners to gain maximum benefit.

Fred Lockwood
Yelvertoft, 2006

Study guide – how you might use this book

The four parts of the book, summarized in the following table can be studied independently.

The four parts of the book

	Video	Other media and multimedia
Appropriate teaching functions	I	2
Pedagogic design principles	3	4

Each part, described in more detail below, will suit readers with varying interests and responsibilities, as follows.

Part I (Chapters 1, 2 and 3) is on techniques and teaching functions that exploit video's strengths. It considers video techniques and teaching functions that could not be achieved as well by other media. Each pedagogic category, individually, might be familiar to readers experienced in video production. However, the full categorization pulls it all together, providing a comprehensive basis for deciding when to use video.

Target audience for Part I: all course developers who have the option of incorporating video into their teaching resources. The categorization would help to identify the parts of the course for which video would add most value and to choose or commission video packages judiciously.

Part II (Chapter 4) is on matching media attributes to learning tasks. This goes beyond video. It considers the different capabilities and limitations of a range of different media.

Target audience for Part 2: it is appropriate for course developers who are concerned with optimizing media deployment.

Part III (Chapters 5 and 6) is on screenwriting principles. It returns to video for a most crucial topic: the principles of effective screenwriting for educational video. This topic has not been covered in any depth elsewhere in the literature. The screenwriting principles are micro-level (practicable) design principles for educational video.

Target audience for Part III: readers who design educational video should find these two chapters of more immediate practical value.

Following Chapter 5 (the first chapter of Part III), which gives an overview, those readers who are practising designers are invited to postpone Chapter 6 until after they have carried out some real screenwriting work. Chapter 6 discusses all 46 design principles in detail.

Readers who are not practising video designers may not wish to study the details in Chapter 6. Chapter 5 gives a sufficient overview to help course developers choose or commission video that is effectively designed pedagogically.

Part IV consists of the final two chapters (Chapters 7 and 8) on picture–word synergy for audiovision and multimedia. These chapters go beyond video, dealing with screenwriting for audiovision (lower tech audio-print composite packages) and for (higher tech) multimedia packages with audio commentary. The screenwriting principles are micro-level (practicable) design principles for audiovision and multimedia. The lower-tech audiovision has great potential in situations where higher tech multimedia is not feasible for whatever reason (e.g. inadequate budget or infrastructure).

Target audience for Part IV: These chapters are suitable mainly for readers who design audiovision and multimedia. They can also help course developers choose or commission audiovision and multimedia that are effectively designed pedagogically.

Introduction: the added-value categories

The 27 categories of video described in Table 0.1 can add substantial value to educational multimedia (termed *instructional* multimedia in North America). The term *multimedia* is used here to apply both to a computer package that includes video segments and to a multiple media course with video as an ingredient.

The categories are video techniques and teaching functions that exploit video's distinctive strengths and that print cannot achieve as effectively. In fact for most categories, neither can audio alone, inside the multimedia package, nor even a face-to-face teacher outside the package. The categories are divided into three domains.

1 Assisting LEARNING and SKILLS development
2 Providing (vicarious) EXPERIENCES (the role most often assigned to TV in many institutions)
3 NURTURING (motivations, feelings)

The claim that the categories in Table 0.1 add distinctive value to learning has not been researched empirically. Rather, it derives from experts' opinions. About half the categories correspond to the 'distinctive value video list' drawn up in the 1980s by the UK Open University's Broadcast Allocations Committee, with the purpose of ensuring cost-effective use of video. This list comprised the techniques and teaching functions that video could deliver distinctively well compared to other available media (as adjudged by consensus through the years). OU course teams had to make a strong case. They had to convince the committee that the learning outcomes they intended for video really did need one or more of the techniques and teaching functions in the 'distinctive value video list'. That is, they had to demonstrate that other, cheaper media would be much less effective. Through the years, this procedure led to the compilation of 18 functions that were adjudged to exploit the strengths of video and that needed video in order to be achieved distinctively well (Bates 1984: appendix). These 18 have been expanded into the above 27 categories as a result of further deliberation.

The basis of the value-added claim for these categories is the rich *symbol system* of video, that is, video's moving pictures, real-time or slow motion, real-life or

Table 0.1 Added value video techniques and teaching functions

1 Distinctive ways to assist LEARNING and (item 9) SKILLS development
1 **composite pictures**, e.g. split screen, S/I
2 **animated diagrams** exploring processes
3 **visual metaphor/symbolism/analogy**
4 **modelling** a process by a simplification
5 **illustrating** concepts with real examples
6 **condensing time** by editing real life
7 **juxtaposition** of contrasting situations
8 **narrative strength** of TV's rich symbol system
9 **demonstration** of skills by an expert
(e.g. craft, physical, reasoning, social, verbal)

2 Providing (vicarious) EXPERIENCES by showing otherwise inaccessible:
1 **dynamic** pictorial change or movement
2 **places** e.g. dangerous/overseas locations
3 **viewpoints** e.g. aerial, big close-up
4 **technical** processes or equipment
5 **3D** objects, using movement or juxtaposition
6 **slow/fast** motion
7 **people/animals** interacting, real or drama
8 **one-off** or rare events (include archive film)
9 **chronological** sequence and duration
10 **resource-material** for viewers to analyze
11 **staged events**, e.g. complex experiments, dramatized enactments

	3 NURTURING (motivations, feelings)
determination, motivation, activation	1 **stimulate** appetite to learn, e.g. by revealing the fascination of the subject
	2 **galvanize/spur into action**, provoke viewers to get up and do things
	3 **motivate use of a strategy** by showing its success, e.g. exam techniques
appreciations, feelings, attitudes	4 **alleviate isolation** of the distant learner by showing the teacher or fellow students
	5 **change attitudes**, appreciations, engender empathy for people
	6 **reassure**, encourage self-confidence
	7 **authenticate academic abstractions** by showing their use in solving real-life problems

diagrammatic, with synchronous narration and sound effects, camera moves and zooms, big close-ups, shot transitions, visual effects, chronological sequencing and pacing of sound and pictures (e.g. enabling the display of body language and the phrasing of speech), visual metaphor, specially constructed scale models – all of video's presentational attributes. In most circumstances, in all of the 27 categories, these attributes make video more effective than other media.

One exception occurs in domain 3, the nurturing domain. A well-scripted dramatized enactment on audio can sometimes evoke more realism and emotion than video – by stimulating the listener's visual imagination. For instance, under category 3.5, *engender empathy for people*, video is only more effective than audio when it really is necessary to view the human behaviour. This is not always the case. Sometimes it is not even permissible because anonymity is required, for example, when portraying a case of alleged child abuse to trainee social workers.

This example has illustrated that for some categories in Table 0.1, in certain circumstances, there is a better choice of medium than video. At the other extreme, there are some categories for which there is no alternative to video – e.g. 2.6 (*fast motion via time-lapse recording*), whereby real life can be speeded up thousands of times.

Even though there are many such categories that manifestly cannot be achieved without film or video, there are still those who doubt that any medium can achieve added value over any other medium for any learning task. There is a body of thought that follows R.E. Clark (1983) in believing that learning is only influenced by the instructional method, irrespective of which medium is used. His widely quoted analogy was that media were 'mere vehicles that deliver instruction but do not influence student achievement any more than the truck that delivers our groceries causes changes in our nutrition' (p. 445).

This position provoked spirited correspondence in the research literature, which endured for many years (in fact, the issues are still not resolved to everybody's satisfaction). In 1994, an entire issue of the journal, *Educational Technology Research and Development* (volume 42, no. 2) was devoted to the debate. Clark's contribution in that issue was provocatively entitled, 'Media will never influence learning!' However, despite the unrepentant title, Clark's view was now more reasonable, namely that, 'It cannot be argued that any given medium or media attribute must be present in order for learning to occur, only that certain media and attributes are more efficient for certain learners, learning goals and tasks' (p. 22).

Although this view is more reasonable than Clark's 1983 position, it still underestimates the differences in the capabilities of different media. The truth is that Clark's grocery truck may not be appropriate for transporting every type of food. For example, imagine *audio alone* attempting to describe a complicated three-dimensional shape, or *print alone* trying to describe a dance routine (even if many photos or diagrams were used). For a detailed rebuttal of Clark's views, see Chapter 4.

In the same issue of *ETRD*, Clark's principal opponent, Kozma, takes the more proactive view that because different media do have different capabilities, our methods must take appropriate advantage of this. He concludes that we should replace the sterile question, *do media influence learning?* with the productive question, *in what ways can we use the (different) capabilities of (different) media to influence learning for particular students, tasks and situations?*

Going further, it is conceivable that the different capabilities of each medium, still poorly understood, will result in powerful new educational methods (designs). In other words, the more that is learned about a medium's distinctive capabilities (and limitations), new methods will suggest themselves to take better advantage of that medium's potential. Conversely, the more that is learned about a medium's limitations, the fewer will be the attempts to use it for inappropriate teaching functions. (The different capabilities and limitations of different media are discussed in Chapter 4.)

The first three chapters of this book address these issues for the medium of video. They consider those capabilities of video that have been recognized by experienced practitioners in the UK Open University and elsewhere. The treatment is not based on media research theory, but derives from a large body of practical and intuitive knowledge concerning the strengths (and limitations) of video.

Some generic uses of video will be excluded. Video can be valuable as a communications medium, for example, in videoconferencing or interactive TV. It can also have value as a distribution mechanism, for example, in video recordings of classroom lectures so as to achieve wider (or repeated) distribution. Neither of these uses will be covered because they are merely *uses of video* rather than *techniques within video production,* which is the subject matter being addressed. In any case, these two uses would exempt themselves on other grounds, in that they do not usually involve *strong exploitation of video's symbol system* (composite picture techniques, sound effects, big close-ups, visual metaphor, etc.), which is another essential theme of the next three chapters.

The 27 categories in the three boxes of Table 0.1 will be elaborated in the next three chapters, with examples and with justifications of added value.

Chapter 1

Video that adds cognitive value or skills value

Domain 1 of Table 0.1; distinctive ways to assist learning and skills

Learning and the development of skills can be facilitated through the nine media-distinctive techniques in domain 1 of Table 0.1 (in Introduction). These techniques will each be illustrated below with a variety of examples. The examples will confirm that the techniques can be accomplished well only by a time-based medium like video with its particular presentational characteristics. These characteristics include: diagrammatic and real-life moving pictures with synchronous sound effects and commentary, camera moves, shot transitions, visual effects and chronological sequencing. Some pictorial illustrations are omitted (a) when movement is essential and a static image cannot help you to visualize the movement, (b) when the image is easy to visualize.

1.1. Composite-picture techniques

These can aid synthetic, analytic, discrimination skills, for example:

- *fleshing out* biological or archaeological skeletons with 3D graphics, slowly superimposed
- *graphically superimposing* geological strata lines on a freeze of a cliff face. The lines would be absent to start with, then superimposed on then off, then perhaps again on then off: the intention is to encourage and enable viewers to distinguish between the strata even in the absence of the graphics lines (such a skill could be built up progressively as more and more examples of strata are presented in this way).
- *screen inserts* In the scene preceding Figure 1.1, a speech scientist has used a picture book to help tell a child the story of the runaway bus. Now (Figure 1.1) the child now has to retell the story, while looking at the pictures. This looking is allowed so as to reduce the strain on the child's memory; this enables the scientist to concentrate exclusively on the child's language development.

    The composite picture allows us to see the child at the same time as seeing what she is looking at.

Figure 1.1 Screen inserts: child plus picture (LDMU)

➜ This clip also illustrates category 2.9, chronological sequence, as explained in Chapter 2.

- *highlighting (or colouring)* parts of a picture while dimming or greying out other parts. A 25 sec video clip uses this effect to highlight the different members of a human family that would suffer from two different types of radiation, *somatic* (Figure 1.2a), affecting the grandmother, and *hereditary* (Figure 1.2b), where damage to the ovum of the grandmother affects her son and grandchildren.
- *presenter + chroma-key.* Next to the presenter, or behind them (Figure 1.3), is a screen that is painted in a single saturated colour, often blue. The mixing desk is set up so that wherever the camera sees this blue colour, that part of its picture is replaced by another picture. This second picture could be from another camera or from a pre-recorded video tape. The effect is that the presenter appears to be standing beside a giant TV screen on which a second picture is being shown.
- *dissolving slowly* between two similar pictures, the second of which is a *progression* of the first, e.g. a cell's stages of dividing. (Incidentally, this invites the viewer to imagine the in-between pictures.) There are many other kinds of slow transition, e.g. mosaic, wipe, page-turn.
- *split-screen,* e.g. a loaded beam on the left with a shot of the strain gauge on the right, or a shot of an observer describing a scene, split with a view of the scene.

(A) (B)

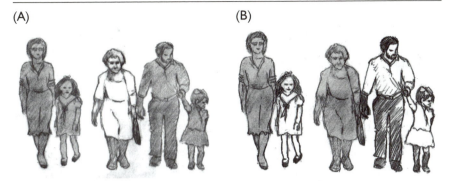

Figure 1.2 (A) Somatic radiation effect, (B) heredity radiation effect (LDMU)

Figure 1.3 Chroma-key

Caution

Although composite pictures are potentially powerful for learning, the viewer needs extra time to process the two components of the composite. This is especially true for the split-screen and screen-insert techniques. So enough time must be given for switching of attention. Even a superimposition of a presenter's name needs extra processing time, so the name should be held longer or the presenter should insert a redundant sentence that does not need a lot of processing.

The basic principle is to try always to get inside viewers' minds – what are they thinking, what are they looking at? You can be sure that they vary – some will look at the left and some at the right of a split screen, then switch attention at different times. Hence repetition or redundancy is recommended. For example, if you have a split screen of a muscle contraction plus its oscilloscope trace, you should show the action more than once. One way of doing this is to duplicate the action during editing. Alternatively, it is sometimes possible to record a sequence of similar actions, e.g. a heart beating several times.

Mind you, some composite pictures do not require much processing, e.g. split screen of two people telephoning each other.

Sometimes you may want to *avoid* a split screen and instead alternate between the pictures, for the purpose of

- getting the viewer to *imagine* the composite
- discouraging detailed comparison, e.g. when the comparison is not a central part of the story, but rather an entertaining side-issue

➔ Splitting the screen is often used prior to recording in a multi-camera studio, during pre-production procedures to match up shots between two cameras.

1.2. Animated diagrams

These can be powerful for explaining dynamic processes: they invite students to share the teacher's imagery.

➔ Within a multimedia package, animations are normally accomplished directly by the computer, rather than being lifted from a video tape – in fact, even for stand-alone video, most animations on video are now done with computer-generated graphics.

- the concept of *iteration* can be portrayed with an animation in which the outputs of a procedure (pictured as a black box) are fed back repeatedly, as inputs into the box, to produce new outputs
- in geology, a water cycle animation, i.e. rainfall, evaporation, rainfall.
- a certain geometrical surface, the *Klein Bottle with a disk removed*, Figure 1.4a, distorts gradually into a different shape, as in Figures 1.4b, 1.4c, 1.4d (the technique is called *morphing*).

In a statistics video, an animation, Figure 1.5, shows a histogram in which the statistical mode (the most frequent value, represented by the highest bar) remains static while those either side go up and down randomly (with heights below that of the mode bar), depicting a variety of distributions, all having the same mode.

This animation is useful for conveying the concept of a *fixed mode despite variations either side* – it would be much less clear with a series of in-text diagrams, because the static mode would not be clearly static.

A common type of animation is the *artist's impression* of real-world processes that are impossible to view for real, for example:

- sub-microscopic processes, such as *the mechanism for a nerve impulse*: positively charged sodium ions flow from the outside to the inside of a section of nerve, then negatively charged potassium ions flow out. This causes the inside of the nerve to become briefly positively charged, then to revert to negatively charged. This local change progresses down the nerve

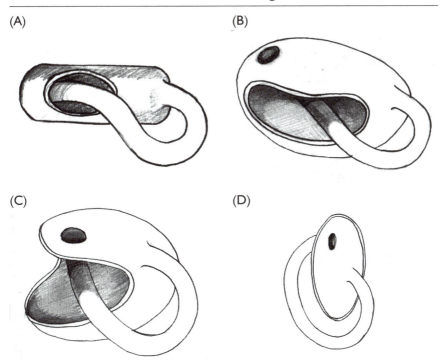

Figure 1.4 (A) The mathematical surface: Klein bottle with disc removed, (B) initial distortion, (C) further distortion, (D) final distortion

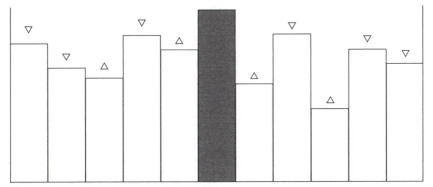

Figure 1.5 Varied histograms, all with the same mode (LDMU)

fibre like a Mexican wave. This progression is the nerve impulse travelling along the nerve.
- cross-sections of volcanic activity, or of a coal-mine, or of a human body, or of a container in which fermentation is taking place.

An example, illustrated in Figure 1.6, is a 40 sec animation of the cross-section of a human throat, showing the breathing problem called *croup* – narrowing of the extra-thoracic airway, causing difficulty when breathing in (since the airway naturally narrows even more then).

Another example: a standard technique in coal-mining is to collapse the ceiling to the right of the working area as miners progress left. An animation shows the collapse (Figure 1.7a), then reconstitutes the ceiling to demonstrate what would happen if the ceiling were not collapsed, allowing the cavity to grow wider and wider. This would cause a dangerous unintended collapse (Figure 1.7b) due to the excessive weight of rock above the wide span of ceiling.

A powerful use of such animation is when it is interspersed with the parts that *can* be seen, for example, the outside of the object.

(A)   (B)

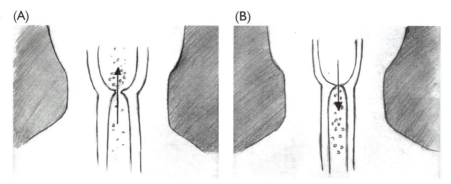

Figure 1.6   (A) Human throat, (B) narrowing when breathing in (LDMU)

(A)   (B)

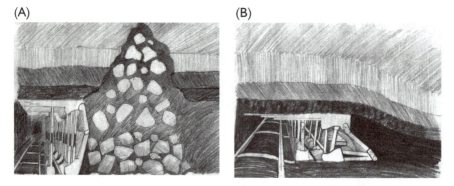

Figure 1.7   (A) Mine ceiling collapsed intentionally, (B) if collapse is prevented, a more dangerous collapse results

(A) (B)

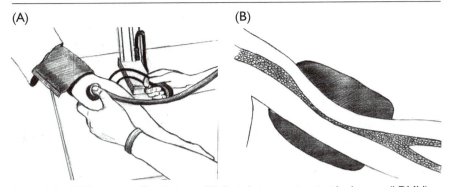

Figure 1.8 (A) Pressure cuff technique, (B) Artist's impression, inside the arm (LDMU)

An example, Figure 1.8a, is when a doctor measures a patient's blood pressure, using the *pressure cuff* technique. The cuff pressure is increased until blood flow ceases. Then the pressure is gradually relaxed until the blood starts to flow intermittently. The doctor hears the pumping sound through a stethoscope and records this pressure as the highest (systolic) arterial pressure. When the pressure is further relaxed, the blood eventually flows freely (so the pumping sound disappears). This is the lowest (diastolic) arterial pressure.

Interspersed with the live shots of this procedure is an artist's impression (Figure 1.8b) of what is happening inside the artery of a patient's arm while the pressure cuff is gradually relaxed.

The interspersion of animation with real life is particularly effective, creating a synergy in which each enhances the other: real life supplies context to the animation while the animation reveals further detail.

As an alternative to animation, there are occasions when you might *contrive* to see a process for real that is normally hidden (e.g. by using a transparent container). However, it might still be instructive to see an artist's schematic representation of what is happening, because this can purposely exclude fine details and focus on the basic process.

Another advantage of schematic representation is when the artist purposely exaggerates a process, for the purpose of clarity. For example, in a medical video, a 20 sec animation shows a cross-section of a human throat and the thorax beneath it. When a person breathes in, the throat narrows while the thorax widens (Figure 1.9a), and vice versa for breathing out (Figure 1.9b). The artist's impression exaggerates these movements.

There are many different kinds of animation:

- schematic or realistic
- two- or three-dimensional
- computer-generated or hand-drawn on cell

(A)   (B)

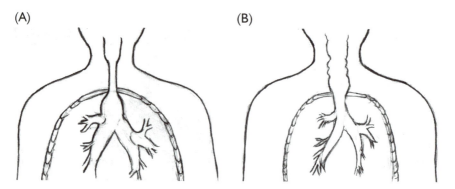

Figure 1.9   (A) Breathing in, throat narrows, thorax widens, (B) Breathing out, throat widens, thorax narrows (LDMU)

The physiology could be explained with two diagrams and some text. However, since it is movement that is being described, video gives a fuller account and greater realism – hence is more informative, as well as being more attractive and arousing.

- single- or double-frame: in *single-frame* the picture changes once per frame (1 frame lasts for 1/25 of a second). In *double-frame* the picture changes once every two frames – this is too jerky in some situations, e.g. for a 1 sec movement across the whole screen width
- stepwise build-up of a diagram (successive segments of a diagram jump onto the screen); this technique is often used to build up a flow-chart. Strictly speaking, this is not animation, in that there is no smooth movement: additional features merely *jump* into an existing diagram. An example is a 30 sec clip from a video showing how axes were made in the Bronze Age (Figure 1.10). A flow-chart is built up, step by step, showing the stages in the construction process.

➔   This clip also illustrates category 1.4, modelling, as explained later in this chapter.

Caveat: do students really learn from animations or are they merely entertained?

Viewers like animations and they say they learn from them. However, an attractive technique is a two-edged sword. Making viewers feel good (rather than bored) *might* stimulate learning. On the other hand they might *fool themselves* that they are learning just because they enjoy the animation.

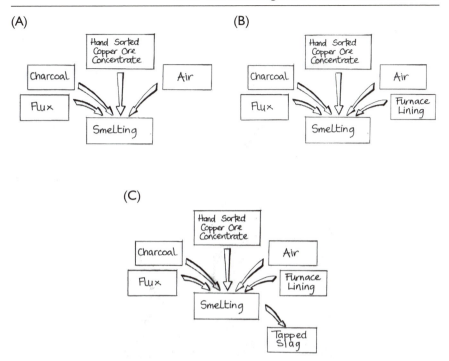

Figure 1.10 (A) Construction of a bronze-age axe, (B) next stage of the construction, (C) final stage of construction (LDMU)

Certainly in the early days of the UK OU Maths output, computer animations were enjoyed by both video producers and viewers. This was despite the fact that the animations were monochrome, and hence difficult to see clearly – for example *tangents* of curves were difficult to distinguish from the curves. It was also despite the animations being rather fast because producers enjoyed the continuous movement and so tended *not to pause* the movement intermittently (and few students had replay facilities).

My minority view was that viewers were kidding themselves (as were producers). I undertook copious calculations to enable coloured animations to be done manually on *cells* by graphic designers. If that were not possible due to the shapes being too time-consuming to draw by hand, I would still resist monochrome computer animations of line drawings. Often, I would replace the animation by a series of stills, dissolving between them, so that the students had to imagine the in-between pictures. I still do not know how far my minority view was justified. Figure 1.11 summarizes the considerations involved in the two points of view.

This question would make an interesting research project. However, the research would not be easy, because the pedagogic quality of an animation can vary enormously. Design principles for animation are included in Chapters 5, 6 and 8.

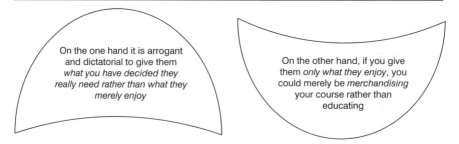

On the one hand it is arrogant and dictatorial to give them *what you have decided they really need rather than what they merely enjoy*

On the other hand, if you give them *only what they enjoy,* you could merely be *merchandising* your course rather than educating

Figure 1.11 Do students learn from animations or are they merely entertained?

1.3. Visual metaphor/symbolism/analogy for abstract processes

For example

- The concept of pressure inside a pressure-cooker (Figure 1.12) can be portrayed by little vibrating arrows pushing down on the liquid and pushing up on the lid.
- The concept of pressure can be symbolized by two sets of footprints in the sand, the set made by the fat man being visibly deeper than those of the thin man.
- A *gravity assist*, accomplished by aiming a space probe to pass close to a planet, is analogous to grabbing the hand of someone running past, in order to bend their path in a slingshot effect.
- In a crime prevention programme, Figure 1.13, viewers are warned how a car thief can seem to *appear from nowhere,* by showing the thief *dissolving* onto the scene – i.e. *appearing from nowhere, like a ghost.*

Figure 1.12 Pressure portrayed by vibrating arrows

Figure 1.13 A car thief appears from nowhere

- An animation (Figure 1.14a) illustrates *going back in time* by removing alternate segments of a time-graph backwards, to leave a dotted graph, that is, half *undrawing* the graph back to a certain point (Figure 1.14b); and then adding a new graph from that point (Figure 1.14c). This technique might be

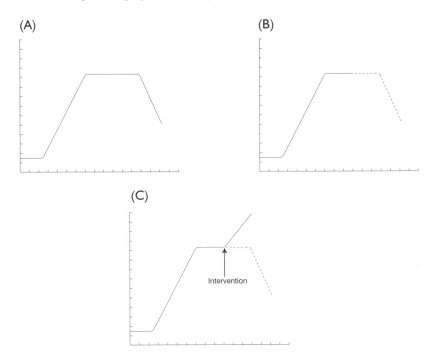

Figure 1.14 (A) Original graph, (B) goiing back to an earlier time, (C) result of intervention at the earlier time

used to consider an alternative progression of events, e.g. to show what the different consequence would have been if an intervention had occurred.

- In a video about change in the workplace, a shot of a snake lunging at the camera, as a metaphor for the narration *change terrifies most of us.*
- In a medical video (Figure 1.15a), a 17 sec clip makes an analogy with a familiar situation – a shot of a person *sucking on a collapsed drinking straw* could be used as an analogy for *a narrowed thoracic airway causing difficulty with breathing in* (the narrowed airway is due to the patient suffering from *croup*). The croup sufferer has no difficulty breathing out (Figure 1.15b), because during this activity the thoracic airway widens.
- Figure 1.16 illustrates a clip in a biology/psychology video about differential sensitivity in different parts of the body. The clip displays a specially built *homunculus* (a distorted model of a human figure), the size of whose body

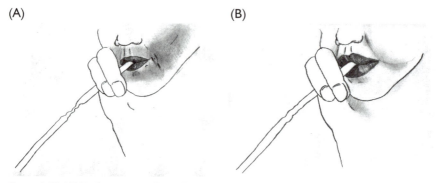

(A)   (B)

Figure 1.15 (A) Sucking on a collapsed drinking straw: analogy for difficulty breathing in, (B) no difficulty breathing out (LDMU)

Figure 1.16 A *homunculus* illustrates differential sensitivity in different parts of the body

parts correspond to their sensitivity. For example, human lips are far more sensitive than the small of the back, so the homunculus has enormous lips and a minuscule back. The figure is shown rotating.

- *Aural analogies* (Figure 1.17) are also possible. In a medical video, students are shown how to diagnose a *pericardial friction-rub* (caused by a condition in which heart tissues rub together). A 40 sec video clip demonstrates how to mimic the sound of this condition: students are shown how to hold the diaphragm of the stethoscope in the palm of their hand and then listen while they rub the back of the hand.

➔   This clip also illustrates category 2.10, resource material, as explained in Chapter 2.

- *Visual effects* can constitute visual analogies, for example a *page-turn* transition can be an analogy for *the other side of the argument* (a *page-turn* transition is where the shot appears to turn like a page and the reverse side of the page is the next shot).
- Another visual effect that is used as a visual metaphor occurs in a 15 sec video clip. The photograph of a nuclear power station *explodes*. Then the photograph reconstitutes itself, as a metaphor for the implied *impossibility* of a nuclear explosion. These effects occur while the commentary talks about the risk of an explosion and then rejects that possibility.
- A statistics video contains a subtle example of a visual metaphor. Figure 1.18 illustrates a 10 sec clip. The narration is introducing the next topic, which is *variability of data*. The next shot is gradually revealed within the bars of a variable histogram. That is, the bar heights vary up and down (but more up than down, resulting in the bars eventually filling the screen). This transition between shots is a visual metaphor for the theme, *variability of data*.

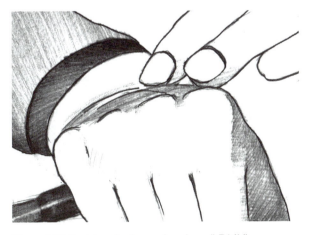

Figure 1.17 Back hand rub: aural analogy (LDMU)

Figure 1.18 Metaphor for variable data (LDMU)

This last metaphor is surreptitious, as are many, so most viewers may fail to notice them consciously. In fact there is little empirical evidence for even subconscious effects, but the industry generally accepts that these do occur – certainly makers of feature films persist in using metaphor and symbolism to create mood and are generally applauded for their style.

A further point that can be illustrated again by the last example is that metaphor is *in the eye of the beholder*: a beginner might not recognize the variable histogram as a metaphor for *variability of data*, whereas a statistician would easily recognize it.

1.4. Modelling a process with a contrived, simplified version

The simplified version shows only the important features, for example:

- through dramatization for sociology (e.g. enactment of parent–teenager interaction)
- through the use of physical models, such as a giant plastic model of a neurone
- through demonstration of major steps for recombinant DNA techniques, omitting minor steps and fine detail
- similarly, a 30 sec video clip demonstrates the major steps in making a Bronze Age axe, building up a flow-chart that omits fine detail.

➔   This clip also illustrates category 1.2, animated diagram, as illustrated earlier in Figure 1.10c.

Everything gets simplified to some extent but the *modelling* described here is a more *purposeful* simplification, as a teaching tactic.

1.5. Illustrating abstract concepts with real-world examples

Evocative real-world examples (e.g. documentaries) are used to make the concepts/principles more tangible. (There is a connection here with domain 2 of Table 0.1, the experiential domain. The presentation of real-world examples would entail experiential categories, such as 2.4, showing technical processes.) Examples of such abstract concepts include the following:

- Supply and demand – e.g. a glut of tomatoes in the street market makes their supply exceed the demand for them, driving the price down; vice versa when there is a shortage of tomatoes.
- From any point on an ellipse (Figure 1.19a), a line drawn through a focus of the ellipse makes the same angle with the ellipse as a second line from that point drawn through the second focus. This can be illustrated with a mirrored elliptic section (Figure 1.19b) by showing a beam of light through the first focus being reflected to pass through the second focus (whatever the angle of the beam).
- In a clip from a statistics video, *random error* and *systematic error* are illustrated with two contestants playing with two sets of darts. Figures 20a, 20b, 20c and 20d show the four outcomes. The white set is biased (it drifts to the right), giving a systematic error. The dark set is well balanced. Both players are aiming for the bull's eye. One player is poor, and his set of three darts contributes additional error, called *random error*. (The poor player's darts spread out much more than the good player's.)

➔ This clip also illustrates category 2.11, staged events, as explained in Chapter 2.

(A)   (B)

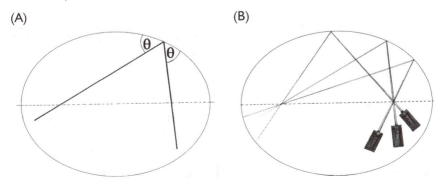

Figure 1.19 (A) Equal angles made by lines through each focus of an ellipse, (B) each beam of light through a focus is reflected to pass through the second focus

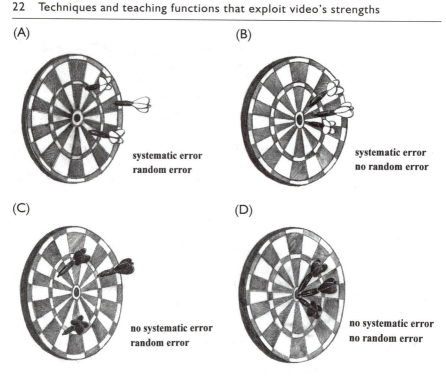

Figure 1.20 (A) Biased darts, poor player, (B) biased darts, good player, (C) balanced darts, poor player, (D) balanced darts, good player (LDMU)

A multimedia package on this topic could well include considerable text, in order to present data for the learner to practice on. However, introducing video into the package enlivens it considerably

- A 20-minute video presents three real-life illustrations of the abstract concept of *statistical estimation*. These are, *height of wheat, concentration of nickel in silver plating, heights of 7-year-old boys.*

1.6. Condensing time

Pruning real-world processes (e.g. editing out non-salient events) brings the duration within the viewer's concentration span.

In an interview, the director often shoots *noddies*, that is, shots of the interviewer nodding, so that some of these can be interspersed in the interview. This is to allow the interview to be edited down without seeing a *jump cut*. For example, if you want to edit out the third paragraph of the interview, then the interviewee's face would usually jump sideways after the edit. To cover up such a jump cut, a common technique is to edit in a noddy at that point. Alternatively, it is now quite common to avoid noddies and instead to *mix* between the second paragraph and the fourth: the interviewee's face then seems to *move slowly* between the two positions, rather than *jumping suddenly*.

Professional integrity dictates that editing a speaker should not result in misrepresentation but rather in clarification of the speaker's meaning in the context of the whole story. (See Table 5.15 for more on professional integrity.)

If you are watching a sculptor at work with an *over-the shoulder* shot, you could cut to a shot of the sculptor's eyes for a few seconds, then cut back to the sculpting but jump ahead in time, i.e. show the sculpting that happened several minutes later. You are not trying to fool the viewer that the process is quick, because this foreshortening technique is a convention that viewers understand. The cut to the man's face is called a *cut-away*.

This technique is illustrated in a 17 sec video clip showing part of the process of making a Bronze Age axe. A man covers an existing axe with facing sand in order to make a mould. Figure 1.21a shows the beginning of the shot of the man's hands sieving the sand. Figure 1.21c shows the end of the shot. A shot of the

(A)   (B)

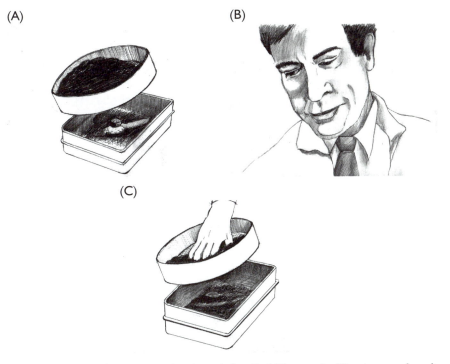

(C)

Figure 1.21 (A) Axe being covered with sand: first 7 of 35 seconds, (B) cut-away of man's face (3 seconds), (C) Final 7 seconds of the 35 second activity (LDMU)

(A)   (B)

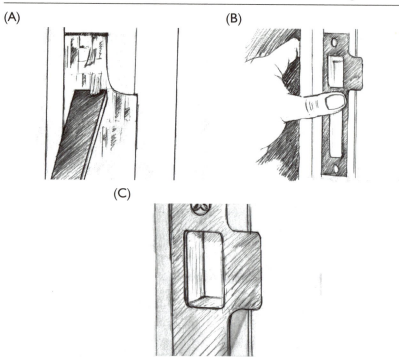

(C)

Figure 1.22 (A) Strking plate channel chiselled out, (B) striking plate positioned, (C) close-up of fitted striking plate (EBS)

man's face (Figure 1.21b) is inserted into the middle of the shot. The time taken to sieve the sand is thereby foreshortened by half.

A more explicit technique for condensing time is used in an 80 sec clip that shows the fitting of the *striking plate* of a mortice lock to a door-jamb (Figures 1.22a, 1.22b, 1.22c). This is edited down from about 30 minutes by *dissolving* between a shot and a later version of that shot, thus editing out some of the action. This happens several times. The consequent foreshortening of the activity is obvious to the viewer.

 This clip also illustrates categories 1.9, demonstration of a physical skill, 2.3, inaccessible viewpoints, and 2.11, staged event, as explained later in this chapter and in Chapter 2.

→ You might want to avoid these foreshortening techniques in some circumstances, for example, if you are giving a demonstration, you might want the viewer to internalize the real-time duration.

1.7. Juxtaposition of contrasting situations/ processes/interpretations

This aids discrimination. For example, in safety training the many different hazardous possibilities in a particular place of work can be presented in quick succession. In real life it is impossible for the learner to experience in such a short time the wide variety of hazardous situations that could be staged in a video. This juxtaposing of situations, compressed in time to occur within the learner's concentration span, hopefully engenders safety consciousness.

Here are three more examples. In a training video on how to give a good interview, an interviewee tries a variety of approaches. The video clip of Figure 1.7 shows what would happen if the coal-mine were not purposely collapsed behind the work-face. A video of hypothetical processes, e.g. *a non-Euclidean universe*, can be shown in which the geometric axioms change.

Another example is a video for medical students: a 45 sec clip shows blood pressure readings of patients in different situations (Figures 1.23a, 1.23b, 1.23c). The students will eventually experience these different situations for real, before they qualify, but this video provides a valuable introduction to the real-life experience since it can condense hours down to minutes, hence bringing a long

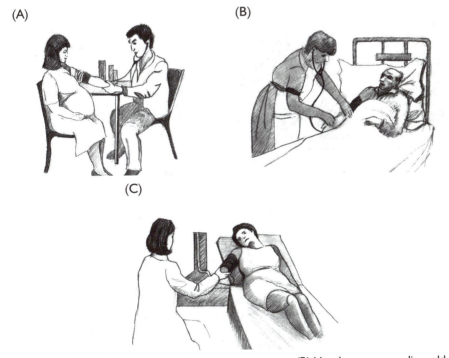

(A)   (B)

(C)

Figure 1.23 (A) Blood pressure reading: pregnant woman, (B) blood pressure reading: old person in hospital, (C) blood pressure reading: in a surgery (LDMU)

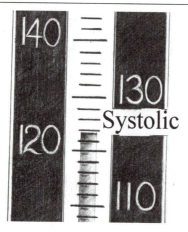

Figure 1.24 Blood pressure reading (LDMU)

series of situations within reach of viewers' concentration spans. This makes it easier for them to compare the situations because it avoids lapses of time when memory of previous situations fades.

Another video for medical students also shows blood pressure readings (Figure 1.24), this time with close-ups of the pressure gauge and with the stethoscope sound on the sound-track. For the first patient, viewers are shown how to judge these pressures according to the sound heard through the stethoscope – the appearance of the word *systolic* signals when they should read off the systolic pressure from the mercury column, similarly for *diastolic*. For the next six patients, viewers have to judge the pressures for themselves. This is just the kind of situation where observing a variety of situations is particularly necessary – because blood pressure measurements are inexact, subjective. Also, the patient's blood pressure is affected by many influences, such as age, mood, temperature.

➜ This clip also illustrates category 2.10, resource material for the viewer to analyse, as explained in the next chapter.

A 20 sec clip shows the difference between a doctor who has a reassuring manner (Figure 1.25a) and one who intimidates (Figure 1.25b). Both doctors are seen speaking to a patient.

➜ This clip also illustrates category 1.9, demonstration, as explained later in this chapter.

All such juxtapositions can either be presented linearly, or students can be given control of the parameters and choose which situations to view and in which order. Enabling such student control converts their experience of juxtaposition into what is termed *simulation*, whereby students change parameters to explore various versions of a process or situation. This usually involves some kind of computer-generated *virtual reality*.

(A)   (B)

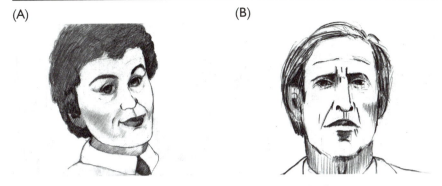

Figure 1.25 (A) Reassuring doctor, (B) intimidating doctor (LDMU)

Simulation is more natural and user-friendly on multimedia (e.g. with a CD-ROM) than on linear video tape or VCD because of multimedia's random access and because of the user's expectation of interactivity. One circumstance where *actual reality*, as portrayed on video, would be preferable to virtual reality is where the behaviour of real people needs to be observed.

1.8. Narrative strength

There is precise control over what the learner experiences in pictures, speech, sound effects, motion, pacing and sequence, which enables a tightly structured educational narrative.

This applies more commonly to linear video tape than to video in multimedia, because narrative needs a substantial duration. However, some of the points under 1.8 are relevant to the whole multimedia package rather than just to the video clips, e.g. an introductory text could *signpost* the next video clip.

Narrative strength derives from facilitating the viewer's attention through educational narrative devices (described fully in Chapters 5 and 6) such as:

- signpost
- seed
- variable pacing to clarify syntax
- texture
- allowing mental elbow room
- picture–word synergy
- varying format, mood, gravity
- link
- consolidate

In a medical video, a 65 sec clip gives an indication of *narrative strength*. The clip describes the symptoms of the disease known as *croup* – narrowing of the extra-thoracic airway, causing difficulty when breathing in (since the airway

Figure 1.26 Narrative sequence: (a) Live action, mother with baby, followed by (b) Animation (see Figure 1.6b) followed by an analogy (see Figure 1.15a)

naturally narrows even more then). The clip is a succession of three other clips consisting, respectively, of (Figure 1.26) live action of the behaviour (category 2.7, Chapter 2), followed by animation of unobservable internal events (category 1.2 – see Figure 1.6b), followed by an analogy (category 1.3 – see Figure 1.15a).

1.9. Demonstration of skills by an expert

Table 1.1 lists five categories of skills and describes them, giving generic examples.

(Incidentally, the demonstration of skill need not always be by an expert. There is value in learners video-recording their amateur performances for the purpose

Table 1.1   Categories of skills

Skill	In order to handle	Examples
a. manual/craft	equipment, materials	• manipulating a home experiment kit
		• woodwork, metalwork
		• drawing/painting
b. physical	body movements	• dance
		• athletic performance
c. reasoning	symbols, techniques	• solving equations
		• brainstorming
d. social	people	• counselling
		• interviewing
		• classroom teaching
e. verbal	vocalization	• learning foreign languages
		• singing/voice production

Figure 1.27 Student learning from *Audiovision*

of self-analysis or for appraisal by the tutor: e.g. a dance performance or a trainee teacher's classroom performance.)

Here are some specific examples.

Manual skill 1

An 18 minute video shows UK Open University students learning from the medium of *audiovision*, audiocassette guiding learners through visual materials. One student (Figure 1.27) is shown listening to a cassette that guides her to examine pieces of limestone, granite, etc, in her home experiment kit.

   This clip also illustrates category 2.4, showing technical processes or equipment.

Manual skill 2

A 30 sec clip, all shot in BCU (big close up), illustrates *anastomosis*, a surgical procedure on the bowel (Figure 1.28): a slit is made in the wall of the bowel and a new piece of intestine is sutured onto the slit The BCU shows the details much more clearly than if students attended the demonstration in person. (The procedure is carried out using a detached piece of pig's intestine, which is similar to a human bowel).

   This clip also illustrates categories 2.3, inaccessible viewpoints, as explained in Chapter 2.

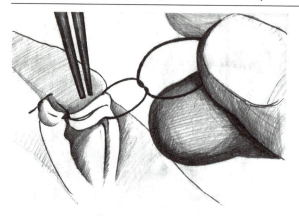

Figure 1.28 BCU of anastomosis (LDMU)

Craft skill

An 80 sec clip demonstrates the craft skill of fitting a *striking plate* of a mortice lock to a door-jamb (see Figure 1.22). Eventually trainees need to see a live demonstration and then to perform the fitting themselves under supervision. However, the live demo will be complemented valuably by the video clip, especially because it satisfies three more categories:

➜ This clip also illustrates categories 1.6, condensing time, as explained earlier in this chapter, also 2.3, inaccessible viewpoints, and 2.11, staged event, as explained in Chapter 2.

Physical skill

In a 20 second clip, an ice-skater, spinning on the spot (Figure 1.29a), demonstrates that her spin quickens when she brings her arms in close to her body (Figure 1.29b)

(A)   (B)

Figure 1.29 (A) Ice skater, arms wide, (B) close arms to quicken spin

Reasoning skill

In a 10 minute video segment, three students attempt to solve a problem set by a tutor: 'Given two equal sized coins, one of which rolls around the other, how many times would the queen's head rotate on itself?'

Social skill 1

In a medical video, a 20 sec video clip shows the social skill of a doctor who has a reassuring manner (see Figure 1.25a, earlier) and contrasts it with that of a doctor who is intimidating (Figure 1.25b)

   This clip also illustrates category 1.7, juxtaposition of contrasts, as explained earlier in this chapter.

Social skill 2

In a video of a bereavement counselling session (Figure 1.30), the interviewee lost his wife only a few weeks earlier and is extremely emotional. An experienced counsellor asks questions, listens and summarizes, acknowledges what the interviewee says. A sympathetic tone and an open body posture encourage the interviewee to speak freely. The combination of all these aspects is very difficult to communicate without using video. Getting the agreement of interviewees to video their session, for professional training purposes, is easier than getting their agreement to be watched live by a group of trainees. Besides, such a live demonstration would need to be restaged for each new group.

   This clip also illustrates categories 2.7, people interacting, and 3.5, create empathy, as explained in Chapters 2 and 3.

Figure 1.30 Bereavement counselling (LDMU)

Chapter 2

Video that adds experiential value

Domain 2 of Table 0.1; providing vicarious experiences

Vicarious experiences can be achieved by showing/documenting phenomena that would otherwise be inaccessible.

2.1. Dynamic change or movement

This is the fundamental reason for video – when movement is necessary for the learning task, for example, to appreciate

- oscillations of a bridge in a high wind
- speed of reaction in mechanical or chemical processes
- the consistency of clay (or other material) when it is being kneaded; e.g. (Figure 2.1), a video clip can show a lump of semi-solid metal as it is sliced and distorted and squashed

➔ This clip also illustrates categories 2.5, three dimensions, and 2.9, duration, as explained later in this chapter.

Figure 2.1 Semi-molten metal, sliced and distorted (LDMU)

Video can also portray complex motion of mechanical parts. For example in Figure 2.2 an engineer demonstrates a borehole drill that has rotating teeth to crush rock; seeing the teeth rotating against the ground enables viewers to appreciate the drill's crushing action.

➜   This clip also illustrates category 2.5, three dimensions, as explained later in this chapter.

Another example of complex motion (Figure 2.3) is in a 30 sec video clip in which an engineering student demonstrates a control mechanism that balances a 12 inch (30 cm) ruler on its end. When the top of the ruler is manually deflected from the vertical, the control mechanism moves just enough in the opposite direction to keep the ruler balanced. Without seeing the complex movements, it is impossible to appreciate the control mechanism.

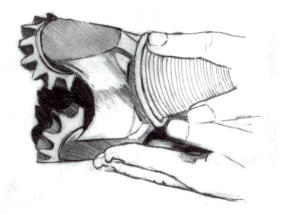

Figure 2.2   Bore-hole drill with rotating teeth (LDMU)

Figure 2.3   Control mechanism, balancing a ruler (LDMU)

In contrast to the above examples, if your information can be conveyed with still pictures, you have to question the need for video. Mind you, there are exceptions when still pictures are acceptable on video, e.g. a sequence of stills as snapshots of a dynamic process which is shown in full movement just before or after the stills.

2.2. Inaccessible places

There are many information-rich locations that are inaccessible because of the danger involved, or the expense, or the distance; video can take viewers on virtual field trips, giving them the vicarious experience of

- deep undersea locations
- overseas locations
- seeing molten metal being poured into a mould in a foundry, as in the 1 minute video clip shown in Figure 2.4. It would be dangerous to take a large group of students into the foundry.

➜   This clip also illustrates category 2.3, inaccessible viewpoints, as explained later in this chapter.

2.3. Otherwise inaccessible viewpoints

For example, aerial views, big close-ups, microscopy, objects of study isolated from their surroundings:

Figure 2.4   Molten metal in a foundry (LDMU)

- A shot of the Alps can be taken from a helicopter flying around a particular geological feature, such as a glacier.
- A 30 sec clip demonstrates a microscope that relays the image to a TV screen. This image is of motile sperm. A video recording can make use of high-quality, expensive microscopes which very few educational establishments possess. Even fewer would possess the facility to project the image onto a video screen, hence enabling group viewing.
- A video about the construction of Bronze Age axes includes (Figure 2.5) a big close-up (BCU) of molten metal being poured into a mould – the view is impossibly dangerous in real life because it would need viewers to stand only 10 cm away from the molten metal.

 This clip also illustrates category 2.2, inaccessible places, as explained earlier in this chapter.

An 80 sec clip shows the fitting of the striking plate of a mortice lock to a door-jamb. The BCU shots and the good lighting are impossible to achieve without specialist equipment. In fact the biggest close-up views could not be experienced by direct observation: they would need trainees to stand dangerously close – only 10 cm (too close to focus anyway). See Figures 1.22a, 1.22b and 1.22c.

 This clip also illustrates categories 1.6, condensing time, and 1.9, demonstration of a physical skill, as explained in Chapter 1; also 2.11, staged event, as explained later in this chapter.

A 30 sec clip, all shot in BCU, illustrates *anastomosis*, a surgical procedure on the bowel: a slit is made in the wall of the bowel and a new piece of intestine is sutured onto the slit. The BCU allows students to see the details much more clearly than if they attended the demonstration in person. See Figure 1.29.

 This clip also illustrates category 1.9, demonstration by an expert, as explained in Chapter 1.

Another kind of inaccessibility is the *purposely restricted view*, in which the object of study is carefully positioned so that surrounding items do not distract the viewer. Such meticulous preparation is typical in video recording and would take exorbitant effort to remount for each cohort of students. For example, a 90 sec video clip could show a complicated chemical process with many pieces of equipment, carefully positioned to exclude irrelevant surroundings.

2.4. Showing technical processes or equipment (especially complex or large-scale)

A 30 sec video clip shows a factory process with several stages in which metal is heated to a semi-solid state and cast into a complicated shape using a very fast compression into a die.

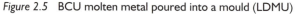

Figure 2.5   BCU molten metal poured into a mould (LDMU)

An 18 minute video shows UK Open University students learning from the medium of *audiovision*, audiocassette guiding learners through visual materials. Several students are seen listening and stopping to carry out activities, e.g. drawing diagrams, manipulating a home experiment kit. See Figure 1.27.

➔   This clip also illustrates category 1.9, demonstrating a skill (by non-experts)

2.5. Showing three-dimensional objects

This is done by moving the object or the camera and/or by exploring the space with the presenter's hand. True, the TV picture is two-dimensional; however, it can realistically convey three-dimensional objects because it can present some (although not all) of the many cues in a real-life scene that enable the viewer to experience 3D

1   binocular vision
2   eyes focusing
3   grain (grain getting smaller in the distance)
4   mistiness in the distance
5   differentiated reflection of light from different planes of the object
6   shadows of protrusions
7   when another object, such as the presenter's hand, explores the outlines of the object
8   parallax: if you move past an object, the nearer parts of the object pass through your field of view faster than the further parts, similarly if the object is moving past you or rotating

The last four, items 5 to 8, and especially 7 and 8, are essentially the ways video can show the realistic three-dimensionality of objects. Hence, to convey three-dimensionality, the best technique is to move the object or camera. Additionally, the three-dimensionality can be enhanced by interposing the presenter's hand, sliding over the object. Appropriate lighting is also effective – to *sculpture* the object by creating differentiated light and shade and also shadows of protrusions.

In Figure 2.1 a lump of semi-solid metal is sliced and distorted and squashed; the movement and the lighting bring out the three-dimensionality.

➔ The clip in Figure 2.1 also illustrates categories 2.1, dynamic change, as explained earlier in this chapter, and 2.9, duration as explained later in this chapter.

A video clip shows an engineer demonstrating a type of borehole drilling bit that has rotating teeth; the engineer rotates the teeth and runs his hands over the whole drill. The three-dimensionality of the object is made realistic by moving the object and having the presenter's hand move over the object. See Figure 2.2.

➔ The clip in Figure 2.2 also illustrates category 2.1, dynamic change or movement, as explained earlier in this chapter.

In a 30 sec video clip, Figure 2.6, various types of ore are displayed; the rotation of the samples (plus the careful lighting) provides good appreciation of their three-dimensionality. This is difficult to appreciate from a static picture (as you can witness here).

2.6. Slow/fast motion

Slow motion

By recording at a fast rate (say 50 frames per second) and playing the recording at the standard rate of 25 frames per second, the motion is seen at slower than normal speed (half speed in this case). Examples:

Figure 2.6   Rotating ore sample (LDMU)

- birds in flight
- predators hunting
- air-bags expanding in a car crash
- a 30 sec video clip shows fast-moving machinery used in a specialized process for casting metal. The clip ends with a repeat of the sequence in slow motion.

Fast motion

Conversely, time-lapse recording involves recording at slow rates (say 1 frame per minute) and playing at the standard 25 frames per second. The motion is thereby seen speeded up (in this case, $25 \times 60 = 1500$ times normal speed). Examples:

- cloud movement
- flowers growing
- bacteria dividing
- a bird, nest-building
- a spider, weaving its web
- a 29 sec video in which the 12 hour tidal cycle is speeded up 1500 times. This is accomplished by the technique of *time-lapse* – i.e. recording one frame then allowing a determined time to elapse (1 minute in this case) before recording the next frame. For normal speed, a new frame gets recorded every 1/25 sec

Such experiences are clearly informative and are impossible to achieve without video – it is no good taking students out on a field trip to watch a flower grow.

Addendum: fast motion for humour

A video shows how different people have individual styles of learning. Four people try to assemble a stool by following printed instructions. Some decide not to follow the instructions precisely. One decides to fill in what he believes to be a missing step in the instructions. Another does not bother to follow the instructions carefully because he finds this boring. A two-minute clip shows the attempts of these last two (Figure 2.7a) and includes a 4-times speeded up sequence of the bored person's messy assembly (Figure 2.7b). However, the purpose of speeding up is not to inform but rather to amuse. Humour is memorable, so it can be a powerful tool for enduring learning.

➔   This clip also illustrates category 2.11, staged event, as explained later in this chapter.

(A)   (B)

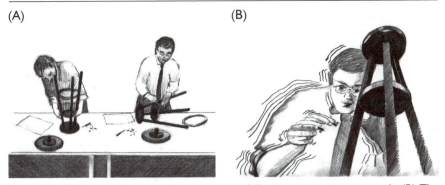

Figure 2.7   (A) Assembling a stool: two men not following instructions correctly, (B) The bored assembler, speeded up (EBS)

2.7. People, animals interacting, real-life or drama

Several sequences can show the stance/demeanour of subordinate animals in dominance/subordinacy relationships. The subtleties of the phenomenon of 'dominance' cannot be appreciated in real life without weeks of careful, skilful observation. A carefully structured 25 minute video can enable the learner to achieve such appreciation.

Important people can be shown being interviewed or interacting with their public: e.g. a week in the life of a government minister (to which an individual student could not gain personal access) or an interview with the author of the course text, who gives further insights into the topic. An individual student cannot access the activities, the interactions, the demeanour of such people, whereas a prestigious teaching institution such as the UK OU might be permitted to trail government officials in their daily work. This can create a sense of importance for the students – they come to know that they are part of a prestigious organization.

A video can demonstrate the tone of voice and body posture of a sympathetic counsellor or of a doctor breaking bad news. For example, in a video of a bereavement counselling session (see Figure 1.30) in which the interviewee lost his wife only a few weeks earlier and is extremely emotional. This shows an experienced counsellor who asks questions, listens and summarizes, acknowledges what the interviewee says. A sympathetic tone and an open body posture encourage the interviewee to speak freely. The combination of all these aspects is very difficult to communicate without using video. Similarly, the interviewee's body language cannot be appreciated without video.

➔   This clip also illustrates categories 1.9, demonstration of skill, as explained in Chapter 1 and 3.5, create empathy, as explained in Chapter 3.

A 10 sec clip shows a baby with breathing problems, as experienced in the disorder called *croup* – narrowing of the extra-thoracic airway, causing difficulty when breathing in, since the airway naturally narrows even more then. Still pictures or sound alone cannot convey the symptoms of croup – the symptoms involve the movements and sounds of the breathing problem. See Figure 1.26.

2.8. Rare or one-off events, including archive film

- There is archive film of the annual Notting Hill Carnival in London, which celebrates West Indian culture.
- There are many examples of rare animal behaviour, such as newts depositing sperm, fish giving birth, foxes burying their kills, the alpha male monkey being chased off by a coalition of high-ranking female monkeys.
- A 10 sec video clip showing Queen Elizabeth opening Britain's first nuclear power station, Calder Hall.

2.9. Chronological sequence and duration

This is important in, for example:

- sequence and pacing of body language
- pauses for interviewing skills
- progress of chemical reactions
- progress of glass melting, buildings collapsing, mud-slides, etc.
- a lump of semi-solid metal is sliced and distorted and squashed. Whereas the distortion could conceivably be depicted with a series of still photos, the pacing of the movements and the length of time it takes for the metal to sag can only be captured on video. See Figure 2.1.

→   This clip also illustrates categories 2.1, dynamic change or movement, and 2.5, three dimensions as explained earlier in this chapter.

See Figure 1.1, showing a child in a composite picture with a picture book that she is looking at. In an earlier scene, a speech scientist has used a picture book to help tell the child the story of the runaway bus. The child now has to retell the story, while looking at the pictures. This looking is allowed so as to reduce the strain on the child's memory; this enables the scientist to concentrate exclusively on the child's language development.

There are three different types of chronological sequence in this clip that help the viewer appreciate the child's stage of speech development:

- the speed of speech delivery
- the duration of pauses
- the sequence of pointing to pictures and speaking.

2.10. Resource material for further analysis by the viewer

A video shows children and teacher interacting in a classroom. Individual trainee teachers or groups of them could replay this and reflect on what is going on. This reflection could be guided by commentary on the video and by printed supplementary notes. See Figure 1.31.

 This clip also illustrates category 1.9, demonstration of social skill, as explained in Chapter 1.

A video for medical students shows a practitioner reading *systolic* (highest) and *diastolic* (lowest) arterial blood pressures, using the *pressure cuff* technique. See Figure 1.24. There are close-ups of the pressure gauge while the stethoscope sound is heard on the sound-track. For the first patient, viewers are shown how to judge these pressures – the appearance of the word *systolic* signals when they should read off the systolic pressure from the mercury column, similarly for *diastolic*. For the next six patients, viewers have to judge the pressures for themselves. This is just the kind of situation where observing a variety of situations is particularly necessary – because blood-pressure measurements are inexact, subjective.

 This clip also illustrates category 1.7, juxtaposing of contrasting situations, as explained in Chapter 1.

In a medical video, a 40 sec video clip concerns a *pericardial friction-rub* (caused by a condition in which heart tissues rub together). The video clip includes the sound, heard through a stethoscope, of a patient's heart with this condition. The real-life sound of a friction-rub in a patient's heart is resource material for students to replay and get familiar with. See Figure 1.17.

→ This clip also illustrates category 1.3, aural analogy, as explained in Chapter 1.

2.11. Staged events/dramatized enactment

It is time-consuming and expensive to stage complex experiments or dramatized enactments for a live demonstration to students. It may well be impossible to restage the events time after time to each new cohort of students. So video might be the only solution, on grounds of economy of scale.

Incidentally, the activity of staging events necessarily occurs for all categories of video production. That is, the producer has to ensure that all performers and props are in the right place, doing the right things and that the conditions are controlled to exclude extraneous noises or intrusive objects or people. (An example was given under 2.3 of a purposely restricted field of view.) However, this kind of staging of events (the normal preparation for recording) is surreptitious – not intended to be noticed by the viewers. In contrast, the *staging* referred to in the present category is explicit – the viewer is meant to realize that the event is staged. Moreover, this *explicit staging* is extra, over and above the normal recording preparation, and hence requires greater expenditure of time and effort.

Here are some examples.

- setting up a complex experiment, e.g. a carefully controlled spray of water under special lighting conditions to demonstrate a rainbow that is in the form of a complete circle
- in a safety training video, a series of staged accidents. In face-to face safety training, it would be impractical for a trainer to stage all the hazardous situations that employees should watch out for and to enact all the ensuing accidents (and to restage everything for each cohort of trainees). Another point is that most accidents so recorded on video would not really have happened – video editing tricks would be used to make the fabricated accidents look realistic – so video is the only way to demonstrate most accidents realistically and forcefully and yet with complete safety.
- dramatized enactment (actors role-playing) of a relationship between an authoritative manager and a difficult employee. It might be imagined that a more natural performance could be achieved from a real manager and employee. However, most people cannot demonstrate their natural behaviour in front of cameras – they look more artificial than professional actors playing the same role.
- In a 75 sec video clip from a statistics video, *random error* and *systematic error* are illustrated with two contestants playing with two sets of darts. The white set is biased (it drifts to the right), giving a systematic error. The dark set is well balanced. Both players aim at the bull's eye. One player is poor, contributing additional error with both sets of darts, called *random error*. (The poor player's darts spread out much more than the good player's.) See Figure 1.20a, b, c, d.

This sequence was highly staged, probably needing many *takes* before achieving the desired placing of the darts. Also, both players were good players in reality, but contrived to throw the darts precisely as they did, one pretending to play badly and both aiming to the right with the alleged biased dark darts.

A multimedia package on this topic could well include considerable text, in order to present data for the learner to practise on. However, introducing video into the package enlivens it considerably

→   This clip also illustrates category 1.5, illustrating, as explained in Chapter 1.

- An 80 sec clip shows the fitting of the *striking plate* of a Mortice lock to a door-jamb. This was plainly staged in a studio, using careful lighting and specialist equipment to achieve the essential big close up shots. See Figures 1.22a, b, c.

➜ This clip also illustrates categories 1.6, condensing time and 1.9, demonstrate a physical skill and 2.3, inaccessible viewpoints, as explained in chapter 1 and earlier in this chapter.

• A video shows how different people have individual styles of learning. See Figure 2.7a. Two people try to assemble a stool by following printed instructions. One decides to fill in what he believes to be a missing step in the instructions. Another does not bother to follow the instructions carefully because he finds this boring. The events are staged, although the individual behaviours are spontaneous.

➜ Part of this clip also illustrates category 2.6, fast motion, as explained earlier in this chapter (Figure 2.7b).

Concluding note: video is indispensable for many experiential provisions

Video is indispensable for many experiential provisions under the above categories, although this has been disputed by some. For example, Laurillard (1993: 114) argues that experiential roles of video are just 'logistical, delivery roles … whereas given enough resources, the students would engage in these experiences directly'. However, there will never be enough resources to take all students to farflung locations in helicopters or bathyspheres, or to restage the events for each new cohort of students, let alone to supply them with telephoto eyes, microscope eyes, heat-resistant eyes (e.g. for close-up shots of molten metal) or slow/fast motion vision. Besides, many such field trips would take several days, whereas video can condense time and employ many other facilitating techniques.

Some such (virtual) experiences would need to be followed up by real life (e.g. lab sessions), but the vicarious video experiences would provide valuable grounding/priming.

Activities

1 For each of the above categories, think about your specialist subject or your current project. Consider whether any of the video techniques would benefit any of the learning tasks in your subject/project.
2 Could a different medium (maybe a cheaper one) provide as much benefit?
3 Could a different medium provide more benefit?

Chapter 3

Video that adds nurturing value

Domain 3 of Table 0.1; nurturing motivations, feelings

There are many nurturing functions for which video can play a distinctive role. This is because the rich symbol system of video provides substantial realism.

In all seven nurturing categories of Tables 0.1, 3.1 to 3.7, the principal intention is that the affective influences (of motivations and feelings) should endure into the future rather than being transitory influences on the student.

Caveat 1. Transitory affective influences, not included in domain 3, that help students learn from the video

Affective changes that are only transitory can nevertheless be valuable if they help students to learn from the video.

One example is to alleviate tedium and re-engage the viewer, by switching between media. That is, in a multiple-media learning package, an inattentive viewer might be re-engaged by switching media, especially from a static to a dynamic medium, e.g. to a moving video image of some real life. Staying too long with a single medium, even video, can result in the *warm bath syndrome*, in which the learner's attention is submersed; that is, the viewer gets passively immersed, without paying much attention.

Other examples are when video entertains, fascinates, delights or amuses. Entertainment is certainly not inimical to learning, nor does it necessitate superficial coverage of the subject. For example, detailed narrative exploration can bring out the intrinsic fascination of a subject, which is a powerful aid to learning, precisely because it is so entertaining. In any case, the occasional lighter, entertaining item can re-engage viewers' attention.

Humour can also be a powerful learning tool. Both entertainment and humour are pleasant and memorable, hence can be powerful for getting a message across and for the learning to endure (whether the message is motivational or cognitive). An important ingredient in humour is the pacing. This ingredient can be enhanced by creative editing. It can also be diminished by a video editor without a sense of rhythm.

There is a danger with entertainment and humour – the technique could swamp the message! If humour is overdone, the viewers could be *entranced* to such an extent that they remember the humour but fail to learn the message. They might even learn the *wrong* message: for example, if the video satirizes the *wrong way to do it*, this might be so memorable that the subsequent *correct way* gets forgotten.

Caveat 2. Some long-term affective influences can also have transitory effects

Although the principal intention of the seven categories below is to engender *sustained* changes in students, lasting into the future, three of the categories might also incorporate an element of transitory change that helps students learn from the video. These are

- 3.1, stimulate appetite to learn; e.g. (in a literacy video) to learn to read in the future, but maybe also (in any video) to learn the specific topic on the video that they are watching now
- 3.4, alleviate isolation; feeling less lonely is beneficial for students' future well-being, but maybe it also helps them to learn the specific topic on the video that they are watching now
- 3.7, authenticate academic abstractions by showing their use in solving real-life problems; this would answer the long-term question of what is the point of all this theory. But answering that question can also have the short-term effect of persuading students to attend and thereby to learn the theory itself, which is the topic of the video that they are watching now; generally, any technique that enhances the relevance of the topic motivates attention.

The nurturing categories (affective influences) are divided into two subdomains, one active (motivational, 3.1 to 3.3) the other passive (engendering feelings, appreciations and attitudes, 3.4 to 3.7).

3.1. Stimulate appetite to learn

Here are some ways of stimulating a student's appetite to learn about a specific topic, sometime in the future.

- by showing the progress of a beginner, *before and after* each stage of learning: adult literacy campaigns on TV could use this technique (and others below) in order to stimulate the appetite to learn reading and writing
- for learning work skills, such as typing, make an analogy with a recreational skill such as juggling or tap-dancing
- by demonstrating the negative consequences of resting on one's laurels
- by revealing the real-life fascination of the subject (not merely *dressing up* the subject with an entertaining style of video), e.g. the concept of a

dominance hierarchy in an animal group will be made more fascinating if the analogy with human behaviour is emphasized

- by exposing learners to a truly inspirational teacher and/or to a famous personality such as a teacher (e.g. BBC Schools TV used the first British female astronaut, Helen Sharman, as a presenter for a science series; Channel 4 Schools used the successful British athlete, Kelly Holmes, as a presenter in a mathematics series)
- by exposing learners to VIPs and their work, e.g. a week in the life of a US Congresswoman (in a course about US politics)
- by exposing learners to a VIP who is also an inspirational teacher. For example, in a video designed to encourage 14-year-olds to appreciate science (Figure 3.1), Richard Feyneman, a Nobel Laureate, radiates enthusiasm when describing the catastrophe of combustion. The effect is heightened by interspersing Feyneman with evocative shots of the phenomena he describes.

➜   This clip also illustrates category 3.5, change attitudes/appreciations, later in this chapter.

3.2. Galvanize, spur into action

- Galvanize viewers to get up and do something, e.g. to filter and boil their water following a health campaign on TV (or a multimedia health campaign for community leaders).
- Galvanize a workforce to cast off their passivity: by showing examples of workers who have taken control of their careers by stretching their abilities, taking initiatives, learning new skills.

Figure 3.1   Richard Feyneman, a charismatic teacher (EBS)

3.3. Motivate use of a strategy by showing its success

- Endorse an exam technique such as 'first read the whole paper through carefully' or, in a mathematics exam, 'jot down what you know about the problem, e.g. what equations do you know that link acceleration, velocity, distance and duration?'
- In a video following four 16-year-old students through their GCSE exam preparation, the most successful student, Tom, explains his strict adherence to his own revision timetable.
- Encourage *lateral thinking* for solving problems, e.g. solving a brain teaser, where nine dots are positioned in a square array and the task is: 'join up the nine dots with four straight lines without taking the pencil off the paper, or retracing your path'. The standard solution is to start with a horizontal line, left to right through the top three dots (Figure 3.2a), but then to *think laterally* by extending this line past the boundary of the square and then starting the second line diagonally down and left so as to draw through two more dots (Figure 3.2b). And so on, as in Figure 3.2c.

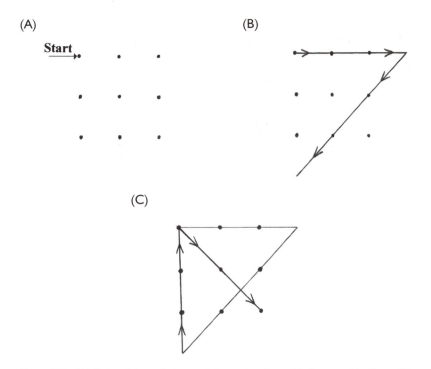

Figure 3.2   (A) Start of the solution to join up the dots with four straight lines, (B) extend the first line past the three dots, then diagonally down/left, (C) complete by drawing upwards then diagonally down/right

This last example literally illustrates *thinking outside the box* (a common metaphor for lateral thinking), meaning, think outside the boundaries that seem to circumscribe your problem – think of deviations and detours, however outrageous. Incidentally, you don't need as many as four pencil lines to solve the problem. There is a solution using a *single* line. Think about it *laterally*. One answer is in section 3.7.

3.4. Alleviate isolation of the distant learner

- By showing the teacher/presenter

Note that the other categories involve imaginative exploitation of video's vast range of presentational attributes, which usually necessitate the speaker being out of vision. In fact the term *head and shoulders* is often used to deride videos that show the presenter in vision, classifying this as static and unimaginative. Nevertheless, the occasional sight of a human presenter (not necessarily in all programmes of a series) can serve to humanize the medium.

- By showing other students: their study problems and solutions

3.5. Change attitudes or appreciations, engender empathy

It is stressful for employees to accommodate change so they are likely to resist it, but they might be encouraged instead to welcome it as refreshing, stimulating, creative – if shown real people who have experienced these positive reactions.

Another example is a video designed to encourage 14-year-olds to appreciate science. Richard Feyneman, a Nobel Laureate, radiates enthusiasm when describing the catastrophe of combustion (he even jokingly ascribes human emotions to the atoms involved). See Figure 3.1.

→   This clip also illustrates category 3.1, stimulate appetite to learn. See above.

To persuade teenagers that physics is not dry and unexciting, a video uses a format that is fast-moving, with frequent cutting, composite shots, and with additional graphics for peripheral stimulation. In addition, the physicists describing their work should be trendy, e.g. in their leisure time they play guitar, go rock-climbing, go to discos, use a WAP phone.

Mind you, a *flamboyant, gaudy* style may induce *fashion fatigue*, hence a short shelf life. Consider this anecdote: I showed the video to a 14-year-old boy, who remarked that it was just like videos they showed at school, the implication being: *you can't fool me, this is just school work*. In addition to this syndrome of *fashion fatigue*, it could be that the real fascination of the subject matter, portrayed well by the video, gets ignored if it is immersed in *gaudiness*, thus defeating the object of the *gaudiness*.

Engender empathy in people who appraise staff by enacting (on video) an appraisal interview in which the appraiser is painfully unsympathetic and comparing this with a more sympathetic appraiser.

Promote empathy for bullied staff by enacting a scene where an authoritative manager berates an employee.

Impart a real feeling for the predicament of those in government by showing the stress involved in a week in the life of a US Congresswoman or UK Minister.

A video for training bereavement counsellors creates empathy for bereaved interviewees by showing recordings of real counselling sessions in which the interviewee breaks down emotionally. The indices of such a breakdown are sometimes subtle. They include body posture, facial expression, tone of voice, pace of speech. See Figure 1.30.

→   This clip also illustrates categories 1.9, demonstration of skill, as explained in Chapter 1, and 2.7, human interaction as explained in Chapter 2.

In a health education video, change attitudes towards hygiene by presenting and interviewing people who have changed attitudes following a family illness or death due to polluted water.

A video for UK schoolchildren compares the life of teenagers in Britain and Ghana; one aim of the comparison is to shake the complacency that Britain is best. The video shows that life in Ghana is slow-moving, self-sufficient, with little choice of travel, food, resources or accommodation. On the other hand Britain is fast-moving, industrial, with little choice regarding traffic, noise, pollution, overcrowding, junk food, threatened environment.

3.6. Reassure, encourage self-confidence

- A video may encourage self-confidence, thereby enhancing readiness to learn by showing other people who've managed badly at first but finally prevailed, such as past students for whom the syllabus eventually clicked.
- A video clip could reassure workers of their ability to deal with change, with the commentary 'we tend to underestimate just how good we are at dealing with change', accompanied by many images of non-threatening change that viewers may have experienced in their everyday lives.
- In a one-minute clip, part of a video concerning taking examinations, an examiner convincingly explains that exams never have trick questions – on the contrary, that all questions are refined repeatedly to be unambiguous.

3.7. Authenticate academic abstractions

This is done by showing their application to solving real problems and is related to the cognitive value 1.5, illustration, which helps understanding. Similarly, showing the *application* of abstract concepts is likely to help in their understanding. However, a stronger, more direct influence of showing such application is *affective*. That is, when a video demonstrates that a concept can be applied to solving a real problem, this has the *affective* consequence of giving *authenticity* to the concept. The viewer now appreciates *the point of all this theory*. Here are some examples:

Use *a geometric theorem* to design a telescope or a searchlight. For example, an astronomical telescope has parabolic and hyperbolic mirrors that are positioned so that together they focus light from a distant object into the eyepiece of the telescope. This invention relies on the following geometric theorem.

> From any point on a hyperbola, a line drawn through a focus of the hyperbola makes the same angle with the hyperbola as a second line from that point drawn through the second focus. Ditto for a parabola.

Use a *quadratic equation* to determine the shape of International Paper Size, i.e. paper sizes A1, A2, A3, A4, . . . All of these are the same shape and each one can be obtained by cutting the previous size in half. (The shape turns out to be the ratio, 1 to the square root of 2.)

Authenticate the concept of *lateral thinking*. (This example has already been illustrated with the brain teaser about drawing a pencil line through nine dots – under section 3.3, promote a strategy.)

A word of warning

Regarding all the categories of Chapters 1 to 3 there is a need for professional quality. When all the above is said and done, the video styles and techniques have to be produced well in order to be effective. So the question of appropriate media/technology is twofold:

1 For each teaching/learning function, select the most appropriate medium/ technology – the one whose attributes best suit the teaching/learning function.
2 Design optimum instructional methods to exploit the particular capabilities of each medium/technology.

This book addresses both questions. Regarding question 1, Chapters 1, 2 and 3 have dealt with 27 teaching/learning categories for which video can add value compared to other media, i.e. for which video is the most appropriate medium. Chapter 4 addresses question 1 for media other than video. Regarding question 2,

The brain teaser set at the end of section 3.3 was, *Draw through nine dots with a single pencil line.* One answer is: fold the paper to position all nine dots on top of one another, then the paper can be pierced with the pencil so that it makes a mark on all nine.

Chapters 5 and 6 give a substantial treatment of pedagogic design principles for educational video.

Activities

1 For each of the above categories, think about your specialist subject or your current project. Consider whether any of the video techniques would benefit any of the learning tasks in your subject/project.
2 Could a different medium (maybe a cheaper one) provide as much benefit?
3 Could a different medium provide more benefit?

Part II
Media selection and deployment

Chapter 4

Matching media attributes to learning tasks and teaching functions

Introduction: the differing potentials of different media

The aim of this chapter is to provide criteria for optimal media deployment. That is, given a set of learning tasks in a particular course, we should assign each task to the medium that is best suited.

Before embarking on this aim, there is an issue that needs to be laid to rest. This is the false impression that different media are all equally effective for all learning tasks – that there is *equipotentiality of media*. This claim has been propounded by some researchers on comparative efficacy of media.

This introductory section therefore sets out to establish that much of the above research has been flawed. Arguments will be proposed that the research has failed to recognize the distinctive presentational attributes of each medium. These different attributes point to learning tasks that can be more effectively presented on one particular medium than on others.

Research studies comparing learning effects from different media have consistently found no significant differences (Clark 1983) or, at best, differences of small size (Spencer 1991, reporting on studies up until the early 1980s). However, there are crippling flaws in most of the studies, as follows.

Naive comparison of so-called like with like

The most serious flaw of the comparison studies is the methodology of the quasi-experimental controlled comparison. In this standard paradigm (derived from botanical experiments), some students experience the media lesson being tested and others do not. The students that do not are given an alternative experience; for example, the same content might be presented in a different medium. The two groups are then tested for any difference in performance on follow-up tasks, or (more sensitively) on differences between pre-test and post-test scores). Authors of such experiments – reported and endorsed by Clark (1983) insist we must compare *like with like* in the sense of ensuring that only the media being compared are different. All other aspects of the treatments, such as the nature of students in the comparison groups, learning environment, teaching method, teaching function, subject matter, time on task, are contrived to be identical, or at least counterbalanced.

However, this practice of balancing conditions and controlling variables when comparing media deliberately ignores their different capabilities. Each medium has its distinctive presentational attributes, its own strengths and its weaknesses. These distinctions must be fully exploited by choosing different treatments of the topic for different media. In fact, it may be necessary to address different teaching functions and learning tasks, and even to choose different topics. (An inventory of such distinctive functions and topics is given in a later section.)

If you try to cover identical topics or teaching functions using identical methods with all the different media, then you deliberately under-utilize every medium's full potential. As Bates (1987) puts it, this practice 'is equivalent to cutting two legs off a horse to see if it can run as fast as a man'.

To conclude, when investigating multiple media learning materials, if you try to compare *like with like* in the above naive sense, you cannot get the most out of each medium. Consequently, the comparison is futile: if topics and teaching functions are ascribed indiscriminately to different media, using identical teaching methods, there is no way of knowing how far each medium's potential has been under-achieved.

Low production quality of video compared to print or face-to-face

The above problem concerns using media for inappropriate topics or learning tasks. However, even when a medium tackles an appropriate topic, the medium may not be tackling it well. This is a second flaw in most comparison studies – low production quality, especially in the case of video.

When comparing the potentials of different media, a primary question should be that of production quality: in order to be fair to each medium, we would need to employ highly creative practitioners and allow them adequate resources and thinking time to exploit the full potential of each medium's presentational capabilities. The point seems obvious. Yet researchers have invariably ignored it, as noted by Bates (1981) who points out that there has rarely been any control of production quality between the media being compared and that most experiments take no account of the professional competence of the production team.

Even those researchers who recognize the problem can do little to solve it: they have to make do with the production resources they are given, which are invariably inadequate. The creative skill and time required to exploit the complex symbol systems of audio-visual media are drastically underestimated in most production centres: salaries are generally low and the productivity required was far too high. For example, a BBC Open University TV producer's yearly load was between 6 and 8 half-hour programmes. Koumi and Hung (1995) point out that this compares with more than 12 at the Indira Gandhi National OU in India and the Sukhotai Thammathirat OU in Thailand, more than 80 at the Chinese Radio and TV University and about 100 at Taiwan's Open University!

Such under-resourcing is just as problematic in comparative studies, where the audio-visual production has usually been carried out in notoriously under-resourced campus-based radio/television centres. It might be argued that if all media are equally under-resourced, then it is valid to compare them. However, compared to video, face-to-face teaching and print have been used in education for far longer, so practitioners are able to exploit these media more fruitfully.

Worse still is a disastrous working practice that stems from unequal status between subject experts and media experts. The standard working practice in many centres is for the subject expert to supply a written script for which the media technician has to provide pictures, with little consultation. This allows no opportunity to optimize picture–word synergy. Such optimization would require an iterative design cycle whereby each new idea for pictures leads to a modification of the words and vice versa, over several draft screenplays (Koumi 1991).

The result of under-resourced video production will be under-achievement of the potential of video. Hence, even if teaching functions that were appropriate to video were chosen for comparison, a result of *no significant difference* could still be expected.

Media-robust topics, teaching functions and learning tasks

There is another crucial respect in which traditional comparison studies have been unsound. As will be argued later, the symbol system of print is as adequate as that of video to cover much of the syllabus in most courses. In other words, there are many (but not all) topics, teaching functions and learning tasks for which print and video do indeed have equal potential. Hence, if print is compared with video for this (large) part of the syllabus, the effect of video will be no better than print. In fact, it may often be worse because there are certainly some, functions for which print is superior to video. This factor has been largely neglected in media comparison research, mainly due to the absence of an adequate media deployment theory.

So, for argument's sake, if researchers have opted for topics, teaching functions or learning tasks for which print and video are indeed equipotential, then of course they should find equipotentiality. Researchers have no theory about which topics, functions and tasks would benefit most from video (not even an intuitive theory based on making team decisions over many years). Hence, they are unlikely to choose functions for which video can add distinctive value.

To continue the horse analogy, the cart has been put before the horse: instead of having a theory to test, researchers have gone ahead with comparison testing, in a theoretical vacuum. In many cases this has resulted in the use of media-robust topics, teaching functions and learning tasks. Because of this, the findings have been non-significant – and the conclusion has wrongly been drawn that no theory is possible!

Differences in learning styles

Even in the studies where appropriate topics have been chosen, individual student differences must obscure media effects.

Many individual differences are likely to be temporary, interacting with the particular topic and style of presentation. These will dilute the size of media effects. On the one hand, the *control* group (or the *traditional teaching method* group) probably contains a proportion of learners who can manage without the distinctive media treatment for this particular topic. On the other hand, the treatment group may contain a proportion of students who find it difficult to learn from the medium (when they are unaccustomed to learning from it, or when they are in this particular mood, or when the medium uses that particular style of presentation). All these factors should lead to research on individual differences with a view eventually to developing techniques to enable individuals to benefit maximally from each medium – by training individuals to get the most out of each medium. Instead, the factors serve to dilute the size of media effects and hence discourage any further media research.

Differences in viewing purpose

The final factor that may obscure differences in outcome for different media is that learners may have attitudes towards some media that result in their not taking them seriously. Clark (1983) and Kozma (1991) report several studies in which the perceived purpose of viewing a TV programme was manipulated: one group was told they would be tested on content while another was told to view for entertainment. The result, as expected, was that those who knew they would be tested learned better. These authors put such results down to differential amounts of invested mental effort. That is, students concentrate harder when they know they will be tested.

In general, since students are accustomed to watching TV for entertainment, they might find it difficult to concentrate on learning from TV unless they are told they will be tested on the material.

Incidentally, UK OU students were never examined on the content of the broadcast media (with rare exceptions), on the grounds that they might miss the broadcast. This policy is likely to throttle the pedagogic potential of broadcast media at the outset – students who know that the material will not be assessed are not likely to treat the media seriously. This tendency is then exacerbated because course developers, for the same reason, choose so-alled *enrichment* roles for media rather than presentation of core material. Students are quick to recognize material that is peripheral to their exam success. Consequently they treat the broadcasts even less seriously.

A proposal for future research

To compare media we could begin from a study of actual, rather than experimental teaching materials, and compare multiple-media packages rather than individual media directly.

Instead of persisting in trying to *prove* media, let us first try to deploy different media to best effect. Let us take that as sensible and get on with the job of being as creative as possible with the distinctive capabilities of each medium. As noted in the Introduction, even Clark, who in 1983 likened media to mere delivery vehicles, relented by 1994 to concede that certain media are more efficient for certain learning tasks. The deployment of different media to the tasks for which they are best suited has been the goal of the UK Open University since it began in 1970. Admittedly the criteria for optimal media deployment have been mainly in the form of unwritten intuitions. The next section tries to formalize these intuitions into a coherent framework, which is offered as provisional guidance for media deployment.

If this framework (or any other formal deployment framework) is utilized reasonably widely in future, a basis would then exist for future research, as follows. One could compare the media deployment success of several multiple-media courses, ideally all on similar topics. That is, compare how different course developers (or different course teams) deploy different media to different parts of the topic and to different teaching functions and learning tasks. One would also be advised to encourage and train students to make the most out of each medium (see the above section 'Differences in learning styles'). Such exploratory *action research* would serve to clarify and refine whatever deployment scheme was being employed. This refined scheme could then serve as the basis for the next course production (and the evaluation of that production) . . . and so on.

So the plea here is: do not try to *compare media*, instead, try to develop and refine the criteria for deploying media to best effect and try to develop and refine the principles of *effective design* within each medium.

Gordon Burt (1997) made a start in this direction by interrogating students of one UK Open University course regarding the media mix in the course. He found that students were generally satisfied with the relative amounts of the different media/components, and there was only a little discrepancy between these judgements and students' assessment of the helpfulness of each medium. So, to this extent, students' judgements appeared to be a valid instrument for measuring the appropriateness of the media mix.

Beyond the question of the relative amounts of different media is the more pertinent one of whether each medium is deployed to the most appropriate learning task. In future research, students' opinions must continue to be sought, but students might find it more difficult to pass judgement on this thornier question of *appropriate deployment based on a medium's distinctive capabilities*. Hence, in addition to students' opinions, further measuring instruments would need to be employed, such as *experts' opinions* and *student comprehension and their performance on transfer tasks.*

Through such research, as more is learned about a medium's distinctive capabilities (and limitations), new methods will suggest themselves to take better advantage of that medium's potential and fewer will be the attempts to use it for inappropriate teaching functions.

This iterative process needs a starting point – a draft scheme for media deployment. One is offered in the next section.

Matching media attributes to teaching functions and learning tasks

As argued in this chapter's introduction, each medium has its distinctive presentational attributes. These attributes, for any particular medium, might be more suitable for some topics and learning tasks than for others. Conversely, each topic and learning task might be more effectively presented on one particular medium than on others. Hence, given a set of learning tasks in a particular course, we should assign each task to the medium that is best suited for it.

However, such assignments are rarely clear-cut. Even if we have managed the difficult task of assigning our set of tasks optimally to the different media, we might then need to modify our choices according to how much production capacity is available in each medium.

Here is a common state of affairs. Suppose that a particular learning task is best tackled with *medium A*, but that *medium A* is fully booked with other learning tasks. Then we might need to use *medium B* instead, the second-best medium for our purpose. However, by suitably modifying our *treatment* of such topics, we might improve the effectiveness of *medium B* and hence rescue the situation to a large extent. In the end, we would hope to have chosen a near-optimal pedagogic deployment of our available media.

Yet in many distance teaching institutions, the deployment of different media for different topics and learning tasks is controlled as much by logistic, economic and human factors as by pedagogic considerations. One reason for this is that user-friendly pedagogic criteria have not been developed to date; at least, there is no consensus on the adequacy of any existing selection models. Another reason is the false impression, conveyed by media comparison research, of equipotentiality between media. The introduction to this chapter has reviewed this evidence for equipotentiality, arguing that the research methodology of most studies has been nonsensical. This section concentrates on pedagogic criteria for optimal media deployment, although logistic considerations are also addressed.

However, the section does not attempt to provide a prescriptive algorithm for media selection and deployment. Rather it compares distinctive attributes of different media, thereby providing a basis for course developers to construct their own selection and deployment procedures.

A framework is proposed that has two ingredients

- a broad categorization of comparative merits of different media (Table 4.1);
- a finer grained inventory of media-distinctive techniques and teaching functions (Tables 4.2 and 4.3).

The framework was developed collaboratively over several years, with the help of theorists and practitioners in international seminars and workshops. Eight media will be considered:

1 radio (broadcast)
2 TV (broadcast)
3 audio (recorded on cassette or disk)
4 video (recorded on cassette or disk)
5 audiovision (audio recorded on cassette or disk, guiding students through specially designed visual materials)
6 print: text, diagrams, photographs, etc. (Incidentally, this book restricts attention to printed documents that are delivered to a body of students. Hence it does not cover the mass medium of newspapers, which has a long history of providing educational material in many countries. For a world-wide profile of the use of newspapers in education, see Steen 2002.)
7 computer package (e.g. CD-ROM)
8 computer-mediated collaboration (via the internet)

In the background is a ninth medium, *human mediation*, against which the first eight media will frequently be compared. In distance teaching institutions, the role of student support by humans is recognized as crucial. This area will be discussed briefly, although a thorough analysis is beyond the scope of this book.

Two further points need to be made concerning our use of the word *medium*. First, it could be argued that our first four media are really only two media. Radio is just audio presentation that is delivered by radio waves rather than by sending students an audio recording. Similarly for TV and video. However, it will be argued that the recorded form affords different teaching functions and student controllability than the broadcast form. Another way of looking at this distinction is to say that both the *medium* and the *delivery technology* must be distinguished, as argued by Bates and Poole (2003: 48). For this reason, I'll continue to distinguish radio and audio as different media; similarly for TV and video.

Second (and conversely), item 7, the *computer package*, is not a singular medium. It can incorporate all the non-broadcast media listed above, that is, text, diagrams (animated or static), recorded video, recorded audio. Hence the selection principles for these constituent media (when considered as standing alone) can be applied to the computer package. The principles would apply when choosing which medium to use on the computer package for each particular topic or teaching function. So, in part, the attributes of the computer package are the sum of attributes of its constituent media. In addition, the computer package has the potential for much more refined *interactive design*.

The analysis of the above media will consider seven types of media characteristics:

- symbol system (or presentational attributes) – the types of symbols the medium uses to communicate, e.g. text and/or moving pictures and/or sound.
- access – the extent to which students are in a position to use the medium for learning
- controllability – how much influence can be exerted by students over the way they make use of the medium
- student reactivity – opportunities provided by the medium for student activity (including mental activity)
- interactivity – an action by a student receives feedback from the medium (according with the definition by Laurillard 1993: 100)
- adaptivity – the medium is able to adapt its provision to suit an individual's needs, emulating the ability of an expert human teacher (according with the definition by Laurillard 1993: 100)
- networking – the medium enables cooperation among learners and between learners and teachers

Comparative merits of media

The concept of *comparative merits* between media is offered as a more fruitful idea than the usual *advantages and disadvantages* of individual media. For example, print is rather impersonal whereas audio-visual media can portray the teacher in person. This pair of evaluations can be expressed as a single comparison, namely:

> Personalizing the teacher is a merit of audio-visual media compared to print.

In the last ten years, participants of workshops held in several countries have helped to build up a substantial list of such comparative merits. Table 4.1 gathers together those merits that such contributors have agreed are important for rational deployment of different media to different learning contexts and tasks.

To get familiar with Table 4.1, consider just one item from each of the first four sections. Each item in the table is a *desirable feature,* something that we want, like *personalizing the teacher*. This appears in section 1 (item 1.4) because personalization of teachers is better achieved by audio-visual media than by print. Notice that the merits in section 1 apply to all audio-visual media, whether broadcast (TV and radio) or distributed as video- and audio-recorded on cassette

Table 4.1   Comparative merits and distinctive teaching attributes of six different media: print, TV and radio (broadcast), video and audio (recordings), audiovision (audio + notes/visuals)

1 Audio-visual (broadcast or recorded) *over* **Print**
1.1   unique ways to help learning, e.g. drama, animation, demonstration
1.2   provision of realistic experiences, e.g. sounds, places, events
1.3   the medium's realism has a strong impact on attitudes, appreciations, motivations
1.4   personalization of teachers
1.5   breaks the tedium of print
      (See Table 4.2 for a finer subdivision of 1.1 to 1.5)
1.6   literacy is not essential

2 Print over **Audio-visual (broadcast or recorded)**
2.1   random access at the student's own pace helps the study of
      • data in quantity, e.g. glossary, study guide
      • fine detail, e.g. equations, photos
2.2   student can browse and select more easily
2.3   print can carry more information
2.4   print is adequate to cover most of syllabus
2.5   easier teacher access/control
2.6   production skills are adequately resourced
      (See Table 4.3 for more detail on 2.1 to 2.6)
2.7   reception is not affected by power outages
2.8   family does not dispute access

3 Broadcast A/V over **Print or A/V recording**
3.1   cheaper for large audiences
3.2   study pacing (obliged by broadcast schedule)
3.3   sense of importance
3.4   sense of community
3.5   sense of immediacy
3.6   non-stop is good for presenting an overview
3.7   recruitment of students
3.8   public/academic exposure
3.9   national resource
3.10 top experts agree to appear

4 Print or A/V recording over **Broadcast A/V**
4.1   student can study when prepared and alert
4.2   student can stop and reflect, annotate notes, hence the medium can carry greater detail
4.3   student chooses repeats
4.4   lessons can have variable length
4.5   lesson can be subdivided into digestible segments, with interspersed activities
4.6   A/V recording is better for group discussion
4.7   frequency of lessons can be varied
4.8   can carry socially sensitive material
4.9   entertainment industry hogs broadcasts

(continued ...)

Table 4.1 Continued

5 TV/video over Radio/audio recording
5.1 more compelling, in general
5.2 more interesting/glamorous to produce
5.3 engages more than one sense (vision and hearing)

6 Radio/audio recording over TV/video
6.1 student access to (cheaper) equipment
6.2 cheaper to produce and deliver
6.3 evoked images are better!
6.4 translation is easier to implement
6.5 portability of equipment
6.6 can listen while driving

7 Video over Audio recording with notes/visuals
7.1 the field of view is predetermined
7.2 when moving pictures are needed
7.3 pictures and sound can be synchronized
7.4 video has picture-search facility

8 Audio recording with notes/visuals over Video
8.1 student choice of when to look where
8.2 cost effective when topic needs pictures but not moving pictures
8.3 adequate production skills easier to achieve

9 Audio recording with notes/visuals over Print
9.1 verbal commentary for diagrams is easier to learn from than margin notes for diagrams
9.2 students can revise more easily from the sparse notes (without replaying the audio)
9.3 (with or without notes) spoken words help pronunciation; pacing/intonation add meaning

or disk. So in section 1 we are comparing a *group of four audio-visual media* with a single medium, *print*.

In contrast, section 3 contains merits of *broadcast audio-visual* over *print or cassette/disk*. One example, 3.7, is the greater potential of broadcast audio-visual for recruiting students. That is, recruitment of students is *better* achieved by broadcast audio-visual media (TV or radio) than by recorded video/audio or print. This is because of the wider exposure that can be achieved by broadcasts. So, in section 3, we are comparing TV and radio with recorded video and audio and print.

Conversely, example 4.4 in section 4 is a desirable feature of both print and audio-visual recording which cannot be accommodated easily by broadcast: namely, *variable length*. (Broadcast schedules normally require standard duration of broadcast slots.)

Incidentally, concerning audio-visual recordings, I'm assuming these are not merely recorded copies of broadcast-style programmes but that their design has exploited the controllability of the cassette player or disk player. For example, a video recording might contain several self-contained segments, separated by captions that advise students to stop the video and carry out activities related to the previous segment. In addition, the recording (whether audio or video) might be accompanied by complementary notes for reference and for guiding interspersed activities. Even without complementary notes, the controllability of recordings confers them with many advantages over broadcasts – all the advantages listed in section 4.

Finally, section 2 contains an example, numbered 2.7, which illustrates the converse of the items in section 1, namely an advantage of print over audio-visual media: the study of print is not prevented (in daylight) by electrical power outages (interruptions of electrical power supply). This advantage of print would of course cease to apply if electrical power outages never occurred, as is almost the case in developed countries.

Such technological differences, as well as institutional and cultural differences, may exist for other comparative merits. For example, it is conceivable that the broadcasting time allocated to your institution is plentiful, so that you are not worried about wasting transmission time. In which case, *variable length* (item 4.4) may be feasible for your broadcasts (not just for your print and audio-visual recordings). Additionally, there may be good educational reasons for broadcasting *fillers* – short programmes to plug the gaps left by variable-length broadcast programmes (although this could be expensive due to the loss of economy of scale).

The first six sections involve the following five media, in various groupings

- print
- four audio-visual media: radio and TV (broadcast), audio and video (recording)

Concerning audio-visual recordings, as mentioned earlier, it is assumed that these are not merely recorded copies of broadcast-style programmes but that their design has exploited the controllability of the cassette or disk player. In other words, students can stop when they are so advised, or whenever they wish, and carry out some activities. The first six sections apply both to the case when audio-visual recordings stand alone and when there are complementary notes for reference and for guiding interspersed activities.

In categories 7, 8 and 9, Table 4.1 makes special mention of such notes for audio-recordings. This is because, unlike video, the notes can convert audio into a very different medium. This is accomplished by presenting the key ideas of the package in the notes, while the audio commentary guides students through these ideas. This composite medium is our sixth audio-visual medium, sometimes referred to as *audiovision*. It has met with considerable success in the UK Open University (Bates 1984: 205). For a description of some examples of the OU's use of audiovision, see Koumi (1994b).

Notice that the sections come in opposite pairs down to section 8. Section 1 is the opposite comparison to section 2, section 3 is the opposite comparison to section 4, and so on. Looking at sections 3 and 4, for example, in section 3 we see that for some purposes broadcast is better than non-broadcast, but for other purposes, in section 4, non-broadcast is better than broadcast.

Computer packages will be tackled in more detail later, but there are some preliminary points related to Table 4.1, as follows. Items 1.1 to 1.5 of Table 4.1 are reasons for including video whether it stands alone or as part of a computer package. (Table 4.2 goes into this in more detail.) Sections 7 and 8 compare video with *audiovision*. However, there is a connection with computer packages. Consider a section of a computer package that contains no video but has an audio-track and also graphics that change at specific points of the audio-track (audio-synchronized graphics). The effect is similar to *audiovision* (where an unlinked audio-recording guides students through a series of graphics). Not all the items in sections 7 and 8 apply to computer packages, mainly because in *audiovision* the visual changes are under the control of the student. However item 7.2 does apply as a reason for preferring video over audio-synchronized graphics. That is, if a particular topic in the package benefits from using moving pictures, then a video sequence is preferable to a sequence of audio-synchronized graphics. Item 8.2 also applies in reverse, as a reason for preferring audio-synchronized graphics over video (when pictures are needed but not *moving* pictures).

For each of the individual merits in Table 4.1, the reason why some media excel over others comes down to one or more of the seven media characteristics mentioned earlier

- symbol system
- access
- controllability
- student reactivity
- interactivity
- adaptivity
- networking

Here are some examples. Most of the merits in category 3 of Table 4.1 derive from the wider *access* afforded by broadcasts (e.g. 3.7, recruitment of students, and 3.9, national resource). Now consider category 2, advantages 2.1, studying fine detail and quantities of data, and 2.2, browsing and selecting. Students' greater *control* over the study of print empowers print with both advantages.

The same is true of most items in category 4 of Table 4.1, advantages of print or audio-visual recording over broadcasting. Most derive their advantage from the greater *control* that students (and/or teachers) have over the way they make use of the medium.

For some items, the advantage derives from more than one media characteristic. This is true of item 4.5, lesson can be subdivided into digestible segments, with interspersed activities. Subdividing into chunks is a consequence of teacher *control* over the length of chunks. Interspersed activities enable *student reactivity*.

Thus far, only six media have been compared. Still to be addressed are the varieties of computer-based media, which are potentially more *interactive* and *adaptive* and which can enable *networking*, although problems of *access* can arise. These comparisons will be discussed after a more detailed analysis of the *symbol systems* of audio-visual media: these systems empower them with distinctive techniques and teaching functions, which print and human teachers cannot match. Questions of *access* and *controllability* will also come in.

Distinctive attributes, techniques and teaching functions for each medium

The purpose of this section is to develop an inventory of the distinctive pedagogic attributes of our six audio-visual media (excluding computers). For each medium we try to determine the techniques and teaching functions that are better served by that medium than by the others. This section goes into finer detail than Table 4.1, which groups together several media and compares this group with another group of media – a *many-to-many* comparison. In contrast, this section embarks on a *one over all others* comparison – it takes each medium in turn and identifies those teaching functions for which it excels over all other media.

The inventory of attributes is intended to supply pedagogic criteria for optimal media selection. From this, course developers can match each topic and learning task with the medium whose characteristics would best benefit that topic/task.

Practices at the UK Open University will be used as a sounding board for the recommendations made in this chapter. Before 1995, the use of multimedia computer packages and the internet were not widespread in the courses of the UK Open University. Hence the practices used before that date are quoted below regarding the first six media.

In order to exploit each medium's presentational attributes fully, the UK OU tries to select that medium which best benefits the nature of each topic or learning task, subject to budgetary and resource constraints. Up until the early 1990s, this aim resulted in a media mix in which UK OU students spent:

- 5 per cent of their study-time working with video (including work on *broadcast notes*)
- 15 per cent working with audio or *audiovision*
- 80 per cent working with printed materials

These are average figures: there were some individual courses where video work constituted as much as 50 per cent of study-time.

Since 1995, the OU's use of multimedia computer packages and the internet has increased rapidly. More and more courses distribute CD-ROMs. By 1999, half of the courses offered computer conferencing and several courses presented their content totally online (via the internet).

However the traditional single media have not been abandoned. Over half of OU courses still distributed audio-recordings in the year 2000. (Although only one course still transmitted radio programmes that year.) As for video recordings, if anything, the proportion of student study-time has increased since 1995. However, trying to present precise figures poses difficulties, for the following reasons.

Many of the CD-ROMs include video and audio, but the time spent by students on these constituent media has not been estimated in general. Hence it is no longer possible to provide an overall estimate of student time spent on all the video offerings. Similarly for audio. Another difficulty with such estimates is that courses have become so diverse that it would be very misleading to quote an *average* breakdown of student time spent on different media.

Returning to our first six media (excluding computer packages and computer mediation), the inventory below is an approximation of UK OU practice, although the OU does not work to an explicit *formula* like this.

Television and video

Table 0.1, in Part I of this book, expands on the techniques and teaching functions that were thought by the UK OU to exploit the distinctive presentational attributes of TV. For convenience, Table 0.1 is reproduced here as Table 4.2.

This array of techniques and teaching functions enable a wide range of learning outcomes. These outcomes will be discussed in terms of the two-dimensional matrix of cognitive outcomes in Figure 4.1. This proposes a taxonomy of six cognitive processes, each of which can be applied to four knowledge dimensions. For example, a learning outcome can be classified as (say) type 4/C: *Analyse* some *procedural knowledge*. A specific example of this type, in the subject of metalwork, could be: 'Differentiate between welding and soldering'. Hence the taxonomy involves a total of $4 \times 6 = 24$ main types of learning outcome.

The full model has several subheadings under each of the cognitive processes and each of the knowledge dimensions. Further elaboration can be found in Appendix A2.1.

Categories of cognitive learning outcomes in bold font in Figure 4.1 can be achieved with non-stop viewing of self-standing video (no supplementary print). Namely, viewers can be enabled to remember and understand all four knowledge dimensions: facts, concepts, procedures and metacognitions (e.g. learning strategies, self-knowledge).

The categories in the table that are not in bold font indicate the kind of learning that cannot easily be achieved through non-stop viewing of video. That is, non-stop video is not an appropriate means of achieving the four highest level cognitive processes, *apply, analyse, evaluate, create* (although all of these are possible to some extent, especially *applying*). Moreover, even for the learning outcomes that are easily achieved, non-stop video is more suitable for providing overviews of the four knowledge dimensions rather than fine detail.

Table 4.2   Added value video techniques and teaching functions

1 Distinctive ways to assist LEARNING and (item 9) SKILLS development
1 **composite pictures**, e.g. split screen, S/I
2 **animated diagrams** exploring processes
3 **visual metaphor/symbolism/analogy**
4 **modelling** a process by a simplification
5 **illustrating** concepts with real examples
6 **condensing time** by editing real life
7 **juxtaposition** of contrasting situations
8 **narrative strength** of TV's rich symbol system
9 **demonstration** of skills by an expert
(e.g. craft, physical, reasoning, social, verbal)

2 Providing (vicarious) EXPERIENCES by showing otherwise inaccessible:
1 **dynamic** pictorial change or movement
2 **places**, e.g. dangerous/overseas locations
3 **viewpoints**, e.g. aerial, big close-up
4 **technical** processes or equipment
5 **3D** objects, using movement or juxtaposition
6 **slow/fast** motion
7 **people/animals** interacting, real or drama
8 **one-off** or rare events (include archive film)
9 **chronological** sequence and duration
10 **resource-material** for viewers to analyze
11 **staged events**, e.g. complex experiments, dramatized enactments

	3 NURTURING (motivations, feelings)
determination, motivation, activation	1 **stimulate** appetite to learn, e.g. by revealing the fascination of the subject
	2 **galvanize/spur into action**, provoke viewers to get up and do things
	3 **motivate use of a strategy** by showing its success, e.g. exam techniques
appreciations, feelings, attitudes	4 **alleviate isolation** of the distant learner by showing the teacher or fellow students
	5 **change attitudes**, appreciations, engender empathy for people
	6 **reassure**, encourage self-confidence
	7 **authenticate academic abstractions** by showing their use in solving real-life problems

Note however that *remembering* and *understanding* an *overview* of a knowledge topic is a useful (and sometimes even an essential) precursor of higher level processing of details. The reverse can also be true – an overview can provide a useful *consolidation* after a learner has undertaken concentrated study of detailed material, but has been left with a fragile grasp of the big picture. Whether or not an overview is better studied before or after studying details depends on the learning task and the individual learner.

Cognitive processes	Knowledge dimensions			
	A. Facts	B. Concepts	C. Procedures	D. Metacognitions
1. Remember				
2. Understand				
3. Apply				
4. Analyze				
5. Evaluate				
6. Create				

Figure 4.1 Anderson and Krathwohl (eds) (2001) revision of Bloom's Taxonomy. The full model has several subheadings under each of the cognitive processes and each of the knowledge dimensions. Further elaboration can be found in Appendix A2.1.

A caveat

For television and video, and indeed for all media, we assume that production resources and staff expertise are adequate to get the best out of each medium. However the judgement of adequacy varies between different institutions. For example, as has been mentioned, a UK OU TV producer's yearly load was between 6 and 8 half hour programmes. Koumi and Hung (1995) point out that this compares with more than 12 at the Indira Gandhi National OU in India and the Sukhotai Thammathirat OU in Thailand, more than 80 at the Chinese Radio and TV University and about 100 at Taiwan's Open University.

Assuming that we do have the resources to get the best out of each medium, there are many circumstances and learning tasks in which media other than TV excel, as follows.

Print

Despite the wide variety of teaching functions for which TV and video is used (above), the UK OU believes that print is adequate for most OU study. The views of most distance teaching institutions are similar. Learning tasks for which print is probably more suitable than other media are

- for the presentation of precise, factually accurate information (Bates and Poole 2003: 175)
- when students need to study information in quantity, e.g. glossary, study guide (which is a crucial function for print)
- concentrated study at an individual pace for analysing fine detail, e.g. equations, diagrams, complex concepts, closely reasoned argument – and further when students are required to evaluate or create such material

➜   In contrast, as noted earlier, non-stop video is more suitable for providing overviews rather than fine detail and for enabling lower level cognitive processes such as *remembering*, *understanding* and, to some extent, *applying*.

- where the student benefits from random access in order to skim and select (e.g. when students revise for an exam they sometimes need to search their printed booklets for scattered information on a particular point)
- text and graphics can carry more information per megabyte than audio or video
- print is adequate to cover most of the syllabus
- substitute for audio-visual media whenever audio-visual production skills and equipment are inadequately resourced (even in cases where video might have superior pedagogic potential)

Occasionally, a learning task that appears at first sight to need video is better presented in print. For example, a series of stills (photographs) in text can substitute for a video animation. Sometimes this is more effective – when the changes at each stage are complicated and need individually paced contemplation, thus encouraging students to visualize the in-between images for themselves.

Returning to the cognitive taxonomy, Figure 4.1, what learning tasks can the print medium enable students to achieve?

An invitation to reflect on learning outcomes that the print medium can enable

First, the four knowledge dimensions, A, B, C, D – can all four be achieved? Think about this before reading on.

My view: it's difficult to generalize, but my feeling is that print may not be as good as video for dimension B, abstract concepts (see Table 4.1, item 1.5) and C, procedures (skills) (see Table 4.1, item 1.9).

Now for cognitive processes: can print do better than video or worse? Again, think about this before reading on.

My view: 'apply knowledge' (3) is better achieved through print, due to reflection-time. The same holds for 'analyse' (4) and 'evaluate' (5).

What about 'create' (6)?

My view: the ability to create may be severely limited by the fact that we have a one-way medium. The potential of interactive, dialogic teaching and learning is examined later in this chapter.

Recorded video (usually with supplementary notes), designed to be viewed in short segments

The contrast was made above between the suitability of print for concentrated study and of non-stop video or TV for providing overviews and lower level processing of knowledge. There are also learning tasks that are intermediate between *concentrated study* and *overview*, for example, *tasks that need concentrated study but flexible access to dynamic visual material.*

Materials requiring such tasks used to be distributed by the UK OU on video cassettes, or broadcast in the early hours, for students to record, with supplementary notes distributed in advance.

These videos are not intended to be viewed non-stop – they are deliberately designed to exploit the stop–start facility of the video player, incorporating student activities during the stops. To this end, the videos include captions every few minutes that ask the viewer to stop the tape and carry out an activity described in the supplementary notes. For example, the caption could read

2nd Video Stop. Carry out the activities in section 2 of your Video Notes.

The videos are indexed, for example, with scrolling numbers in top right of screen showing the video's duration in minutes and seconds. This allows the video notes to reference segments of the video. For example, the notes in section 2 might read:

Section 2. Laboratory techniques in segment 2 of the video (video index 05.05–11.40)
• Activity A for Tape Stop 2. Penicillin is a microbial (fungal) product that inhibits the growth of some bacteria. However, penicillin does not affect fully mature bacterial cells. Bearing this in mind, recall the film report of Fleming's discovery (video index 07.05–08.47) and discuss what Fleming claimed he had observed.
• Activity B for Tape Stop 2. At the beginning of the video segment, Dr Dring inserted the necks of tubes into a flame before transferring material from one to the other. He said he wanted to prevent contamination. Can you think of TWO ways in which this procedure prevents contamination?

An Appendix in the video notes would include 'model answers' for these activities.

The proportion of UK OU video that was designed in this form had been increasing steadily, reaching 30 per cent by 1994, and still rising in 2000. (After about 2002, the Open University moved away from long-form narrative video to using short clips, termed *video assets*, inside digital multimedia packages. This interactive medium has largely replaced the video-print package and is covered in Chapter 8.)

The teaching functions of video and TV are as in Table 4.2, but greater detail can be tackled with recorded video plus notes than with TV or self-standing video. Crooks and Kirkwood (1988) point to three areas for which recorded video is more effective than broadcast television, resulting from the facility to search, pause, stop, rewind and replay:

1 providing vicarious experiences
2 imparting visually or conceptually dense information
3 triggering reflection or group discussion

Whereas all three areas are valid, there is a problem for area 2. In truth, the visual and conceptual density could not be increased very much, because video is a time-based medium, and this fact restricts the visual density and pace that viewers can comfortably process, even when the video segments between stops are short.

Incidentally, the average duration of each UK OU video is 30 minutes but students have to spend about 2½ hours studying the video as guided by its *notes*. Broadcast TV programmes and self-standing videos (intended to be viewed once, without stopping) also have *broadcast notes* but these typically add only 20 to 30 minutes to the 25-minute viewing time.

A second version of the print–video package

There are two distinct versions of the above print–video package. One is *video-led*, in which the video does most of the teaching but where the supplementary print enables additional reflection and practice by the learner. This is the type illustrated above.

An alternative is a *print-led* package, where all the study guidance is in print, relating to successive short segments of the video recording. For example, a teacher-training package might be in this style, with the video-clips being pure *actuality* (recording of actual, unrehearsed behaviour, such as video observation of classroom activity), without commentary on the sound-track. This comes under teaching function 2.10 of Table 4.2, *resource material for the viewer to analyse*. The printed material would contain pedagogic rationale for the classroom methodology and would suggest reflective activities related to the observational video. For example:

> Continue viewing the video from index 10:56 until 13:59. There is a caption at this point that tells you to stop and carry out the activities in this section (write your comments below each question):
>
> The teacher divided the mixed ability group of 4 pupils into two pairs of 2 each. If this is done randomly, one of the pairs might have both pupils of high ability and the other pair might have both pupils of low ability. Is this appropriate for the tasks that the teacher assigned, or should she ensure that each pair is mixed ability? …

Learning outcomes for the above three types of video, self-standing, video-led, print-led

Having introduced three types of video, all with supplementary notes, we could think of each type as a *hybrid* medium or a *composite* medium. Hence the augmentation of learning that is afforded by the supplementary print has to be taken into account. With this in mind, let's return to the question of learning outcomes that can be achieved with the three types. First, a summary of the three types.

1. Self-standing video or TV (non-stop viewing)

A video that does all the teaching by itself (a type sometimes referred to as *long-form narrative*), without the support of printed material. However, if desired, some video notes could prepare students for the video and summarize it. And, most valuably: the notes could suggest post-viewing self-test questions.

2. Video-led print–video package

A package consisting of a *scripted* video plus printed video notes. All the teaching is done on the video by the commentary (with a few points elaborated in the notes).

The video is in sections, designed to exploit the stop–start facility of the video player. Between sections, viewers stop the video and answer the questions in the video notes. The notes supply answers, which may sometimes elaborate, giving extra information that is not contained in the video.

3. Print-led print–video package

Again, the video is in sections with interspersed questions. However, instead of scripted scenes, the video contains *actuality* (actual behaviour), such as the interactions between a teacher and students. There is no commentary on the video. All discussion of the contents of the video is carried out in the printed study guide, through question and answer.

Figure 4.2 summarizes the features of the three types of video package

Learning outcomes achievable through the three types of video package

Now that we have an idea what outcomes are achievable with the print medium, let's return to Figure 4.1 and consider how far the supplementary print has extended the possible learning outcomes of our three types of video.

For the first type, non-stop viewing of self-standing video, the supplementary notes could include post-viewing self-test questions, which could augment the

	1. SELF-STANDING VIDEO	2. VIDEO LED PRINT-VIDEO PACKAGE	3. PRINT LED PRINT-VIDEO PACKAGE
Commentary on video	YES – all teaching done on video	YES	NO
Video in sections, to be stopped and started	NO	YES	YES
Print suggests pre-video and post-video activities	YES	YES	YES
Print suggests activities related to the video content	Not usually	YES	YES
Print contains all the analysis of the video content	NO	NO	YES

Figure 4.2 Checklist for the three types of video package

range of teaching functions to include the third and fourth cognitive processing levels of Figure 4.1, *apply* and *analyse*. However, the *knowledge* would still involve no fine detail. This is because it is difficult for learners to reflect on the knowledge since all of it would come from the non-stop, time-based video medium, not the print medium. (The notes can't easily add detail because they refer to a large amount of video content, e.g. half an hour.)

In the second type (video-led) because only *short* video segments are viewed, the *depth* of knowledge can be somewhat greater – finer detail and conceptually more dense. That's *without* the supplementary print. Now take that into account – the questions and answers in the print can extend the learning outcomes to the fifth cognitive process: *evaluate*.

For the third type (print-led) the video is observational, without commentary. So the teaching functions are a combination of the print functions above and the *experiential* functions in box 2 of Table 4.2. (Also item 9 of box 1.) The conceptual density may not be as great as type 2, because of the absence of simultaneous commentary to analyse what the video is showing. On the other hand, because learners concentrate on observing *behaviour*, they may achieve the basics of the final cognitive process, *create*.

Considering the above range of formats for video and the wide variety of suitable teaching functions in Table 4.2, it may seem surprising that only 5 per cent of UK OU students' study-time was served by television and video. In fact, if only pedagogic considerations were applied, the television and video provision could probably have been quadrupled. However, video production is expensive and the 5 per cent figure may have been the maximum enabled by budgetary and resource allocation judgements.

In addition to the competition from other media for this allocation, a large proportion of the OU budget goes to student support services and tutorial provision. This fact brings to the surface the issue of *human media*. While it is recognized that human mediation is essential for the quality of distance learning, an adequate treatment is beyond the scope of this book. The topic is addressed briefly in the final section of this chapter.

Warning regarding the limitations of one-way media

Don't be too ambitious. Cognitive processes 4, 5, 6 (analyse, evaluate, create) are very difficult to achieve with a one-way medium. You really need dialogue with a teacher who can *adapt* to the individual learner.

Audiovision

Other learning tasks that require close attention to detail but need verbal guidance and *static* visual material have been presented by the UK OU on *audiovision*. This is audio-cassette/disk guidance through specially designed visuals, such as notes or diagrams. The diagrams can be on a computer screen rather than on paper, as in a multimedia package supplied on CD-ROM (more on this later).

Here is a summary of teaching functions and learning tasks that audiovision can achieve distinctively well:

- for topics/audiences where attention might wander with audio alone: visual points of reference can anchor attention, help *active* listening;
- when audio needs visual mnemonics (memory aids), e.g. in learning tasks such as comparing numerical data or studying long lists of items or understanding a complex argument.

  Unlike print, the first sentence on *audio* has physically disappeared when the second sentence is spoken. Hence if the first sentence is difficult to remember, it needs to be supported by a visual reminder. Similarly, if several sentences describe items for comparison, a visual reference list will refresh listeners' memories of the earlier sentences. In all such cases, where auditory memory might be overloaded, *audiovision* is the solution – the visuals act as memory aids.

These two generic items, *visual points of reference to anchor attention* and *visual memory aids*, form the basis for widening the scope of audio. These are the reasons why audiovision can tackle many more teaching functions than audio alone. Some specific functions are the following:

- Informal guidance through a *step-by-step process* (e.g. a build-up to a complex concept or a summary of previous work) which is outlined by specially designed printed materials. The printed materials contain the key teaching points and the audio fleshes out these points.
- Talking students through practical procedures (e.g. home experiments, computer operation), so that hands and eyes are free for practical work.

- When students need to sense *teacher looking over their shoulder.* Visuals enhance the sense of personal tuition, as if the teacher were looking at the same visuals over the student's shoulder. There are many situations that benefit from this sense, e.g. students not accustomed to distance learning might feel isolated, or if the learning task particularly needs a sense of personal tuition. One example here is the *remedial tutorial.*
- The objects of study are visual resource materials, e.g. rock samples, supply and demand curves, architectural site plans, transcripts of law court cases, printed words to be studied in a literacy course.
- For interactive designs: visuals can express student activities in rigorous detail.
- Substitute for video when static pictures are sufficient: when the topic benefits from the use of pictures but does not need moving pictures.
- Substitute for video when the diagram is too large to be legible on TV (and when the diagram needs to be studied as a whole, so cannot be presented by panning the camera over successive parts of the diagram).
- Substitute for video for reasons of cost or staff expertise: adequate production facilities and staff expertise are more achievable for audiovision than for video.

The average study-time spent by UK OU students per 30 minute audio is 2½ hours. Over half of the 265 audio programmes studied by a UK OU graduate prior to 1995 were in the form of audiovision.

Audio recordings and radio

Finally, there are teaching functions that benefit from a purely radio or recorded audio presentation, without notes. (Note however that there are important differences between radio and recorded audio, with comparative advantages on both sides, as noted in sections 3 and 4 of Table 4.1.) The benefit over print derives from hearing the voice – the intonation, the phrasing, the pacing. Some appropriate uses of audio, without the need for notes, are as follows:

- experts' opinions
- personal experiences of interviewees
- human verbal interaction (real or dramatized)
- documentaries/recorded events (e.g. that illustrate abstract concepts with real-world examples), for listeners to analyse, evaluate, discuss
- informal study guidance (e.g. course introduction, remedial tutorial, exam advice), given by a personalized, sympathetic voice of a course tutor
- aural experiences and models of good practice: where the objects of study are the sounds themselves, e.g. music, language pronunciation, dramatic or poetic performance

Table 4.3   Summary of teaching functions and learning tasks, for media other than self-standing, non-stop video/TV or computer

Print

For presenting precise, factually accurate information (Bates and Poole 2003: 175)

When students need to study quantities of information (e.g. study guides – crucial)

Concentrated study at an individual pace for analysing fine detail, complex concepts or losely reasoned argument – and further when students are required to evaluate or create such material

Where the student benefits from random access in order to skim and select

Text and graphics can carry more information per megabyte than audio or video

Print is adequate to cover most of the syllabus

Also, print might substitute for video for reasons of cost or staff expertise

Video recordings with interspersed activities

Tasks that need concentrated study but flexible access to dynamic visual material (the range of teaching functions is the same as that for non-stop video or TV, in Table 4.2, but stop-start video enables a more detailed analysis than TV, especially when supplemented with notes). Also see Table 4.1, sections 3 and 4.

Audiovision

Informal guidance through a *step-by-step process*

Talking students through practical procedures

In situations that benefit from *teacher looking over the student's shoulder* (e.g. remedial tutorials)

The objects of study are visual resource materials

For topics/audiences where attention might wander with audio alone (visual points of reference anchor attention)

When audio needs added visuals to avoid memory overload

For detailed specification (in text) of student activities

Substitute for video when static pictures are sufficient

Substitute for video when the diagrams are too detailed to be legible on video

Also, audiovision might substitute for video for reasons of cost or staff expertise

Audio recordings and radio

Experts' opinions

Personal experiences of interviewees

Human verbal interaction (real or dramatized)

Documentaries/recorded events

Informal study guidance

Aural experiences and models of good practice (e.g. music studies, foreign language)

When multi-language versions are needed

illlterate audiences can be catered for

Errata, remedial tutorials, topical information: enabled by the speed of production (radio only)

- when multi-language versions are needed, language translations are easier than for video
- illiterate audiences can be catered for
- topical errata, remedial tutorials enabled by the speed of production and delivery (radio only)

Caveat

The summary in Table 4.3 concerns purely cognitive issues – *which learning tasks suit which medium?* These are questions for the teacher (the instructional designer). From the point of view of the learner, there are also issues of media preference. Which medium is preferred can depend on individual learning styles. In fact, even a single individual may learn better from video on some occasions than others. This is one good reason for a *multi-pronged attack*, that is, covering the same topic by several media, each medium contributing a distinctive emphasis. Driscoll (2000: 388) notes that

> multiple modes of representation have now received support as an instructional strategy from cognitive information-processing theory, educational semiotics, and biological theories, as well as from constructivism.

Symbol system, access, control, reactivity, interactivity, adaptivity

The *symbol system* of a medium refers to its presentational attributes, i.e. the types of symbols that the medium uses to communicate – text and/or moving pictures and/or sound, etc. For example, video can use both still and moving pictures, real-time or slow motion, real-life or diagrammatic, with synchronous commentary and sound effects, camera moves and zooms, big close-ups, shot transitions, visual effects, chronological sequencing and pacing (e.g. enabling the display of body language and the phrasing of speech), visual metaphor. Table 4.2 above concerns the exploitation of the *symbol system* of TV/video.

This section considers several further characteristics of media, other than their symbol systems. A second type of characteristic that is crucial in education is *access*. This is the extent to which students are in a position to use the medium for learning, including whether they possess

- the resources and costs involved in its use;
- the knowledge and skills necessary to use the medium effectively.

For example, most of the advantages in category 3 of Table 4.1 (broadcast over print, audio-visual recording) stem from the wider access afforded by broadcasts (e.g. 3.7, recruitment of students, and 3.9, national resource).

A third type of media characteristic is the degree of *student control* – how much influence can be exerted by students over the way they make use of the medium. Students' greater control over the study of print empowers print with the advantages in 2.1 of Table 4.1, studying fine detail and quantities of data, and 2.2, browsing and selecting.

Then again, most of the listed advantages of print or audio-visual recording over broadcasting (category 4 of Table 4.1) derive from the greater control that students (and/or teachers) have over the way they make use of the medium.

For some items in Table 4.1, the advantage derives from more than one media characteristic. This is true of item 4.5, *lesson can be subdivided into digestible segments, with interspersed activities*. Subdividing into chunks is a consequence of teacher *control* over the length of chunks. Interspersed activities enable a fourth type of characteristic, *student reactivity* – that is, opportunities provided by the medium for student activity (including mental activity), in response to a media presentation. It will be shown in Chapters 5 and 6 that, whereas audio-visual recordings enable such reactivity more explicitly than do broadcasts, there are *activating* techniques that can compensate for the inability to stop the broadcast.

This consideration leads to two further types of characteristics, *interactivity* and *adaptivity*. The term *interactivity* refers to the situation when an action by a student receives feedback from the medium. The term *adaptivity* refers to the ability of the medium to adapt its provision to suit an individual's needs. The six media considered so far appear to lack both of these capabilities (although when there are interspersed activities during a video or audio package, and answers are supplied, these answers do constitute a generalized feedback).

Two classes of media that have the potential to be both interactive and adaptive are those that utilize computers (our seventh and eighth media, *the computer package* and *computer-mediated collaboration*). Computers will not be covered in depth, but the major comparative features are included below.

Computer packages and multimedia

Tutorial programs

Just like video and audiovision, teaching packages on the computer can be in the form of tutorial programs. These provide graphical and textual information, test students' comprehension and supply feedback on their activities. However, the computer's storage and processing power provides the potential for more individualized learning: the material can be organized in a network structure, enabling learner choice of a variety of paths through the material.

Various elaborations of the basic model introduce the potential for more interactivity and adaptivity.

Tutorial simulation

By incorporating *simulation,* a computer package enables students to explore how processes change when parameters are varied. They can choose which parameters to change and by how much (Koumi and Daniels 1994). This constitutes a far greater degree of interactivity than is possible through print or stand-alone audio-visual media.

Interactive multimedia (e.g. using CD-ROM)

There is also the advantage of a multimedia package all on one machine. Using CD-ROM or through the internet, extended segments of good-quality audio and video can be incorporated into computer packages. Hence, learners do not have to switch machines whenever the medium switches. Hawkridge (1993: ch. 8), discussing such packages, notes that a limited number of intriguing multimedia programmes had been developed as early as 1993, for example, to aid language development.

Caveat

The capacity for *interactivity* in such multimedia packages does not necessarily imply capacity for *higher learning outcomes* than are afforded by audiovision. For example, if the visual materials of an audiovision package are printed on paper, learners have random access to study, analyse and compare large quantities of data. In Chapter 7 it will be shown how learners can compare eight diagrams on two facing pages. Such cross-referencing between eight diagrams' worth of information would not be possible on a multimedia package – that much information would be illegible on a single screen. Hence audiovision is better suited than interactive multimedia for tasks that require comparison and analysis of large quantities of information.

Nevertheless, the above three types of computer package are all capable of good *interactivity*. As for *adaptivity*, this is supposed to be a central feature of an elaboration of the above tutorial programs and tutorial simulations.

Intelligent tutoring systems

Intelligent tutoring systems derive from the field of artificial intelligence. These attempt to *model* the students by monitoring their responses, i.e. to *infer what they know and don't know about the relevant domain* and hence to decide *which instructional action, if any, to take next* (Ohlsson 1991: 11).

Murray (1999) distinguishes several distinct ITS authoring systems that have been used to produce learning packages. He notes that they fall into two broad categories, *pedagogy-oriented* and *performance-oriented* (elaborations of tutorial programs and tutorial simulations, respectively). Pedagogy-oriented systems are based on a traditional curriculum (or courseware) metaphor and focus on how to sequence and teach relatively canned content. Performance-oriented systems embody a *learning environments* instructional metaphor and are geared toward device simulation (e.g. virtual laboratories). Some recent systems combine aspects of both perspectives: they focus on providing rich learning environments in which students can learn skills by practising them and receiving feedback.

In the latter category, diagnostic engines have been developed that can match the learner's performance with a model that they develop of the subject matter. De Koning *et al.* (2000) developed an experimental version of a *general diagnostic engine* to represent and analyse the reasoning behaviour of learners. Specifically, their version was able to determine those reasoning steps that the learner cannot have applied correctly, given the observations of learner behaviour. The results of the diagnosis were used to focus the dialogue with the student on those topics that correspond to erroneous behaviour. By focusing on behaviour errors in a systematic way, the learner's ability to self-repair was stimulated.

Multimedia intelligent tutoring system

If multiple media are incorporated into ITS, we get a *multimedia intelligent tutoring system*, which would appear to offer the best of all worlds, although development time would be very high.

 Chapter 8 gives a comprehensive framework of design guidelines for multimedia packages.

Next, something that is truly *adaptive*, because it involves communication with people, which automatically incorporates the seventh media characteristic, *networking*.

Telecommunications and computer-supported collaboration

Collaborative learning is potentially very powerful. Brown *et al.* (1989: 19) note that

> Groups are not just a convenient way to accumulate the individual knowledge of their members. They give rise synergistically to insights and solutions that would not come about without them.

The authors do not suggest a mechanism for this effect. However, it is intuitively plausible that synergistically generated insights would be triggered by hearing the differing slants of others' thoughts and hence being stimulated to think *laterally*.

Computers can facilitate such communication with various types of computer conferencing.

Visually enhanced telephone conferencing

Audiographic conferencing involves a telephone conference unit in each site plus a computer with an electronic tablet. This allows the teacher and/or student to draw diagrams that appear simultaneously on all computer screens in the centrally connected network.

The computer can also offer simulations or micro-worlds within which the collaborative activity is undertaken. This can be combined with videoconferencing, which includes a video camera in order that collaborators can see each other. The camera can facilitate collaborative problem-solving by adding non-verbal signals such as facial expression and gesture.

In the above cases, participants of the conference are online and the communication is *synchronous*, that is, each participant receives the message at the same time as it is being transmitted.

Conferencing with text messages

A text version of online conferencing is the *chat room* whereby participants type their messages and the messages appear one below the other on screen. This communication is (almost) synchronous.

A widespread method is *asynchronous* conferencing through *electronic bulletin boards*. This is an enhanced web-based version of emailing, supported by software such as WebCT, FirstClass, Blackboard and EBBS (Stratford 1998). The text messages are sent to a website, in which the sender's ID is positioned on screen in a hierarchical tree structure to indicate the succession of messages in the discussion thread. Each message can be opened by clicking on the sender's ID. A participant can type a response to any message or can start a new discussion thread. Participants can also attach documents to their messages.

Henri and Rigault (1996) contend that asynchronous computer mediated conferencing (CMC) provides more intense communication than face-to-face, because CMC frees participants from the struggle for *the right of audience* (p. 10). This enables them to react to the content, and not the author, with more reflective communications.

Bullen (1998) makes a similar point, that CMC has a democratizing effect, compared to face-to-face discussion, because it prevents domination by verbose speakers, also that asynchronicity provides time for composing thoughtful rather than spontaneous responses.

Stacey (1999) found various kinds of socioaffective support in a collaborative group. She also found that the sense of group responsibility was a motivator: individuals do not want to let down their collaborators, so they give of their best.

The above socioaffective benefits of asynchronous conferencing are likely to result in cognitive benefits. For example, a worry about precise meaning or implication of a concept might be insufficient to stimulate further reflection. But when the issue arises in a discussion, one is spurred to address it, that is, to spend time clarifying the concept in one's mind. This claim is made from the author's personal experience. But there are many more direct cognitive benefits. Various researchers have found significant, *direct* cognitive benefits of *collaborative learning* between students through the strategies in Figure 4.3 for *co-construction of knowledge*. Also in Figure 4.3 (at the bottom) are recommendations by other researchers for tutors' strategies of *dialogic teaching* that significantly enhance learning. Central to these strategies are the theories of Vygotsky (1962, 1978), summarized in the centre of Figure 4.3.

Co-construction of knowledge through collaboration
- asking and answering questions for clarification of ideas [A, B, E, H]
- obtaining feedback [A]
- exchanging ideas [A, B, I]
- sharing diverse perspectives [A]
- making and judging inferences [E, H]
- discovering/exploring dissonance [B]
- negotiating compromise/synthesis [A, B]
- personal cognitive adjustment towards the group consensus [A, H]
- group responsibility is an individual motivator [A]

Dialogic Teaching

- *Vygotsky's theories* [C, D]
    - Zone of Proximal Development (ZPD) = the region between what (knowledge construction) the learner can achieve unaided and what the learner can achieve with the help of a teacher or more knowledgeable peer
    - Theory of Social Cognition: we construct knowledge by internalising conversation and social interaction (e.g. in a collaborative group of peers, **as above**)
- *Roles of CMC tutors*
    - encouragement, reinforcement [E, F, G, H]
    - validation and support [E, F, G]
    - prompting and probing [G, H]
    - clarification [E]
    - redirecion [E]
    - summaries [E]
    - respond selectively to students comments, but when asked for feedback, respond quickly (*just-in-time tutor help*) [A, E, F]
    - regular (not clustered) responses encourage activity [E, F]
    - challenge assumptions, diagnose misconceptions [J]

Figure 4.3 Learning by interaction with teachers and peers (A. Stacey (1999); B. Gunawardena *et al.* (1997); C. Vygotsky (1962: 103); D. Vygotsky (1978); E. Bullen (1998); F. Tagg *et al.* (1995); G. Andrusyszyn *et al.* (1997); H. Henri *et al.* (1996); I. Kanuka *et al.* (1998); J. Anderson *et al.* (2001))

Allocating different treatments, teaching functions, learning tasks, topics to different media

Consider first the six media discussed in depth – print, TV, radio, video, audio, audiovision. The ten categories of broad comparisons (Table 4.1) and the inventory of media-distinctive techniques and teaching functions (Tables 4.2 and 4.3) are recommended as a basis for media selection and deployment. The strategy is elaborated in the next section.

Concerning computers, whenever a package incorporates an audio segment, the distinctive attributes of audio come into play. Similarly for video. In addition, the computer can offer more substantial individualized *control* and *interactivity*. It is also easier through the computer to *adapt* to students' individual needs by pre-empting their intellectual predicaments.

Of course computers have *access* problems. This is not only the question of access to equipment by the students. There is also the problem of access by teachers/producers to the enormously complex skills required to design successful multimedia intelligent tutoring packages. The required skills were apparently rare in the early 1990s (Hawkridge 1993: ch. 8). Even by 2000, the production process of such packages is like a *black hole* for resources, sucking an enormous amount of time and effort from the production team.

As for CMC, a lot of work is going on to identify designs that are conducive to collaborative learning and dialogic teaching. How far do CMC technologies actually live up to their promise? Do email and computer conferencing in fact promote active learner participation and interaction – and above all, learning? How must online conferences be structured and monitored to work well? Are they more useful with certain groups than with others?

Human media

Human tutors have been discussed above in relation to computer mediated communication. However, in general, there are many more mediating functions that can be served by human beings in a distance learning course. As noted earlier, none of the non-human media above can yet claim to be truly *adaptive*, as can human mediators – able to adjust their provision to suit an individual learner's needs.

A comprehensive treatment of student support (by humans) in distance learning is beyond the scope of this book. However, some brief headings are offered below, largely derived from a book by Rowntree, who notes (1990: 266–72) that learners studying at a distance may be in touch with tutors, mentors or other learners, by

- writing to one another
- telephone
- computer conferencing

- the exchange of audio-recordings
- face-to-face contact

Incidentally, these various means of communication are fruitfully thought of as *different media*. Certainly face-to-face conferencing, by speaking to one another, must have different attributes and affordances than asynchronous written conferencing.

The various roles for human mediators include

- counselling on learning and social issues
- remedial tuition
- face-to-face tutorials
- laboratory practical work
- feedback on learners' performance in assignments
- self-help groups of learners

Pedagogic criteria for media selection

There are many worthy media selection algorithms/schemes in the educational media literature. (For a survey, see Romiszowski 1988.) However, those that attempt to be exhaustive are invariably so complicated that they are too cumbersome. Another common problem (e.g. see Kemp 1985) is that the characteristics of media are described in terms that are too *broad* to inform the decision process adequately, such as

- Does the topic require a three-dimensional presentation?
- Is colour necessary?
- Is movement necessary?

One reason for this lack of depth is that the models attempt to predict all possible questions that all course/topic authors might ask. This results in a great many questions at the global level, but the model makers rarely proceed to the finer levels of media characterization in which the micro-features of each medium are addressed.

Table 4.4 describes a three-stage scheme for resolving this dilemma, for each individual institution or even each course developer. This is the major purpose of this chapter.

A temptation to be avoided in the media selection procedure

The following points concentrate on the use of video. However, they can be easily adapted to any medium. Because video can be so powerful in achieving many types of educational objectives, there is a danger that *extra* course objectives will be invented to justify the use of video. On the whole this practice is not recommended. It is self-indulgent to use video for objectives that are only peripheral to the academic content. It is also expensive.

This practice of *inventing media-suitable objectives* happens quite frequently, for various reasons. One reason could be favouritism for video. Another reason might be that it has been decided to allocate eight video programmes to a course (through some less-than-objective criteria) and consequently the course development team have to justify that allocation to themselves and to others.

Table 4.4   Three-stage scheme for media selection

---

1 List Comparative Merits and Distinctive Teaching Functions

Consult a table of comparative merits and an inventory of media-distinctive teaching functions. The comparison table (Table 4.1) and the inventory of media-distinctive teaching functions (Tables 4.2 and 4.3) are offered as being of reasonable pedagogic depth. You may also want to include extra comparative merits and teaching functions, appropriate to your culture, institution and the skills and preferences in your course development team.

Additionally, concerning computer systems, take account of the interactivity that's possible with computer packages and the adaptivity of computer conferencing. (For additional reading on this see Laurillard (1993: chapters 6–10), Ohlsson (1991), Eisenstadt and Vincent 1998.)

Also take account of the adaptivity that can be achieved by other forms of human mediation (as summarized in the last section, following Rowntree, 1990).

2 Devise a procedure for media deployment based on your list (above)

Devise *your own* algorithm/procedure for media selection and deployment based on such a categorization of comparative media merits; that is, a categorization that is substantial enough to be of genuine pedagogic utility. Knowing your own course, the media selection process comes down to matching each topic/task with the medium whose characteristics would best benefit that topic. This is still very difficult to achieve, but since we are at the level of an individual course, the questions that need to be asked are few enough to be manageable.

Having managed this procedure, you might then need to modify your choices according to how much production capacity is available in each medium.

3 Fully exploit the potential of each medium

The above procedures will be ineffective if the potentials of your media are under-achieved. Hence, institutions need to exploit the medium maximally, by using expert producers with sufficient time and resources. Chapters 5 and 6 discuss principles of pedagogic screenwriting for video, Chapter 7 for audiovision and Chapter 8 for multimedia packages.

Even then, some students will not learn well from some media in some situations. Statistically, this dilutes differential media effects. Do not take this as evidence to reduce media variety. Rather think of those students that are helped: multiple media, addressing topics from distinctive angles, can accommodate individual differences in learning styles. Also, try to develop all students' ability to learn from a variety of media.

Caveat 1

The invention of extra objectives may not always be academically unethical. When access to media does result in decisions to modify the syllabus, this is not always a bad thing: the availability of video and the knowledge of what it can do might enable the inclusion of objectives that are genuinely important to the academic content of the course, but that would have been impossible without video. In this event, the course developers would broaden their horizons in an academically respectable/cogent direction.

The extent of this broadening depends to some extent on the creativity of the audio/video production staff and on the facilities they are afforded to exploit video's strengths. That is, the better the producers recognize the potential of video, the greater the variety of uses of video that will suggest themselves.

Caveat 2

Besides, maybe the courses are not yet chosen. At an early stage, why not choose subjects and courses which make evocative use of the available media. For example, in development, if lots of things need developing, they cannot all be tackled at the same time. So why not start with the ones that suit the available media?

Conclusion

It comes down to the course developers being honest with themselves on the following. Does every objective for each medium have genuine academic and pedagogic importance/cogency (even though the objective may have been an afterthought)? Or are some objectives no more than peripheral, having been invented purely to justify the use of the media? I will close this chapter with an example.

A chemistry course team is considering the use of video to take students on virtual field trips to industrial plants, in order to show how laboratory activity can be scaled up to industrial production. Apart from this potential use of video, the rest of the course deals with the theory of chemical reactions (mainly using the medium of print) and laboratory demonstration of the reactions (in occasional laboratory work by students, e.g. in weekend schools).

Is this a justified use of video or is the objective *understanding industrial scaling up* just an invention to justify the use of video? This depends on the views of the course team, as follows.

The ethical course team

The course team might always have been of the opinion, from the outset, that theory and laboratory work could never provide a rounded exposure to the subject and that knowledge of industrial production was also necessary. In this case, it would be academically respectable to use video to show industrial processes.

The unethical course team

However, suppose at the outset that the course team wanted to concentrate on theory and lab work because they judged that they could not do justice to the topic of industrial applications in such a short course. Let us say they even judged that the subject of industrial applications needed a whole course of its own. In this case, if they still chose to use video to present (say) an overview of industrial processes, they would be inventing objectives that were peripheral to the course they really believed in.

The course team that broadened its horizons

A third possibility is a course team that was initially intent on excluding industrial processes, but who grew convinced that their inclusion would add *essential* value to the course. And the reason for this conviction was its collective recognition of the potential of video to present industrial processes so realistically. So much so that the team decided that video could circumvent that feeling of being lost that some team members had themselves experienced on leaving university to work in industry.

Part III

Pedagogic screenwriting principles for video

Chapter 5

Screenwriting for video in educational multimedia

An overview of the pedagogic screenwriting principles

One fundamental principle of education is that teachers should endeavour to create an enduring fascination for the subject matter. If they succeed, then the job is half done: the more the students love the subject, the less help they need in their learning.

Most educators accept that video can impart such fascination. However, some believe that it cannot actually teach – that is, that it cannot achieve serious cognitive objectives, enabling viewers to learn concepts, principles, problem-solving strategies and helping them to think critically. But you cannot sustain students' fascination unless they achieve a really penetrating understanding of the subject. This chapter and the next concern how to structure the video learning experience to accomplish this.

Educational video producers and screenwriters are happiest if they can envisage their video provoking *eureka* experiences – viewers' eyes lighting up with delighted revelation as they suddenly grasp a difficult concept.

Introduction

In an effective video design, words and pictures need to be carefully interwoven, in order to create synergy between them, resulting in a whole that is greater than the sum of the two parts. This is why the title of this chapter uses the word *Screenwriting* instead of the standard *Scriptwriting* – because *script* suggests just the words, rather than the combination of words and pictures.

A treatment of pedagogic design principles is necessary in order to underpin the good intentions of Part I of this book – the catalogue of video techniques and teaching functions that exploit the strengths of video, enabling students to acquire robust cognitive structures, realistic experiences and desirable attitudes/appreciations. The video techniques will fail in these tasks if they are not implemented well, that is, with due attention to pedagogic effectiveness,

However, producers prefer to make programmes rather than enter into academic debates about the craft of screenwriting. Hence, until now, there has been no comprehensive practitioner-based framework for effective screenwriting of educational video. This chapter and the next offer such a framework. This attempts to formalize the main principles underlying practitioners' intuitively constructed programmes.

The main ideas of the screenwriting framework are in part (b) of Table 5.1. Part (a) of the table concerns preliminary considerations that interact with the elements in part (b). Briefly, *target audience* and *learning context* affect the style and depth of the screenwriting treatment, while *teaching intentions* underlie the whole story.

Table 5.1 (b) contains just one example for each of the 10 categories, but actually each category contains several design principles to choose from, depending on the storyline. The full expansion of the table will be given later, but here is a preview of some further design principles.

The example given in Table 5.1 (b) for category 2, signpost, illustrates the design principle *chapter heading* (what's coming next). Two other types of signpost are:

- *Focus* (what to look out for). Here's an example of a sentence of narration advising viewers what to look out for: 'In the next clip, concentrate on the arms of the spinning skater.'
- *Context/rationale* (why we are presenting the next item). For example, 'We are going to look at the sport of boxing because this illustrates what we want to investigate – the variety of arguments that people propose to justify the use of violence.'

The entry in Table 5.1 (b) for category 10, link, is the design principle that the content of each chapter of the video should be linked to the next chapter. Another kind of link is between the video content and other learning materials, such as printed booklets. For example, the designer needs to cross-check that the terminology is consistent between video and other learning materials. It is easy to make the mistake of introducing modified terminology during the many stages of the design process.

Further design principles are advocated later, in Table 5.3.

The provenance of the screenwriting framework

Existing literature

The literature on screenwriting for educational video is of limited value. The effectiveness of television or video as a medium of education has been frequently discussed, but most often from the point of view of completed programmes. Surveys of the research such as Bates (1988) and Greenfield (1984) demonstrate the power of video as a learning medium and also reveal various limitations depending on its intended usage.

However, the reported research studies rarely suggest explicit, practicable design features that could improve the pedagogic effectiveness of video. Instead,

Table 5.1 The pedagogic framework of narrative screenwriting principles (part (a) is expanded in Table 5.2 and part (b) in Table 5.3)

(a) How will the video be used?		*Examples*
By whom	**A. Target Audience**	Second year undergraduates
In what context	**B. Learning Context and complementary learning**	Supplementary video notes
For what purpose	**C. Teaching Intentions**	
	1 Cognitive Learning Outcomes	1. Argue a scientific theory
	2 Provision of Experiences	2. Take viewers on a virtual field trip
	3 Nurturing (motivations, feelings)	3. Influence attitudes
(b) Pedagogic screenwriting structure for each chapter		*Examples*
Make them want to know	**1. Hook** (capture and sustain attention)	Shock close-up of moist human brain. Narration: *This is a real human brain*
Tell them what you will do	**2. Signpost** (information about what's coming)	Scene: four monkeys eating. Narration: *let's concentrate on social behaviour*
Do it pedagogically	**3. Facilitate Attentive Viewing**	Presenter says: *helium in this balloon, carbon dioxide in this one. What will happen when I release the balloons?*
	4. Enable Individual Construction of Knowledge	e.g. don't blanket the shot with words – leave slack for contemplation
	5. Sensitize	e.g. timely occurrence of music
	6. Elucidate	e.g. uncluttered, simplifying graphics
	7. Texture the Story	e.g. vary mood, gravity
	8. Reinforce	e.g. repetition from a different angle
Tell them what you have done	**9. Consolidate/ Conclude**	e.g. summarize key features, helping viewers to stand back from the story
Connect it	**10. Link**	e.g. link each chapter to the next one

most recommendations have been at a philosophical macro-level. For example, three researchers, Salomon (1983), Bates (1987) and Laurillard (1991), separately came to similar conclusions, which can be encompassed as:

> Strong links should be made between the events portrayed and the ideas they represent.

At the other extreme, recommendations have dealt with individual minutiae, such as the presenter's 'direction of gaze' or 'the type of background visible behind the presenter' (Baggeley 1980; Lin and Cresswell 1989).

This is not to suggest that studies of macro-level design factors or of individual variables should be abandoned. However, if such studies are to be useful to practitioners, their methodology and recommendations need to be founded on a comprehensive framework for educational video design. Otherwise, they just float in a theoretical vacuum, swamped by the many other powerful design factors that must be included in a practicable framework.

The acknowledged pedagogic sophistication of the above researchers can provide a valuable backdrop to the skills of educational screenwriters but cannot supplant these practitioners' insights. This becomes clear when the researchers' recommendations are compared with the complexity of Table 5.3 – a collaborative accumulation of insights derived from decades of screenwriting.

The discordance between research designs and actual practice is represented even more starkly by *media comparison* research. Kozma (1991) cites 11 studies that compared a video program with its decomposed audio-only and vision-only presentations to determine the role of these two sources of information. Most of the studies found that the intact video programme resulted in more recall. This finding is not only trivial, it is also fruitless. Good media producers would rescript the words if denied the pictures and would use different pictures if denied the words. They might even refuse, on principle, to use an inappropriate medium, e.g. to present a highly visual topic with words alone.

To avoid such fruitless research, what is needed is a comprehensive theoretical framework for educational screenwriting, one that embraces both micro- and macro-level design principles. While this framework needs to concur with established learning theories, it must also derive from *practitioners* in order to ensure the practicability of the principles espoused.

To my knowledge, no micro-level framework has been attempted until now, with two exceptions. This author published an earlier version of the framework (Koumi 1991). Subsequently, Wim Westera (1999) published another screenwriting framework, which overlapped with the 1991 version to an extent. The framework here has benefited from Westera's paper. One of his micro-categories is *post-synthesis*, which essentially involves *consolidation*. This concept previously featured only in the title of category 9 of Table 5.3. It has now been included as a separate principle, 9b, consolidation. This is defined as a short sequence that integrates key features into an intact whole; for example, in a foreign-language video, the disparate elements of each sequence can be consolidated by being spoken in a single final paragraph.

A module in a series chaired by Parer (1993) consists of a handbook of tips and hints, complemented by a video compilation. The second half of the 16,000-word handbook consists of five readings, reproduced from various journals. The module is a useful introduction, but seeks to cover a great many topics in short space, including production techniques and formative evaluation.

Stuart DeLuca's (1991) book is good on ways of working, production procedures and techniques such as storyboarding. It does not address pedagogic design.

A book by Grant Eustace (1990) gives good advice on writing for corporate video, in a situation in which there is a separate writer, producer, director and maybe even a programme designer. However, the book concentrates on the words and is therefore weak on the synergy between words and pictures.

The pedigree of the framework: practitioners devised it

Fortunately, the opportunity and the necessity to develop a model of educational screenwriting arose at the BBC Open University Production Centre in 1982. That was the first year in which the British Council invited us to conduct our annual three-month EDTV Course, Television Production in Education and Development. This was delivered by a course team of BBC producers, with some input from OU academics. It catered mainly for overseas educational video producers and screenwriters, on scholarships awarded by international funding agencies.

We were thereby forced to stop and deliberate on the unwritten principles behind our intuitively constructed programmes. The original skeleton of our collective ideas has undergone several major revisions, the last of which adapted the ideas to *video in multimedia*. This was summarized in Table 5.1 and is expanded below in Table 5.2, Usage, and Table 5.3, Pedagogic screenwriting. Table 5.3 has an appendix dealing with video as an ingredient of a multimedia package.

→ This chapter and the next reproduce segments of screenplays (picture–word scripts) as illustrations of effective screenwriting principles. Due to copyright restrictions, it has not been possible to provide the corresponding video segments. However, this should not detract greatly from readers' appreciation of the principles, for the following reason. When making a detailed analysis of a segment of video, relating each word, pause and picture to the whole segment, it is often more helpful to study the printed screenplay rather than the time-based video. This is because the static, printed screenplay enables self-paced, measured reflection of the segment.

The framework in Tables 5.2 and 5.3 is based on screenwriting workshops and lectures, delivered by this author between 1982 and 2002. These were conducted

Table 5.2 Three usage dimensions

A. Target Audience

1 **Culture**

2 **Age**

3 **Previous experience/knowledge**

4 **Commitment of viewers**: eavesdroppers, students, students whose video learning is examined

5 **Facilities**, e.g. does learner have exclusive use of hardware that runs the package?

B. Learning Context and Complementary Learning

1 **Other media**
e.g. class teacher, print, audio-tapes, other students, other computer packages

2 **Pre-work, post-work**

3 **The package surrounding the video**

4 **Does the learner control how the package is run?**

C. Teaching intentions

1 **Cognitive Learning outcomes/objectives**
e.g. remember/understand facts, concepts, procedures, strategies, metacognitions

2 **Providing Experiences**
e.g. concretize, explore, demonstrate

3 **Nurturing (a) motivations, (b) feelings**
a) stimulate appetite to learn, galvanize into action, motivate use of a strategy
b) fascinate, alleviate isolation, change feelings/attitudes, build confidence, enhance relevance

Note

Specific examples of how the three dimensions of Table 5.2 interact with the screenplay will be given after an introductory discussion of Table 5.3.

The screenwriting framework in Table 5.3 includes a choice of several principles or techniques for each of the 10 categories. This is not intended as a prescription. The framework is meant to be used flexibly, rather than as a recipe. No chapter of a video need include all 46 techniques nor even all 10 main categories. For instance, it is counterproductive to *signpost* what's coming (category 2), if the next item is meant as a surprise.

Normally, it is appropriate to apply one or two techniques for each of the 10 categories, as befits the story and the screenwriter's style.

In any case, the word *chapter* is defined loosely as a *self-contained section*. This definition involves subjective judgement. One screenwriter's *section*, necessitating a *signpost* and a *conclusion*, may be another's *subsection*, which may only need a *link*.

Table 5.3 **A Pedagogic Screenwriting Framework** for each chapter of the content narrative

Make them want to know	**1. Hook** (capture attention and sustain it)	a Shock, surprise, delight b Fascinate, entertain/amuse, appetise, create suspense
Tell them what you will do	**2. Signpost**	a Set the scene/Introduce b Distant signpost: what is coming later c Chapter heading: what is next? d Focus: what to look out for e Context/rationale: why are we doing it?
Do it pedagogically	**3. Facilitate Attentive Viewing**	a Pose questions b Encourage prediction c Do not mesmerize (do not *over-absorb* the viewers)
	4. Enable Individual Construction of Knowledge	a Words not duplicating pictures b Concretize, activate existing knowledge c Do not obscure the geography d Do not blinker, disclose the context e Pause commentary for contemplation f Invent visual metaphors g Scaffold the construction of knowledge
	5. Sensitize (Facilitate receptive mindset)	a Seeding b Music style/occurrence by Design c Signal change of mood or topic d Consistent style e Conform to video grammar f Reassure, build confidence
	6. Elucidate	a Specify logical status b Vary tempo to indicate syntax c Do not overload d Restrict picture–word density e Moderate intellectual depth f Maximize (intellectual) clarity g Enhance legibility/audibility
	7. Texture the Story	a Vary the format b Non-linear/non-sequential c Vary gravity using lighter items
	8. Reinforce	a Repetition (from a different angle) b Re-exemplify

(continued ...)

Table 5.3 Continued

		c Compare/contrast d Denouement/dramatic climax e Synergy between words and pictures
Tell them what you have done	**9. CONSOLIDATE/CONCLUDE**	a Recapitulate b Consolidate/Summarize key features c Generalize d Chapter Ending
Connect it	**10. LINK**	a Content-Link between items b Story-Link/Pick-Up c Indicate assumed external knowledge d Integrate with complementary learning materials

Notes

This appendix to Table 5.3 applies to video in multimedia (not to self-standing video).

The pedagogic principles in Table 5.3 are intended to apply to each multimedia section or *chapter* that includes a video clip, i.e. a video clip together with related text and graphics that make up a self-contained section. So the principles are not meant to apply just to the video clip by itself, but rather to the whole section (or chapter) containing the video clip

But, there are two deviations from this idea, at opposite ends of a spectrum. First, when the video clip by itself forms the *chapter*. Second, when the multimedia chapter *disintegrates* because the learner has chosen to study its elements in the 'wrong' order. Here are the implications of these two deviations

1. If the video clip itself is self-standing as a *chapter*, the structuring principles also apply to the clip on its own. (Normally such a self-standing video clip would be quite long, e.g. over 3 minutes.) This is also the situation for broadcast TV programmes or videos that are self-standing (i.e. not contained within a multimedia package).
2. Suppose that a sequence of elements of the package comes with a recommended order of study – for example, the sequence might consist of some text, then a video clip then some graphics, then some concluding text. The author's intention is that the sequence, studied in that order, forms a self-standing coherent chapter of content. However, also suppose that the package allows the learner *total freedom of random access*. Then an adventurous learner might choose to experience the elements of the chapter in the *wrong* order. Hence, the narrative coherence of the sequence would disappear and there would no longer be a *chapter*. Nevertheless, the above structuring principles would help those learners who do follow the recommended order. Those more adventurous learners who stray from the recommended order might be the type of people who do not need as much structuring as the others. That would be just as well because their straying must have disrupted the intended narrative coherence.

An alternative characterization of these adventurous learners is to view them not as *disrupters* but rather as *constructors*. In this view, discussed by Gibson (1996: 19), the acceptable norm in future will be for multimedia authors to incorporate many different layers in a single work and to enable 'a wide variety of paths through (the material)', so that learners can piece together their own, idiosyncratic stories. In this view, the construction of these stories entails collaboration between the story-teller and the audience.

The design considerations for such multi-layered works are rather more complex than the framework proposed in Table 5.3, in that the diverse possible narrative structures of the viewers need to be borne in mind when devising the hyperlinks in the multimedia package. Nevertheless, the centrality of *narrative* remains. As Gibson notes 'when we seek to understand the meaning of an event, our most effective way of doing so is to place it within a context of related events, telling ourselves a narrative' (p. 8). Chapter 8 discusses multimedia techniques and design features whereby narrative coherence can be salvaged.

at several overseas educational media production centres and also at the BBC up until 1994, during the ten presentations of our EDTV course.

The development of the pedagogic screenwriting framework of Table 5.3 was grounded in

- our continuing experiences of producing videos for the OU and evaluating them
- our evaluations of UK Schools TV, both BBC and Channel 4
- our evaluations of course exercise videos produced by EDTV students

Whenever we judged that a segment of video was educationally effective, we re-examined the structural framework (Table 5.3) to discover whether it provided reasons for the effectiveness. Conversely, if a video segment was judged to be ineffective or counterproductive, we examined the framework to see if it identified what the video lacked.

The judgement that a particular video was effective or otherwise was not derived empirically but rather by consensus of expert witnesses – educational video producers and subject experts at the OU, all regarding themselves as educators. So the framework was built up and refined, over several revisions, from examining more and more educational videos and their screenplays and from analysing the judgements of expert witnesses.

Additional development of the framework was effected by action research, in the following sense. The teaching effectiveness of the framework was continually scrutinized – did EDTV students (trainee video producers and screenwriters) learn to make effective videos by following its principles? Through such scrutiny, principles that confused trainees or that failed to improve their productions were weeded out or refined.

Hence, the development of the framework progressed through a combination of action research and the judgements of expert witnesses. Some ten years into this development, the fourth version of the framework was published by this author (Koumi 1991).

The framework presented here is the result of two further revisions. These were again based on videos judged to be effective or otherwise and on the framework's success in developing the skills of trainee video producers. In addition, refinements were made in response to recent developments reported in the educational literature, regarding cognitivist and constructivist learning theories. Most of the refinements in these last two revisions were no longer made by consensus of expert witnesses, but rather, independently by this author.

Readers who wish to study the design principles of Table 5.3 without preamble should skip the next section and proceed to the subsequent main section, 'Illustrations of the screenwriting principles'.

The relationship of the framework to theories of learning and teaching

In addition to the grounding of the framework in videos judged to be effective by practitioners and to its refinement through action research, the framework is also consistent with reputable theories of learning and teaching.

A blend of structured exposition and constructivist learning opportunities

Most categories in Table 5.3 structure the learning experience for the learner. However, category 4 returns control to the learner. So does category 3 to some extent. In summary: in categories 3 and 4 the screenwriter *gets out of viewers' minds*, enabling them to function as independent learners, whereas the categories other than 3 and 4 involve the screenwriter getting *into* the viewer's mind. There is no actual contradiction. Both precepts are sympathetic, in the following sense. In the latter, the producer has to feel *with* the viewers, trying to predict what they are thinking and looking at on the screen. In the former, the producer has to feel *for* the viewers as thinking human beings who must not be led by the nose on a tight leash but should be given opportunities for independent thought. These opportunities have two purposes:

- to cater, in parallel, for individual differences
- to encourage and enable active/mindful viewing, and hence to avoid *mesmeric immersion* but instead to stimulate analytic viewing and *constructive* learning

Constructivist theories of learning

In recent years, the constructivist movement has had a strong influence on teachers of both children and adults. Roughly speaking, constructivism asserts that knowledge is not passively received but actively built up by the learner, who selects information and organizes it in a way that is individually meaningful. This results in a knowledge structure that is personal and unique in its details. However, as Driscoll (2000) notes, most would say that the knowledge structure captures the essence of common knowledge. A widely accepted modification of this position is *Social Constructivism* which asserts that knowledge is a product of social processes and not solely an individual construction – that robust understanding and knowledge are socially constructed through collaborative dialogue – that meaning is socially negotiated. For a fuller account of constructivism, see McCormick and Paechter (1999) and Driscoll (2000).

The constructivist conception implies that a classroom teacher should not attempt merely to impart information to a group of learners and expect understanding. Instead the teacher has to be aware of each learner's knowledge and learning strategies and then assist each learner in restructuring their knowledge (e.g. by asking clarifying and provocative questions). Additionally, the learning situation should include a social dimension, involving discourse between teacher and student and also between students.

A zealous adherence to this philosophy would appear to disqualify the use of one-way media such as educational video, because of the absence of dialogue. Moreover, the video usually seeks to impart a specific body of knowledge to a group of learners. The aspiration of the video producer is that more or less the *same* knowledge should be assimilated by all the learners.

In contrast, a constructivist would predict individual differences of interpretation of video sequences, depending on viewers' individual cognitive structures. Hoijer (1990) investigated this prediction. She found clear individual differences in comprehension and interpretation of TV programmes depending on viewers' perceptual, cognitive and emotional characteristics. Concerning the process of analysing verbal and visual discourse and attaching meaning to it, Hoijer concludes:

> ... it is a creative and constructive process whereby the viewer ... uses her earlier knowledge and experiences as they are represented in her cognitive structures. It is in the light of what the viewer already knows that he or she interprets television discourse.

It should be noted that Hoijer was investigating *informative television discourse* rather than instructional (educational) video. So her examples were probably more amenable to individually differing interpretations than a pedagogically structured video would be. In any case, we do not need to disqualify video on the above grounds, provided it is structured as recommended in our framework, as argued below.

From earlier remarks it can be seen that the framework amalgamates *structured exposition* with *constructivist learning opportunities and encouragement*. That is, it advocates a balance between the following aspects:

- opportunity and encouragement for students to construct their own, idiosyncratic knowledge (categories 3 and 4 of Table 5.3).
- structured, narrative exposition of knowledge (remaining eight categories of Table 5.3)

Bruner (1999) can be interpreted as supporting a balance between these positions. He accepts the constructivist position that the learner is 'an active, intentional being; (and that) our knowledge about the world and about each other gets constructed and negotiated with others'. However, he also recognizes that

> Nobody can sensibly ... argue that the accumulation of factual knowledge is trivial. And it would take a bigot to deny that we become the richer for recognizing the link between reliable knowledge from the past and what we learn in the present.

This reliable knowledge needs to be discovered by the learner. An efficient way of doing this is through the transmission of a structured exposition of the knowledge by an expert, for example, through the medium of instructional video.

Sherry (1996) notes that the information processing approach subscribes to the theory that:

> The teacher represents an abstract idea as a concrete image and then presents the image to the learner via a medium. The learner, in turn, perceives, decodes, and stores it.... . The learner then develops his own image and uses it to construct new knowledge, in context, based on his own prior knowledge and abilities.

Hence, the general philosophy of the screenwriting framework is a blend of constructivist and information processing approaches.

Merrill (2002a) also posits such a blend. In a synthesis of reputable instructional design theories, he expounds five *first principles of instruction*:

1   Set learners' real-world problems (of progressive complexity).
2   Activate learners' prior knowledge as a foundation for new knowledge.
3   Demonstrate new knowledge to learners (rather than telling them about what is to be learned).
4   Learners apply new knowledge to solving the problems.
5   Learners integrate new knowledge into everyday life.

Educational video has the potential to serve the second and third principles, activation and demonstration, and the screenwriting principles of Table 5.3 can realize this potential, as follows.

Merrill's third principle, *demonstrating new knowledge*, is served by the structured exposition that is the purpose of eight out of the ten categories of Table 5.3 (other than categories 3 and 4, as noted earlier).

Merrill's second principle, *activation of prior knowledge*, is served by several of the principles in Table 5.3. Principle 4b, concretize/activate existing knowledge, explicitly addresses activation. But four other principles also serve activation, 2a, set the scene, 3a, pose questions, 3b, encourage prediction, and 10c, indicate assumed external knowledge. All of these cases are elaborated in the next chapter.

Cennamo (1993), in reviewing literature regarding video learners' invested mental effort, would condone techniques that activate prior knowledge and hence reduce the effort of searching memory for that knowledge. She concluded that

> Expending effort for (searching memory for) related knowledge may result in a breakdown of comprehension … However when additional effort is devoted to the process of elaboration and creating meaning from the content, parallel increases in achievement scores may result.

Notice that her second sentence shows that Cennamo is yet another researcher who would recommend that the video design should include *constructivist learning opportunities*, which is the purpose of categories 3 and 4 of the pedagogic screenwriting principles of Table 5.3.

Fully fledged constructivist opportunities require time for reflection and/or dialogue. Yet little time is available while a video is running, unless a video cassette is stopped and started by viewers (see Chapter 4). But even with non-stop viewing, the video should be structured to permit viewers to engage in *some* constructivist learning (personal construction of knowledge). The result, as envisioned by Gibson (1996), is that the story becomes a collaboration between the story-teller and the audience.

Scaffolding

Merrill's third principle follows Van Merriënboer (2001) in that it also recommends *portrayal* of required skills. For example, showing learners a worked example of the problem to be solved. Such learner support is also included in Merrill's expansion of his first principle, where he recommends several ways to support learners' problem-solving – for example, as also recommended by Van Merriënboer (2001), setting simpler problems first or showing half the solution.

These techniques provide scaffolding for learners' own construction of knowledge. *Scaffolding* is a metaphor that is used by constructivist theorists to describe supporting learners to construct knowledge that is beyond their reach, withdrawing the support little by little as learners progress. This withdrawal is crucial and must be done judiciously so as to prevent long-term dependence on the part of the learner – the aim is for learners to become self-directed, independent performers in future encounters with tasks similar to the learned task. For more on scaffolding see McLoughlin *et al.* (2000), Van Merriënboer (2001) or Merrill (2002a).

This *scaffolding* aspect of Merrill's first and third principles is involved in the whole of category 4, which proposes encouragement and support for learners' construction of knowledge.

Structured exposition, teaching intentions, learning outcomes

Exposition, structured to resolve students intellectual predicaments

Returning to Bruner, some of his earlier work (1977) condones some more specific aspects of the framework. He advocates predisposing students towards learning (as in Table 5.3, category 1, hook), and structuring a body of knowledge so that it can be most readily grasped by the learner (the purpose of Table 5.3 as a whole).

Macmillan and Garrison (1994) have a particular view of structured exposition that includes the pedagogic strategy of trying to predict students' intellectual predicaments

> It is the intention of teaching acts to answer the questions that the (student) epistemologically ought to ask, given his or her intellectual predicaments with regard to the subject matter ... Our definition emphasizes the relation between student, teacher, and subject matter without centering the interaction on any one of them. The students need not actually ask the question. It is simply that given their epistemic state (for example, background knowledge) they ought to ask the question, and could. Here we will only be concerned with the fact that intentionality seems part of the 'essence' of teaching.

Predicting and answering the questions that students ought to ask is the intention of five out of the eleven categories of Table 5.3: signpost, elucidate, reinforce, consolidate/conclude, link.

Teaching intentions and learning outcomes

Incidentally, the concept of the *intentionality* of teaching also appears in Table 5.2 as the title of dimension C, *Teaching intentions*. This might seem to fly in the face of the swing in recent years from a teacher-centred to a thinking-learner-centred perspective. This was a necessary and laudable shift to counter the philosophy of the teacher being the font of all knowledge, with the student the passive recipient. One strategy that accords with this swing is, ironically, to specify what the learner should know and be able to do at the end of a teaching/learning session. This specification is phrased in terms of educational (or instructional) *outcomes* or *objectives*. The reason that this is ironic is that learning objectives are inherited from behaviourist theory, which does not concern itself with the thoughts of students but only with their behaviour.

Specifying learning outcomes is certainly a way of informing learners what they are expected to achieve, and hence is learner-centred. Nevertheless, the title of dimension C, *Teaching intentions*, is unashamedly teacher-centred. The reason for this is the necessity for us (teachers) to be honest with ourselves. When producing an educational video, the teacher who is producing the video has *teaching intentions*.

Hence, although *learning outcomes* are included in dimension C (as part 1), the starting points for these outcomes are the teacher's *intentions*; these intentions underpin what the video is meant to accomplish. Indeed, the word, *accomplish*, being an action word, is revealing. A teacher performs *actions* and implements *techniques* that are meant to help students learn. In the teaching/learning collaboration, the teacher *acts* first (or designs instruction first) and the student *learns* as a consequence. Admittedly, students learn lots of thing that are not intended by the teacher and many of these things are valuable. But we the teachers are charged with designing the learning experience. It is therefore intrinsic for teachers to talk first about what teachers intend and do in order that students can learn in reaction. In the words of Macmillan and Garrison (1994), as quoted earlier, 'intentionality seems part of the "essence" of teaching'.

Pratt (1997) would agree with this sentiment. He has found that teachers feel passionate in their statements of intent, which points towards an agenda, a sense of purpose, a commitment. As Pratt puts it (chapter 2)

> An instructional objective is a distant and microcosmic representation of an intent ... The behavioural straightjacket of objectives is not at all like the flexible and passionate statement of intent (that) educators express ... Intentions therefore are clearly more than the collection of one's objectives ... they are an enthusiastic statement of commitment.

Progressive disclosure of learning objectives

Another issue concerning learning objectives is the timing of their disclosure to the learners. Several other theorists have questioned the traditional practice of presenting learning objectives at the outset of the learning materials. Keller (1987) suggests that students can be overwhelmed by a detailed specification of performance requirements and evaluative criteria. He recommends progressive disclosure, or telling students what is expected of them as they are ready and able to understand the requirements. Reiser and Dick (1996), cited by Driscoll (2000: 61), suggest that students be given simpler, perhaps more general, statements of objectives to guide their learning.

With regard to educational video, the narrative technique involves progressive disclosure of objectives, so the above point applies particularly to long-form narrative video. This is because statement of precise objectives would prejudice the suspense that narrative tries to inject (and suspense is a good motivator for learning). In fact, even when objectives are disclosed, this is often done implicitly, in the form of signposts or rhetorical questions. (This technique is illustrated in the next but one section, with regard to a particular long-form narrative video.)

When should the developer specify learning objectives?

Of equal importance to the learner-centred issue is the teacher-centred question of when, during the development timeline, should the learning outcomes be specified? Anecdotally, most video producers experience difficulty in specifying objectives up front. When they do attempt this, they invariably find that they need to revise the objectives so that they match the content. This is because the design process involves several drafts as the storyline is developed and refined. The purpose of this process is to end up with a coherent narrative that has an effective pedagogic structure. This process involves many twists and turns as the storyline is developed, driven by the endeavour for pedagogic efficacy. This endeavour would be prejudiced if the designer attempted to adhere steadfastly to pre-specified objectives that could not be accommodated in a pedagogically coherent video structure. Hence the specification of learning objectives should be a multi-stage iterative process, whereby the story and the objectives are successively refined to correspond.

Merrill (2002b: 3) makes a similar point:

> Traditional ISD (Instructional Systems Design) advocates early specification of instructional objectives. The problem with this approach is that instructional objectives are abstract representations of the knowledge to be taught rather than the knowledge itself. Often the specification of the actual content is delayed until the development phase of ISD. Many designers have experienced the difficulty of writing meaningful objectives early in the design process. Often, after the development starts, the objectives written early in the process are abandoned or revised to more closely correspond with the content that is finally developed.

Narrative structuring of the subject matter

In addition to the above considerations, there is another reason why Table 5.3 advocates narrative structuring of the subject matter. This is consistent with the concept of Pedagogical Content Knowledge (PCK) – how teachers know and understand the subject matter in order to choose appropriate teaching strategies. Sigrun Gudmundsdottir (1995), citing many researchers, reports that experienced teachers who exhibit PCK do so through narrative techniques. Narrative seems an obvious choice for them as an organizing, interpretive structure to give meaning to knowledge, to transform knowing into telling.

A particular manifestation of narrative in Table 5.3 is the fact that the subdivision of the story into chapters is taken for granted. This is because such subdivision is a fundamental narrative technique. The result is positive. The subdivision into chapters facilitates the task of predicting learners' intellectual predicaments, by *subdividing that task*. In other words, the teacher–screenwriter can update his/her model of the learner at the end of each chapter, can reconsider learners' intellectual predicaments at several points (ends of chapters) and supply a consolidation (category 10) that resolves these predicaments.

As noted earlier, Gibson (1996) takes it for granted that learning material needs the coherence that derives from narrative structuring. Laurillard *et al.* (2000) put it as follows: 'Narrative provides a macro-structure, which creates global coherence, contributes to local coherence and aids recall through its network of causal links and signposting.'

Illustrations of the screenwriting principles

Chapter 6 covers all the 46 principles of Table 5.3 thoroughly. However, a taste of what is involved can be gleaned from the 12 principles that will be discussed in the present chapter in a specific context – namely as they apply mainly to a particular educational TV programme. This is a UK Open University programme, *Dominance and Subordinacy*, which was number 13 (of 16) in a second-level undergraduate course, Biology Brain and Behaviour. Ideally, this 24-minute programme should be available for your viewing before it is analysed. Unfortunately this was not possible due to copyright restrictions, so the shots that are analysed are given only in the form of a printed *screenplay*, that is, a printed storyboard describing the images and audio.

Table 5.4 Outline of the TV programme, Dominance and Subordinacy

Part 1. Library Film of Primates in the Wild (6 min)

(a) Introducing TV 13/14/15: Dominance/Infant care/Sexual behaviour

Social groups of primates: monkeys, apes, humans
Primate organization: single-male, multi-male, nuclear family
Competition, care of infants, mating

(b) Introducing TV 13 (this programme)

Competitive situations: food, sexual activity, shelter
Aggressive/submissive gestures
Dominance and subordinacy

Part 2. Shot in a research compound: rhesus in captivity (18 min)

Many illustrations of subordinacy behaviour (avoids injuries)
Establishment of dominance relationships
Defining and recognizing dominance
Dominance does not imply greatest number of victories
Determining dominance hierarchy/ranking
Hierarchy is not precisely linear: triangular relationships occur
Alpha animal (rank 1) is male in most species (but not in all)
Rank can be dependant on mother's rank
In adolescence, youngest daughter rises in rank above older sisters (mother
    defended her in infancy)
Reproduction depends not just on male rank but also on female preferences
Evolution: survival strategies include dominance/subordinacy behaviour

In a multimedia package the usual practice is to have short video segments, lasting from 1 to 3 minutes, so it might seem inappropriate to use a 24 minute programme as an illustration. However, the principles of Table 5.3 apply to short segments of the programme as well as to the programme as a whole – and it is such short segments that this chapter analyses.

The first pedagogic screenwriting category that will be illustrated comes under section 6 of Table 5.3, elucidate, that is, make the storyline clear. One of the elucidating techniques is 6b, vary tempo to indicate syntax (*syntax* refers to questions like, 'Is this a continuation of the last topic or is it a new topic?'). The technique concerns how to vary the tempo of the programme in order to make its syntax clear. For example, in Table 5.5, consider the pauses in the narration.

At the end of the narration for shot 1, there is a long pause lasting 3½ seconds, whereas after the picture changes to shot 2, there is a very short pause lasting only a ½ second. (Viewers probably do not register ½ sec as a pause. In any case, their attention is taken up by the change of shot. The 1 sec pause at the end of shot 2 may also not be registered as a pause.)

The reason for this uneven tempo is to help viewers to appreciate that shot 2 concerns a new topic. Specifically, the long pause in narration at the end of shot 1 allows viewers to finish assimilating the first topic, individual animals in laboratories, and to recognize that the topic has ended. If they are in any doubt that it has ended, the immediate narration after the change of picture *interrupts* any lingering thoughts about the previous topic. This interruption signals that a new topic is starting. (Viewers discover what the new topic is, namely, social group living, after a few words.)

The transition between shots 1 and 2 is in contrast to that between shots 3 and 4. Between shots 1 and 2, the topic changes. But from shot 2 to shot 3 the topic remains the same: both shots concern *social behaviour*. This continuation of topic is signalled by a different variability in the tempo. The pause in narration at the end of shot 2 is short (1 sec), whereas the pause after the picture changes to shot 3 is long (3 sec). This transition between shots 2 and 3 is precisely opposite to that between shots 1 and 2.

Table 5.5 Shots 1 to 3 of the TV programme, Dominance and Subordinacy

Picture	Narration
1. Chimp, hanging upside, down pressing buttons on a console	So far in this course, we've concentrated mostly on individual animals, often in contrived laboratory situations LONG PAUSE (3½ SECONDS)
2. Three gorillas, joined by a fourth	SHORT PAUSE (½ SEC) But many animals live for all of their lives in social groups SHORT PAUSE (1 SEC)
3. Four monkeys eating	LONG PAUSE (3 SECONDS) This is the part of the course where we concentrate on social behaviour

This time, the short pause at the end of shot 2 identifies shot 3 as a further illustration of shot 2's topic. The reason for this is: when a new shot starts very shortly after some commentary, viewers interpret the picture as illustrating that commentary. Moreover the long pause at the start of shot 3 reinforces this interpretation: the viewer recognizes that time is being allowed for contemplation of this further illustration of shot 2's topic. Table 5.6 summarizes the two contrasting tempo signals.

Incidentally, the appropriate duration of pauses in narration depends critically on how *busy* the pictures are. For example, a pause of 3 seconds may feel like only 1 second if there is a lot of movement in the picture (needing a lot of visual processing by the viewer).

An apocryphal story

One of our EDTV students made a TV programme about a motorway service station. During the last shot of a sequence showing different restaurants, his commentary said 'So there are many different places to eat.' Then, without pause, the picture changed to the interior of a washroom! The other students all laughed, telling him he had said that people ate in the washroom. He denied this, insisting that the commentary about eating was during the restaurant shot, not the washroom shot, and that his subsequent commentary (rather late into the washroom shot) was, 'And there are also public conveniences.' He was soon persuaded that his tempo had given the wrong signal.

Incidentally, he is now a good educational video producer. Maybe that is due to natural talent, but maybe there is a lesson here for trainers: people often learn from their mistakes, so they should be given the opportunity to make those mistakes, i.e. they should be encouraged to make their own decisions rather than being led by the nose. Of course, feedback and remediation then become necessary. In the above case, remedial advice came through the post mortem discussion between students and instructors. The consensus resolution was that the commentary 'So there are many different places to eat' should be positioned one shot earlier, at the end of the penultimate restaurant shot, giving viewers a few seconds, without commentary, to contemplate the final *place to eat*. Then the words 'And there are also public conveniences' should come at the end of that final restaurant shot, cutting to the washroom during or immediately after the word 'conveniences'.

Table 5.6 Summary of the *varying tempo* signals in shots 1, 2, 3

Shot 1	Words Long pause (3½ sec)	
Shot 2	Short pause (½ sec) Words Short pause (1 sec)	New topic
Shot 3	Long pause (3 sec) Words	Same topic as shot 2

Table 5.7 gives more detail regarding the signals given by varying the tempo, expressed by contrasting the techniques, *loose editing* versus *tight editing*.

Returning to the TV programme *Dominance and Subordinancy*, following shot 3, the next 30 seconds illustrate several screenwriting principles and techniques. The picture–word transcript is given in Table 5.8.

Shots 10 to 14 illustrate a combination of two *reinforcement* techniques: repetition and comparison, numbered 8a and 8c in Table 5.3.

When comparing two items, X and Y, it is not adequate to show them only once each (X–Y), because while the viewer is studying Y, the memory of X is fading. So the minimum necessary is to repeat X, i.e. to show X–Y–X, and better for balance: X–Y–X–Y. In shots 10 to 14 the items being compared were human and animal faces: and the sequence was

H–H–A–A–H–A–

Incidentally, shot 13, the human face which *aped* the ape, was meant as a joke to delight, and thereby to capture the viewer's attention: design principle 1a in Table 5.3.

In the same vein, the commentary just prior to the human face, 'The monkeys and the apes are our closest relatives', was purely to fascinate the viewer (1b of Table 5.3). That is, the sentence is not actually needed for the academic content of the story – it is purely a narrative device to captivate viewers, so that they remain interested in the rest of the story.

Table 5.7 The signals given by the 4 possible tempos

Outgoing commentary	Incoming commentary	Incoming topic same/new?
loose	tight	new topic (specified by the incoming commentary)
tight	loose	same as topic of outgoing words – and the loose incoming words allow time for viewers to contemplate the new shot in the context of the outgoing words. Note that these words may be *more than* tight – the final word may straddle the cut or even fall after it
loose	loose	same topic as outgoing picture
tight	tight	topic is related to the outgoing words but the new words may modify the topic or elaborate on it

Definition. A *loose outgoing shot* refers to a long pause after the commentary (or after the action) before the cut to a new shot; and a *loose incoming shot* is one with a long pause between the cut and the start of the commentary or action. Conversely, *tight editing* has short pauses.

Table 5.8 Shots 4 to 14 of Dominance and Subordinacy

Picture	Narration
Shots 4 to 9	
Various shots of primates i.e. of monkeys macaque	And on TV, we focus on primates, like these Japanese macaques. There are many different kinds of primates. First, there are the monkeys; these Japanese macaques are old-world
rhesus marmoset	monkeys – that is, monkeys from Asia and Africa; and so are these rhesus monkeys. Rather different are new world monkeys, like
and of apes gorillas, chimps	the marmosets from South America. The primates also include the apes, like these gorillas you saw earlier, and these chimps. And of course
10. Shots of human family, ending with a close-up of the **mother's** face and a final close-up of the **baby's face**	human beings are primates *pause*: which is one of the reasons why behavioural scientists are
11. Macaque face	so interested in primates. The monkeys
12. Chimp face	and the apes, are our closest relatives.
13. Human face (mimicking the head-movements of the previous animals)	[*pause*]
14. Gorilla face	[*pause*] Another source of scientific interest in primates is the wide variety of social
15. Long shot, troop of Japanese macaques	organizations among the various species

Usage

Before discussing further screenwriting principles from Table 5.3, it is time to return to Table 5.2 and consider *usage* parameters. These must be considered at the outset. The parameters in the three dimensions should all inform the screenwriting in a variety of ways.

Dimensions A and B, *target audience* and *learning context*, both affect the style and depth of the story. These issues will be addressed later. The parameters of dimension C, the *teaching intentions*, have a direct relationship to the screenplay. The cognitive learning outcomes, especially, must underlie the whole story. That is, the TV programme must attempt clear visualization/demonstration of the facts and processes that are specified as cognitive objectives. For example, the TV programme showed how an observer recognizes dominance and ascertains the dominance hierarchy (the ranks) (part 2 of TV outline, Table 5.4). The reason for demonstrating this process was that it was one of the cognitive objectives (b9 in Table 5.9) – ability to describe how an observer assesses ranks. Table 5.9 gives all the other specific values of the three usage dimensions with respect to the programme.

Table 5.9 Specifications (values) in the three Usage dimensions for the TV programme Dominance and Subordinacy

---

A. Target Audience Characteristics
Culture: British, mostly middle-class.
Age: Mostly 30 to 40, but some as old as 70.
Commitment: OU undergraduates studying the course, Biology, Brain and Behaviour.
Previous experience/knowledge: The present course is a 2nd level Science Course; so its students have passed the Science Foundation Course.
Facilities: Own colour television set (but not necessarily a video recorder).

B. Learning Context and Complementary Learning
The broadcast notes for TV 13 include a taxonomy of primates, as pre-work. The post-programme notes include a summary of the programme (about 1000 words), together with some alternative methods whereby certain behaviours can become established, concluding with a Self-Assessment Question which asks students to rank a group of animals in a dominance hierarchy, given data on winners of competitive encounters.

The text for the week's work covers a more general heading, *Aggression*. Students are advised to read some of this text before viewing TV 13.

TV programmes 14 and 15 complete a *mini-series*; TV 14 is on 'Infant Care in Primates' and TV 15 on 'Sex and Hormones in Primates'.

C. Teaching Intentions
Intended cognitive learning outcomes/objectives
Outcomes expressed initially as overall intentions and refined later during the production process:

a. Overall intended outcomes at the outset of the production	b. Final refined objectives once the storyline is well advanced
a1) Orient thinking away from individual animal behaviour towards social behaviour, particularly competition	b1) to b8). Understand the dominance phenomenon as follows: b1) a relationship between two animals (in which one invariably defers to the other) b2) the relationship avoids serious fights
a2 Distinguish between the terms • dominance • rank • dependent rank	b3) results in a linear hierarchy (ranking), with an alpha animal (rank 1) b4) non-linear 'triangular' relationships also occur b5) dependent rank (e.g. dependent on mother's rank) b6) mother supports daughters against older daughters, hence adult daughters are ranked in inverse order of age
a3) Describe a method by which an investigator could assess which of two animals was dominant over the other	b7) female preference (not just male rank) influences reproduction b8) reduces risk of injury to (intelligent) subordinates b9) Describe how an observer can assess ranks

Experiences provided
Observation of the behaviour that is described in text.
Nurturing feelings
Create fascination with the animal behaviour in the programme.

Note: The teaching intentions of the TV programme are supported by the related text (Item B of Table 5.9). Memorable TV images are expected to *concretize* the text. Conversely, the text is expected to evoke and anchor memories of TV images.

Caveat 1

The relationship between the objectives and the story is not one-directional. It was noted earlier that the specification of objectives should be a multi-stage iterative process: first decide on overall teaching intentions (overall instructional goals), then work on a pedagogically coherent story that meets these intentions, then refine the teaching intentions to develop more specific learning outcomes that match the story, then tweak the story to better meet the objectives, and so on.

Table 5.9 shows the initial and final versions of these learning outcomes. There were nine final objectives but notice that the initial teaching intentions made no reference to four of the final objectives, b2, b6, b7, b8. These emerged as the storyline was developed over several drafts (even including some final modifications made during video editing). In fact, the objective b9, mentioned earlier, ability to describe how an observer assesses ranks, was only specified in such precise terms after a good deal of story development – after the designers realized that a clear understanding of the phenomenon of dominance (the major teaching intention) could not be achieved without clearly demonstrating the method of identifying dominance (a3 in Table 5.9) and assessing ranks (b9).

Caveat 2

I mentioned another educational objective earlier, in a different context. The term, fascinate, appeared at the end of the previous section as a narrative screenwriting device (1b of Table 5.3). It also appears in dimension C of Table 5.2, being one of the possible educational objectives under the affective (nurturing) domain. Hence, the whole video programme might have as one of its objectives *to fascinate the viewer*. This is true of most educational videos, and it was particularly true for this *Dominance and Subordinacy* programme, in that the video images of animal behaviour were intended as a *fascinating* complement to the Open University course text on *Dominance and Subordinacy* (as noted in Table 5.9).

The following are some of the ways in which the specifications in Table 5.9 interact with the screenplay. We have already made a start on dimension C, educational objectives. So let's continue with this dimension. A good discipline when writing the outline of a TV programme (or of a video clip) is to take each teaching intention in turn and to justify the use of TV/video for meeting that intention. You need to ask, why is your TV/video treatment better suited than other media to achieve that intention? The answer, for each intention would involve one of the items of Table 4.2 in Chapter 4, added value video techniques and teaching functions.

For the experiential and cognitive intentions in Table 5.9, one reason that video is the best medium is that it gives students the experience of seeing the behaviour that is described in their text. This reason appears in Table 4.2 as function 2.7 (showing animals interacting).

Another reason why video is the preferred medium, for three of the cognitive objectives b3, b4 and b6, is that some carefully designed animations build up to a visual overview, enabling students to visualize the complex phenomena. This appears in Table 4.2 as function 1.2 (animated diagrams exploring processes).

For the nurturing intention in Table 5.9, to fascinate the viewer, the reason that video was thought to be the best medium is that the experience of seeing the animal behaviour is likely to fascinate viewers. This could be classed under function 3.1 of Table 4.2 (reveal the fascinations). However, good screenwriting always aims to fascinate the viewer.

Remember that, iteratively, the narrative was developed to match the final detailed objectives and vice versa. However, the detailed objectives were not revealed to students pre-broadcast. Instead the broadcast notes contained just two of the three 'overall objectives' that initiated the design process – a2 and a3 of Table 5.9. If the specific objectives, b1 to b9, had been revealed pre-broadcast that would have spoilt the story, in which these aspects of dominance and subordinacy were revealed in a fascinating narrative progression.

However, objective a1 of Table 5.9 and the detailed objectives b1 to b9 were disclosed implicitly during the progress of the TV narrative. This was accomplished in the form of narration that initiated the subsequent content, for example using signposts (Table 5.3, category 2) or posed questions (Table 5.3, category 3a) – as follows.

a1. Orient thinking away from individual towards social behaviour, particularly competition

Narration that implicitly discloses objective a1:

> This is the part of the course where we concentrate on social behaviour. And on TV, we focus on primates.

The subsequent segment (as noted in Table 5.4, part 1(a)) covers the following content:

- social groups of primates: monkeys, apes, humans
- primate organization: single-male, multi-male, nuclear family
- competition, care of infants, mating

Following this, part 1(b) of the video is initiated by narration that emphasizes competition:

> The (aspect of behaviour) we'll concentrate on is Competition. First of all, let's be clear why competition arises at all in primate social groups … just how (does) an animal resolve the problem of competing for resources?

The disclosure of overall intended outcome a1, as above, is summarized in Table 5.10, which goes on to list the disclosure of specific objectives, b1 to b9.

Table 5.10   Video sections, narration that initiates each section and implicitly refers to objectives (disclosures of objectives described in more detail below in this table)

Segments of Dominance And Subordinacy (as in Table 5.9)	Narration that initiates each segment	Table 5.4 objectives implicitly addressed
Part 1. Library Film of Primates in the Wild (6 min)		
(a) **Introducing TV 13/14/15:** Dominance/infant care/sexual behaviour		
i) Social groups of Primates: monkeys, apes, humans	This is the part of the course where we concentrate on social behaviour	a1
ii) Primate organization: single-male, multi-male, nuclear family	On TV, we focus on Primates ... number of adult males and females varies with species	
iii) Competition, care of infants, mating	... animals within a group compete for resources, they mate, they care for their young	
(b) **Introducing TV 13 (this programme)**		
i) Competitive situations: food, sexual activity shelter	... why competition arises at all in social groups ...competition for resources ...	a1
ii) Aggressive/submissive gestures	conflicts are seldom resolved by full-blooded fights; instead... both animals perform displays indicating likelihood of running away or attacking.	b2
iii) Dominance and Subordinacy	... how consistently does one of the pair submit to other one? ... the rest of the programme ... the concepts of dominance and subordinacy.	b1
Part 2. Shot in a research compound: Rhesus in captivity (18 min)	To accomplish repeated observations ... scientists have studied animals in captivity	
i) Many illustrations of subordinacy behaviour (avoids injuries)	... watch these two animals as an orange is thrown towards them. (BEHAVIOUR SHOWN) Animal A didn't have to fight animal B to get the food ...	b1, b2
ii) Establishment of dominance relationships	How did such a relationship become established? When this group was first put together, aggression was much more violent	
iii) Defining and recognizing dominance	... we need to be very careful about the definition of dominance ... let's consider how we measure it	b1 b9
iv) Dominance does not imply greatest number of victories	... the measure of aggression is not the same as dominance ...	

(continued ...)

Table 5.10 Continued

Segments of Dominance And Subordinacy (as in Table 5.9)	Narration that initiates each segment	Table 5.4 objectives implicitly addressed
v) Determining dominance hierarchy/ranking	see if we can find some principle of Hierarchy of Dominance indicating the structure of a social group	b9, b3
vi) Hierarchy is not precisely linear: triangular relationships occur	... linear hierarchy may not always be appropriate ... triangular relationships have been observed	b4
vii) Alpha animal (rank 1) is male in most species (but not in all)	Nevertheless there is usually a number one, a single animal ...	(rank 1) part of b3
viii) Rank can be dependant on mother's rank	... not always the outcome of a fight between two animals ... mothers are the most reliable of allies	b5
ix) In adolescence, youngest daughter rises in rank above older sisters (mother defended in her in infancy)	interesting counter-intuitive point ... relationship between age and acquisition of dominance	b6
x) Reproduction depends not just on male rank but also on female preferences	a low ranking male may have to attract a female to join him away from the majority of the group	b7
xi) Evolution: survival strategies include dominance/subordinacy behaviour	what advantage there could be for a submissive animal in the relationship?	b8

On the left is a reproduction of Table 5.4, the outline of the video, listing the video sections. In the centre are the segments of narration that initiate each video section. On the right are the learning objectives that are referred to implicitly by each segment of narration.

These disclosures of objectives are reiterated below in chronological sequence, displaying fuller versions of the narration fragments of Table 5.10.

b2. (Understand that the dominance relationship) avoids serious fights

The fact that serious fights are avoided is revealed incidentally as animals are shown competing for various resources. The scenes are repeated in a subsequent consolidation segment starting with the narration.

> One thing that has become clear and which is illustrated by the examples you've seen is that conflicts are seldom resolved by full-blooded fights;

instead … both animals perform displays indicating likelihood of running away or attacking.

Subsequent scenes in the video show several more examples of deference behaviour.

b1. (Understand the dominance phenomenon as) a relationship between two animals (in which one invariably defers to the other)

This objective is addressed twice during the narrative:

> Given any pair of animals … how consistently does one of the pair submit to the other one?
> … watch these two animals as an orange is thrown towards them.

A few seconds later, following the shot of the two animals' reactions to the thrown orange, the narration observes

> Animal A didn't have to fight animal B to get the fruit.

Then after several examples of competitive encounters in which one of the pair always wins, the exclusively pair-wise relationship is re-emphasized:

> Now we need to be very careful about the definition of Dominance.

Subsequently it is pointed out that it is a relationship acceded between each *pair* of animals.

b9. Describe how an observer can assess ranks

An implicit reference to this objective is the narration

> Now we need to be very careful about the definition of dominance … let's consider how do we measure it

– followed after a few shots by the narration

> see if we can find some principle of Hierarchy of Dominance indicating the structure of a social group

This second item of narration also refers implicitly to another of the objectives, b3.

b3. (Understand that the dominance phenomenon) results in a linear hierarchy (ranking), with an alpha animal (rank 1)

This objective is implicitly disclosed by the narration

> see if we can find some principle of Hierarchy of Dominance indicating the structure of a social group

The last part of the objective, concerning the *alpha animal*, is referred to more explicitly by the narration

> Nevertheless there is usually a number one, a single animal

This sentence is actually preceded by one that refers to objective b4, as follows.

b4. Non-linear triangular relationships also occur

This objective is implicitly disclosed by the narration

> But such a linear hierarchy (ranking) may not always be appropriate; triangular relationships have also been observed

b5. Dependent rank (e.g. dependent on mother's rank)

This objective is implicitly disclosed by the narration

> Let's return to consider how animals become dominant or subordinate ... not always the outcome of a fight between two animals ... a coalition of animals that help each other in a fight ... mothers are the most reliable of allies ... an infant's rank is highly dependent upon the rank of its mother. This is called Dependent Rank.

b6. Mother supports daughters against older daughters, hence adult daughters are ranked in inverse order of age

This objective is implicitly disclosed by the narration

> An interesting and counterintuitive point concerning the relationship between age and the acquisition of rank ... sometime between the ages of one and four, a female rises in rank above her older sisters.

b7. Female preference (not just male rank) influences reproduction

> A low ranking male may have to attract a female to join him away from the majority of the group before he will [dare to] mate with her ... primate females may display partner preferences based on more than just male ranks.

b8. Reduces risk of injury to (intelligent) subordinates

This objective is implicitly disclosed by the narration

> You may wonder what advantage there could be for a submissive animal in the relationship ... avoids risk of serious injury.

The above examples illustrate how one might depart from up-front disclosure of blunt statements of behavioural objectives. Stating such objectives at the outset would serve to spoil the suspense of the narrative. In any case, if all the objectives were lumped together at the outset, in one indigestible, unmemorable block, learning would be more hindered than helped. This latter objection would apply to long-form narrative video, but would be less true of *stop–start* video, in which short segments of video are studied: since the segments are short, there would not be many learning objectives for each segment.

Dimension A of Table 5.2: audience characteristics

The manner in which objectives are disclosed to students should not prejudice the requirement that the video design must be tied to the objectives. Furthermore, to ensure that the video meets the objectives, it is also necessary to know the characteristics of the target audience, dimension A of Table 5.2. The programme needs to target a well-defined audience, otherwise it will lack focus.

In the present example, all members of the target audience, 2nd level OU undergraduates, have completed a science foundation course, so many technical terms are used without interpretation. Also, the producer and the academic narrator knew the science foundation course and had met its students many times. So the general *flavour* of the programme was designed (intuitively) to suit the target audience. In particular, note that the education is *formal*, that is, the target audience consists of dedicated students of a formal course, culminating in a final exam. Hence the programme is more didactic than would be a programme for informal education.

However, since the programme was broadcast nation-wide, Open University students are not the only viewers. A secondary target audience is the general British public, therefore some account has to be taken of their tastes and sensitivities. For

> Caveat. If you try to please everybody, you might end up pleasing nobody. The narrower your target audience, the more focused you can design the TV programme.

example, as implied at several points of Table 5.4, sexual behaviour (of monkeys) is shown in the TV programme. The duration and size of framing of such behaviour is the choice of the programme director/producer, who must therefore make this choice so as to avoid offending the audience (including the secondary audience – the general public).

Dimension B of Table 5.2 – the learning context and complementary learning experiences

Item B of Table 5.9 notes that the broadcast notes contain pre-work in order to prepare the primary target audience for the TV programme. Hence the amount of information and its rate of delivery can be higher than for an uninitiated primary audience. (The next chapter discusses broadcast notes in general, including the rationale and the possible ingredients for pre-, during and post-activities.)

Other important factors of the learning context include that the programme is intended for individual viewing, all the way through without stopping, in the absence of a teacher or other students. These factors certainly have substantial effects on the design of the programme and the complementary learning materials – the video treatment must contain reasonable pacing and a degree of redundancy (conveying information in more than one way).

Finally concerning dimension B, if the package surrounding a video sequence is a multimedia package, then there are various implications. For example, if the video sequence is to be viewed quarter-screen, figures in the shot should not be so distant that they are difficult to distinguish. Also, the duration of the sequence should normally be short (say under 3 minutes), in the expected multimedia style. (This issue does not apply to the TV programme, *Dominance and Subordinacy*, since this was not an ingredient of a multimedia package: rather, it was broadcast as a self-standing long-form narrative video, intended to be viewed non-stop.)

Returning to the screenwriting principles of Table 5.3

Following the first mention of sexual activity in the *Dominance* programme, the question of maternal care is introduced, and the way this is done illustrates design principle 4a of Table 5.3, Words not duplicating Pictures. The words are generalizing or telling a parallel story rather than describing the pictures literally, as shown in Table 5.11.

Table 5.11 Illustration of principle 4a: words not duplicating pictures

Picture	Actual narration – generalizing from the pictures (not duplicating them)	A literal description would have been the narration
The shot shows a rhesus monkey mother suckling her baby while simultaneously grooming an older offspring.	Individual animals care for their young, and they may do so for several years.	Individual mothers suckle their babies and groom their older offspring.

So the literal description (final column) would have contained only the information that can be seen in the pictures, nothing more. In contrast, the actual sentence that was used (middle column) is a generalization of the events in the picture – it adds information to the picture. Also, this generalization encourages viewers to contribute their own interpretation to the pictures and words. They should deduce that suckling is one way of caring for the young and that grooming is another – and that the animal being groomed is an older child.

The whole point, for all the items in categories 3 and 4 of Table 5.3, is to encourage mindful, constructive viewing, rather than passive reception. In this way, each viewer effectively becomes a co-author of the story. That is, each viewer's idiosyncratic version of the story is a collaboration between the viewer and the screenwriter.

The most extensive of the 46 principles in Table 5.3, is 8e: synergy between words and pictures. That is, words should reinforce pictures and vice versa, to maximum effect.

An implication of this is that a subject specialist should not write the commentary of a video programme without thinking of the pictures, and then expect a video producer to find the most effective pictures. That is because the most effective pictures for the topic might necessitate considerable changes in the proposed words. The reverse also applies: thinking of a sequence of pictures first and hoping that effective words can be composed as an afterthought may not work well.

Instead, what is required is an iterative process of picture–word composition whereby one draft of the words leads to a draft of the pictures, which in turn leads to a second draft of the words, and so on. Even more sophisticated and sometimes achievable by experienced screenwriters, is for words and pictures to be thought of together, as an integrated whole, at each successive drafting.

The utmost opportunity for the full implementation of picture–word synergy occurs in the production of *animation*. Here, the producer/screenwriter has total control of the design of the pictures as well as of the words (subject to financial constraints). Therefore, words and pictures can be meticulously planned to synchronize appropriately and to reinforce each other maximally.

There were several animations in the video, for which maximal picture–word synergy was endeavoured. Unfortunately, it is difficult, in print alone, to describe a specific animation adequately so as to illustrate the picture–word synergy (but see Chapter 8 for design principles). However, a valuable related question can be addressed at the opposite extreme. When the pictures are unpredictable location recordings, how can the words be composed so that pictures and words reinforce each other maximally, especially if the recording is of animal behaviour, the most notoriously unpredictable?

Table 5.12 gives the transcript of one shot in the *Dominance and Subordinacy* programme and the picture–word synergy is then analysed.

There are four essential elements in the narration that are being illustrated by the pictures:

- the female
- her brother
- her dominance
- her smaller size

It was not possible to compose a sentence whereby all four of these elements synchronized with their appearance in the shot. The sentence that was actually composed (Table 5.12) ensured that two out of the four elements synchronized with their appearance.

Two elements that synchronized

The first element that did synchronize was *the female*: she was mentioned in the narration at the same time as she was being pictured. The second element that synchronized was *her smaller size:* when this was mentioned, the female's brother had just come into view and he was twice her size.

Two elements that did not synchronize

However, when *her brother* was first mentioned, he had not yet come into view; and even further out of synchronization was the mention of *her dominance* in the middle of the sentence. At that stage of the shot, there had been no evidence of her

Table 5.12 Transcript of an animal behaviour shot: in Dominance and Subordinacy

Pictures (Single Developing Shot)	Narration
Camera follows walking Rhesus monkey (mother holding baby).	In five years time, the seven year old female may still be dominant over the six year old male, even though she's now smaller than he [pause]
Mother's younger (but larger) brother comes into view. Mother displaces him from his resting-place.	

dominance. Her dominance was not apparent until the very end of the shot, when the brother deferred to his sister by moving away from his resting place when she approached. She then went and sat in his place. This displacement occurred after the whole sentence had ended.

The rationale: two elements were not obvious from the pictures alone

The reason for contriving to achieve picture–word synchronicity for the two elements, *the female* and *her smaller size*, was that these elements were *pictorially the least obvious of the four*. This is because the baby being held by the female (identifying her as a mother) was not easily visible. Secondly, her size difference was only visible for a few seconds between her brother coming into view and his moving out of view again. Hence the viewer's visual attention needed to be directed towards these indistinct features by synchronizing the words with them. The other two pictured elements, *her brother* and *her dominance* were much more obvious visually and hence did not need the corresponding words to be synchronous.

From the above example, it can be seen that decisions on the precise wording of the commentary have to be made after the video recording has been painstakingly viewed and evaluated. If the best shot illustrating the above behaviour had happened to feature the four elements in a different order and with different clarity, the most effective narration may have been entirely different, for example:

> In five years time, the six-year-old male will be much larger than his seven-year-old sister, but may still be subordinate to her.

Incidentally, the optimal procedure of recording final commentary *after* viewing the recording was not in fact followed for this TV programme. The commentary was recorded in the US location and brought to the UK, with the pictures, for editing. If there had been the opportunity, some additional editing with additional commentary, recorded after viewing the shots, would have improved the programme. For example, the shot is rather fast and should have been repeated, with some new commentary: 'Watch that again. The smaller sister merely walks up and her brother gives up his seat to her.'

A second example of wording contrived to best reinforce a picture

Another example of *unnatural* word order so as to maximize the picture–word synergy, comes from another video in the same course that includes an ethologist studying the behaviour of newts. There is a close-up as the newts are released into some muddy water. The newts quickly disappear from view as they swim downwards, and the narration is as shown in Table 5.13.

Table 5.13 Unnatural word order, to maximize picture–word synergy

Picture	Actual words used
Newts in scientist's hand Cut to shot of water, as newts are dropped into the water Newts disappear after 1 sec	However, newts are difficult to observe in their muddy natural environment [*pause 1 sec*]

One consideration is to position the sentence, relative to the pictures, so that the muddy water is clearly identified as the natural environment of newts. The positioning in the table achieves this purpose. But in addition, the phrase 'muddy natural environment' finishes before the newts have disappeared. So viewers have a silent moment to anticipate the disappearance, i.e. to accept the implicit challenge in the commentary that they should look hard to try to observe the newts for as long as possible.

A more natural word order would have been: 'However, the natural environment of newts is rather muddy, so they are difficult to observe.' As before, this sentence should be positioned, relative to the pictures, so that the muddy water is clearly identified as the natural environment of newts. However, the only positioning that achieves this purpose is as in Table 5.14.

So this word order would mean the newts disappeared *before* the viewer has been challenged to try to observe them. (The newts disappear just before the words 'to observe'.) Note here that the actual words used (Table 5.13) reinforced the picture by manipulating the viewer's perception of the picture – the words prepared the viewer to perceive the picture *actively*.

The principles of the pedagogic screenwriting framework (Table 5.3) that have been discussed so far have been quite complex. To conclude, here are some further principles that are fairly simple, but just as important.

Returning to the video, *Dominance and Subordinacy*, some way through the programme, there is a transition in the story, signalled by the narration:

Now that we've defined dominance, let's consider – how do we measure it?

The first half of the sentence, 'Now that we've defined dominance', is an example of a type of consolidation/conclusion (category 9 of Table 5.3), called a *chapter ending* (9d). The educational objective of such a chapter ending is that the viewer mentally *closes the book* on the chapter or topic (and knows which book has been closed, because it has been named). The topic has thus been labelled and *filed away* in the viewer's mind, which is now *cleared* to receive the next topic. The other three types of consolidation listed in Table 5.3 (9a, b, c) are more substantial, extending back into the chapter to recapitulate or summarize, or even going outside the chapter to generalize.

The second half of the sentence, 'let's consider – how do we measure it?', is an example of a type of signpost (category 2 of Table 5.3) called a *chapter heading*

Table 5.14 A more natural word order, but the words do not match the pictures

Picture	More natural wording, but does not work as well
Newts in scientist's hand	However, the natural environment of newts
Cut to shot of water, as newts are dropped into the water,	is rather muddy, so they are difficult
Newts disappear at this point	to observe

(2c). The educational objective of such a chapter heading is that the viewer *opens a mental channel* to receive the next item and labels the channel with the name of the subject matter. This also connects the channel with anything the viewer already knows about the subject, in which case the new ideas are assimilated into the existing mental framework.

A chapter heading is one of four distinct kinds of signpost listed in category 2. Another, more global kind of signpost is 2a, *set the scene* or *introduce*. For example, shot 3 in Table 5.5 sets the scene for the programme: it puts the programme in the context of the current part of the course.

Only 12 of the 46 elements of Table 5.3 have been covered in this introductory chapter. Many of the remaining items of Table 5.3 are self-explanatory, to the extent that readers can make good guesses as to what they entail. For readers who want a full coverage, all the principles in Table 5.3 are covered in depth in the next chapter.

However, those readers who are practising screenwriters are recommended to postpone reading the next chapter until they have undertaken some real screenwriting, using this current chapter to modify their usual designs, that is, reappraising their usual techniques in light of the principles in Table 5.3.

This recommendation derives from some proponents of cognitive apprenticeship theory (see Cash *et al.* 1997), who advocate practical work immediately after an overview of a theory but before the details of the theory. This enables learners to activate relevant existing knowledge and to construct new knowledge (of the overview) through the activity of implementing their interpretation of the overview. Following this, the details of the theory can be studied with less danger of overloading the learners. These details would hopefully resonate with their new knowledge.

This introduces the possibility that readers will interpret the overview in this chapter rather differently from the intentions of this author, which are detailed in the next chapter. That eventuality should not be a problem. Whenever readers' interpretations of the overview disagree with their later study of the detailed principles, they would learn by reflecting on the discordance. Their reflection would result in some degree of compromise between their interpretation of the overview and the detailed framework. If substantial discordances remained, that is still not a problem. The framework would benefit if its exposure to a knowledgeable readership resulted in constructive criticism, leading to a modified framework in a future publication. Contributions from readers will be attributed appropriately.

There is one last section, before inviting readers to undertake the above challenge. So far, no ethical issues have been discussed in any depth. Table 5.15 addresses this crucial area and the six principles are elaborated below.

Item a. Choose learning tasks that are suitable for video

Lazy thinking could result in using video for a task that under-utilizes the potential of video, for example, a task that could have been achieved with audiovision, at a much lower cost. Use Table 4.2 to determine for which tasks video is better suited than other media.

Item b. Screenwrite to achieve full pedagogic potential

The iterative process of screenwriting is arduous (each new design for pictures suggesting new words and then vice versa, over and over). It might be aborted prematurely through fatigue, or through knowing that a pilot segment will be produced and evaluated before the screenplay is finalized. Such a premature cessation should be resisted. Having completed a *final* screenplay, a conscientious screenwriter should go through one more iteration, considering whether all the screenwriting categories in Table 5.3 have been sufficiently developed.

One circumstance in which this *post-final* appraisal might be skimped is for a video that does not need to hit a precise duration. However, if a precise duration is mandatory, as is the case for broadcast TV, a post-final draft script or two are invariably required after it is discovered that the current *final* draft is overlength. The process of cutting down the duration usually forces extra refinements that improve the screenplay.

Item c. Are you inventing learning objectives to justify using video?

Having chosen learning tasks for which video is suitable (item a) and then written a meticulous screenplay (item b), there is still the question of whether the tasks (the objectives) are central to the curriculum. Do not *invent* objectives that are

Table 5.15 Professional Integrity

a.	Choose suitable learning tasks for video
b.	Screenwrite to achieve full pedagogic potential
c.	Are you *inventing* objectives to justify using video?
d.	Design for students, not colleagues
e.	No false promises when hooking
f.	Unbiased exposition, not propaganda or misrepresentation

peripheral to the course objectives just because TV can achieve the objectives effectively. The academic content must come first.

However, the knowledge that video is available can lead to the inclusion of perfectly respectable objectives that improve the course but that would not have been thought of if video had been absent. An expansion of these points is the section entitled 'A potential trap in the media selection procedure' at the end of the last chapter.

Item d. Design for students, not colleagues

Resist designing the programme just to please your colleagues, if this is detrimental to your target audience. There is a strong danger of this, since careers depend on reputations and also since producers thrive on compliments from peers. The content and the style must be relevant to the needs and the tastes of the students

Item e. No false promises when hooking

The following sentence of narration might ensure a suspenseful, attentive audience: 'After you've seen the techniques in this programme, your memory will improve four-fold.' But note that the suspense must eventually be relieved – there must be no false promises. In this example, the promise is clearly false – four-fold memory enhancement could not be that simple.

Creating a false preconception with the hook is unethical.

Item f. Unbiased exposition, not propaganda or misrepresentation

A producer cannot be totally objective, yet must endeavour to be – must consciously endeavour for objective, unbiased exposition. Do not propagandize, even when seeking to counteract an existing prejudice; instead, persuade by reasoned, balanced argument. For example:

- In a video that tries to promote the subject of physics to teenagers (who previously regarded it as dry and unexciting), do not force the scientists you interview to remove their safety overalls, on the grounds that 14 year olds dislike uniforms.
- It is not enough merely to claim that 'high standards of quality are strictly observed under the new management'. The claim needs to be justified with *evidence* of high quality and of how it is achieved.
- Do not merely say 'giving up smoking is a good thing'. Give evidence that it is good and why.
- When making comparisons, ensure that the examples are representative. For example, when comparing two teaching techniques, *transmission of*

information compared with *activity learning*, carry out sufficient research to find reasonably good exemplar of each technique.

- When editing an interviewee's contribution (say in the interests of clarity or brevity) ensure that the result still faithfully represents the speaker's meaning in relation to the video story. Editing decisions can pose difficult ethical considerations.

Challenge activity

Before reading more details (in the next chapter) about all 46 design principles of Table 5.3, it is advisable to consolidate what you understand so far about the design framework. A good way of doing this is to apply the ideas of the current chapter to your next production. This will be challenging because even the current chapter contains a lot of material. A good strategy is as follows:

- Start your design (e.g. write an outline screenplay) before rereading this chapter – just rely on your first impressions from the chapter.
- Reread and reflect on this chapter. If you find that your outline has not taken account of some useful elements of the chapter, make the appropriate modifications.
- After your next draft of the screenplay, interrogate this chapter again to see if any of the principles can improve your design.
- Repeat for your final screenplay.
- Contact the author if the above activities convince you that some of the proposed screenwriting principles need revision.

Chapter 6

Screenwriting for video in educational multimedia

In-depth coverage of the principles of Table 5.3

Until now, there has been no comprehensive framework for effective screenwriting of educational video. This chapter and the previous chapter offer such a framework. This attempts to formalize the main principles underlying practitioners' intuitively constructed programmes.

The framework, given in Table 5.3 of the last chapter, is based on screenwriting workshops and lectures, delivered between 1982 and 2002. These were conducted at several overseas educational media centres and also at the BBC Open University Production Centre, Milton Keynes, UK, during our annual three-month EDTV course. This course catered for overseas educational television producers, scriptwriters and managers.

Usage (Table 5.2)

It was noted in the last chapter that the values of Table 5.2 (Usage) must interact with the principles in Table 5.3 in the design of an effective educational screenplay. Of direct effect is dimension C, *Teaching Intentions*, which must underlie the whole story. (Remember however the proposal that specifications of learning outcomes need to be reappraised and refined as the content is developed.)

Some examples of interactions with all three dimensions were given as they applied to a particular TV programme, *Dominance and Subordinacy*. Here are one or two further examples and some general points.

Consider the following example of how an element of dimension A of Table 5.2 can interact with an element of category 4 of Table 5.3. Specifically, how the *age of the audience* can affect how to implement item 4b, concretize. When illustrating that a parabolic mirror provides a parallel beam, a young audience would find *a car's headlights* to be a tangible (concrete) illustration, whereas their grandparents, who remember the Second World War, would find archive film of *searchlights* much more evocative and tangible.

More generally, there are four features of the screenplay that need to match the *age* and *previous knowledge* of the target audience (items 2 and 3 of dimension A). These are

- load (number of teaching points)
- picture–word density (pace of information flow)
- intellectual depth of concepts
- intellectual clarity

These features appear in category 6 of Table 5.3, elucidate, where the advice is to reduce load, pace, depth and to maximize intellectual clarity. (This advice is elaborated in the next section on the principles of Table 5.3.) However, in the context of harmonizing with the target audience, the advice is also the opposite, namely that you should not *underestimate* the sophistication of the target audience. That is, load, pace and depth *should not be too low* for the target audience. Nor should the clarification be overdone.

If load, pace and depth are too low, you will be failing to keep viewers stimulated and attentive. Similarly they will become bored or irritated if you overdo the clarification (i.e. if you over-explain things). However, these consequences may be of secondary importance. Perhaps more important is the resulting under-utilization of video. If the load is too low for the audience, this means you could have taught more within the same video duration (and kept the audience attentive at the same time). Similarly, if the pace or depth is too low. Also, you waste time if you over-explain things (and you possibly irritate the viewers during this period of time).

In fact, while you are trying to match the intellect of the audience, if you accidentally aim *slightly* high in terms of load, pace or depth, it is not necessarily a bad thing, because if the viewer is a little over-extended, learning may endure longer. However, this is dangerous because you may lose some of the viewers. If you are worried that you may have aimed slightly high, follow that item with a clear summary.

Turning to dimension B of Table 5.2, complementary learning, a summary was given in Table 5.9 of the specific content of the broadcast notes for the programme *Dominance and Subordinacy*. Here are some general points about broadcast notes.

Broadcasts are transitory; after viewing, the student needs some hard copy to annotate and with which to revise. Also, before viewing, the notes can put the programme into context – how to view and use it. Even programmes on cassette or disk need this back-up – because it is difficult to search back and forth to find the section you want, and then to compare it with other sections. (Video segments in a multimedia package have their video study guide incorporated into the package – most of the items below refer to complete, self-contained video *programmes*.)

The notes can be in the main text or in a separate booklet. Table 6.1 lists some ideas about potential content.

Note that the items in Table 6.1 necessitate careful integration with print and other media. Hence it is essential to devise a linked print-media production schedule that allows cross-fertilization between the media.

Table 6.1   Broadcast Notes for TV – an important example of complementary learning (Table 5.2, dimension B)

A.   For studying before viewing
Outline of content and its treatment
Teaching intentions and learning objectives of TV programme
Recommended preview activity/study (this controls entry-knowledge)
Study guide for programme: what to look out for, how to view the video

B.   For studying before and/or after
Study guide showing relevance and relationship to other media

C.   For studying after the programme
Summary of programme
Advice to look back at the pre-work, especially the learning objectives, to consolidate memory of the TV while it is still fresh
Text-appropriate elaboration, i.e. elaboration of video material that is better achieved in print and was therefore omitted from the video
Additional examples and alternative explanations which had to be omitted from the video due to insufficient space
Reproduce complex diagrams, graphs and tables (and elaborate these if necessary)
Numerical data quoted
Key formulae (e.g. chemistry, maths)
Technical terms and jargon used
Other significant items and definitions
Key images to jog the memory
Names and relevant qualifications of principal speakers
References and bibliography
Plans and elevation of scenes depicted (e.g. architectural)
Flow-chart (e.g. for observed process)

Post-viewing activity, including self-assessment questions
Rationale for self-assessment questions:
1   reinforcement/consolidation of TV learning
2   pre-knowledge of post-viewing assessment encourages switching on the TV
3   pre-knowledge of post-viewing assessment encourages attentive viewing
4   sharpens producer's teaching intentions
5   links TV/text *learning modes*
6   the answers can be collected in a survey as evidence for evaluating the programme.
7   teaching on the same topic that is not suitable for TV can be relegated to print
8   through the latter, direct TV/text integration can be achieved

Printed study-guides for *print-led* video packages – a special example of complementary learning (Table 5.2, dimension B)

As mentioned in Chapter 4, one type of video is pure *actuality* (recording of actual, unrehearsed behaviour, e.g. video observation of classroom activity), without commentary on the sound-track. The commentary is supplied instead in the form of a printed study guide, which students read before and after viewing the video. The study guide asks questions about the video-recorded actuality and suggests issues to reflect upon and compare with students' own experiences.

For example, in the design of such a package for INSET teacher training, the study guide for each observational video might include an introductory section and five main sections:

0   An introduction, identifying the video and when it should be viewed. (This section might also include a brief summary of the related printed unit, e.g. 'Teaching Using Group Work')

1   One or two main points to look out for on the first viewing (all the way through, without stopping): the classroom teacher's intentions regarding methodology and learning outcomes, comparison with student's own experiences.

2   Post-viewing, a reminder to discuss the points noted in section 1.

3   The main section, consisting of several subsections, each one specifying some activities relating to a short segment of the video. Teachers view the video again, stopping after each segment (at the 'stop-tape' caption) to carry out the activities. (Some examples were given in Chapter 4.)

4   Feedback regarding the activities of the third section.

5   Suggestion for classroom practice of the techniques on the video, followed by group evaluation of the practice.

In this type of package, the pedagogic design resides mainly in the printed study guide. Hence the principles of Table 5.3, Pedagogic screenwriting, should be applied mainly to the study guide, where appropriate. It is important to note that not all the principles are appropriate for the print medium. Table 6.2 identifies which principles apply to which medium of the package.

The table clearly contrasts *print-led video* from *long-form narrative video*, for which the screenwriting principles of Table 5.3 were originally formulated. However, the table should not be taken to imply that long-form narrative video should accomplish all the principles, without help from printed video notes. This is not quite true, as can be seen in Table 6.3 which augments Table 6.2 by comparing all three types of video that were discussed in Chapter 4. The summary of the three types is reproduced here.

1. Self-standing video (non-stop viewing)

A video that does all the teaching by itself (a type sometimes referred to as *long-form narrative*), without the support of printed material. However, if desired, some video notes could prepare students for the video and summarize it. And, most valuably: the notes could suggest post-viewing self-test questions.

Table 6.2   Applying Table 5.3 to the print-led video package, in which printed material guides the study of Actuality Video (e.g. video observation of classroom activity)

The design principles of Table 5.3		Whether it is the PRINT or the VIDEO that achieves each design principle
1	a	Shock/surprise/delight	PRINT (and VIDEO sometimes)
	b	Fascinate (or entertain)/appetize	PRINT (and VIDEO sometimes)
2	a	Set the scene/Introduce	PRINT
	b	Distant signpost: what's coming later	PRINT
	c	Chapter heading: what's next?	PRINT
	d	Focus: what to look out for	PRINT
	e	Context/rationale: why we are doing it	PRINT
3	a	Pose questions	PRINT
	b	Encourage prediction	PRINT (and VIDEO sometimes)
	c	Don't mesmerize (don't *over-absorb* viewers, don't *submerge* their minds)	Take care! Long actuality segments, without commentary, can be soporific (cause mental lethargy)
4	a	Words should not duplicate pictures	PRINT should not duplicate the VIDEO pictures
	b	Concretize/activate existing knowledge	Important role for PRINT
	c	Do not obscure the geography	VIDEO
	d	Do not blinker, disclose the context	PRINT (and VIDEO sometimes)
	e	Pause commentary for contemplation	There is no narration
	f	Invent visual metaphors	Not possible with actuality video
	g	Scaffold learners' construction of knowledge	PRINT
5	a	Seeding	PRINT (and VIDEO sometimes)
	b	Music style/occurrence by design	Should not use music
	c	Signal change of mood or topic	VIDEO – using fades and dissolves
	d	Consistent style	VIDEO (and PRINT)
	e	Conform to video grammar	VIDEO
	f	Reassure/build confidence	PRINT
6	a	Specify logical status	PRINT
	b	Vary tempo to indicate syntax	VIDEO (to some extent)
	c	Don't overload	VIDEO
	d	Restrict picture–word density	VIDEO
	e	Moderate intellectual depth	PRINT
	f	Maximize (intellectual) clarity	PRINT
	g	Enhance legibility/audibility	VIDEO
7	a	Vary format	*Actuality* restricts the format
	b	Non-linear/non-sequential	Possibly for the series of VIDEOS
	c	Vary gravity using lighter items	PRINT (and VIDEO sometimes)
8	a	Repetition (with a different angle)	VIDEO
	b	Re-exemplify	VIDEO
	c	Compare/contrast	VIDEO
	d	Denouement/dramatic climax	VIDEO
	e	Synergy between words and pictures	PRINT should synergize with the VIDEO pictures
9	a	Recapitulate	PRINT
	b	Consolidate/summarize key features	PRINT
	c	Generalize	PRINT
	d	Chapter ending	PRINT

(continued ...)

Table 6.2 Continued

The design principles of Table 5.3	Whether it is the PRINT or the VIDEO that achieves each design principle
10 a Content-link between items	PRINT
b Story-link/pick-up	PRINT
c Indicate assumed external knowledge	PRINT
d Integrate with complementary learning material	PRINT and VIDEO

2. Video-led print-video package

A package consisting of a *scripted* video and printed video notes. All the teaching is done on the video by the commentary (with a few points elaborated in the notes). The video is in sections, designed to exploit the stop–start facility of the video player. Between sections, viewers stop the video and answer the questions in the video notes. The notes supply answers, which may sometimes elaborate, giving extra information that is not contained in the video.

3. Print-led print-video package (the type involved in Table 6.2)

Again, the video is in sections with interspersed questions. However, instead of scripted scenes, the video contains *actuality* (actual behaviour), such as the interactions between a teacher and students. There is no commentary on the video. All discussion of the contents of the video is carried out in the printed study guide, through question and answer.

Elaboration of the principles of Table 5.3, pedagogic screenwriting

1. Hook – capture attention (1a) and sustain it (1b)

1a. Delight, surprise, shock (in order to capture attention)

The unexpected, whether negative (shock), neutral (surprise) or positive (delight), will *arouse* and *engage* the learner.

For example, viewers will certainly be aroused if the video starts with the shock close-up of a moist human brain, with the narration, 'This is a real human brain [*pause 4 sec for contemplation*].' Mind you, too great a shock might cause viewers to switch off, e.g. showing the state of the lungs of a heavy smoker might cause the smoker to *block out* the image, rather than be persuaded to stop smoking.

Table 6.3   How the pedagogic video design principles (Table 5.3) apply to the video and print components of the three types of video package

Design principles	Self-standing video	Video-led package	Print-led package
1 a Shock/surprise/delight	**V**	**V**	**P** (and **V** sometimes)
b Fascinate, entertain, appetize, create suspense	**V**	**V**	**P** (and **V** sometimes)
2 a Set the scene/introduce	**V** and **P**	**V** and **P**	**P**
b Distant signpost: what's coming later	**V**	**V**	**P**
c Chapter heading: what's next?	**V**	**V**	**P**
d Focus: what to look out for	**V**	**V**	**P**
e Contex /rationale: why we are doing it	**V**	**V**	**P**
3 a Pose questions	**V** and **P**	**V** and **P**	**P**
b Encourage prediction	**V**	**V** and **P**	**P** (and **V** sometimes)
c Don't mesmerize (don't *over-absorb* viewers, don't *submerge* their minds)	**V**	**V**	Long actuality segments, without narration, can be soporific
4 a Words should not duplicate pictures	**V**	**V**	Print words should not duplicate the video pictures
b Concretize/activate existing knowledge	**V**	**V**	Important role for print
c Do not obscure the geography	**V**	**V**	**V**
d Do not blinker, disclose the context	**V**	**V**	**P** (and **V** sometimes)
e Pause commentary for contemplation	**V**	**V**	There is no commentary
f Invent visual metaphors	**V**	**V**	Not possible with actuality
g Scaffold viewers' construction of knowledge	**V**	**V** and some **P**	**P**
5 a Seeding	**V**	**V**	**P** (and **V** sometimes)
b Music style/occurrence by Design	**V**	**V**	Should not use music
c Signal change of mood or topic	**V**	**V**	**V** – using fades/ dissolves
d Consistent style	**V**	**V**	**V**
e Conform to video grammar	**V**	**V**	**V**
f Reassure/build confidence	**V**	**V**	**P**
6 a Specify logical Status	**V**	**V**	**P**
b Vary tempo to indicate syntax	**V**	**V**	**V** (to some extent)

(continued ...)

Table 6.3 Continued

Design principles	Self-standing video	Video-led package	Print-led package
c Don't overload	V	V	V
d Restrict picture–word density	V	V	V
e Moderate intellectual depth	V	V	P
f Maximize (intellectual) Clarity	V	V	P
g Enhance legibility/audibility	V	V	V
7 a Vary format	V	V	Actuality restricts format
b Non-linear/non-sequential	V	V	Possibly for the series of videos
c Vary gravity using lighter items	V	V	P (and V sometimes)
8 a Repetition (with a different angle)	V	V	V
b Re-exemplify	V	V	V
c Compare/contrast	V	V	V
d Denouement/dramatic climax	V	V	V
e Synergy between words and pictures	V	V	Print words should synergize with video image
9 a Recapitulate	V	V	P
b Consolidate/summarize key features	V and P	V	P
c Generalize	V	V	P
d Chapter ending	V	V	P
10 a Content-link between items	V	V	P
b Story-link/pick-up	V	V	P
c Indicate assumed external knowledge	V and P	V and P	P
d Integrate with complementary learning materials	V and P	V and P	V and P

Note:

V indicates that the **VIDEO** achieves the pedagogic design principle, and **P** indicates that **PRINT** achieves it

As noted in the last chapter, Table 5.3 is meant to be used flexibly, rather than as a recipe. No chapter of a video need include all 46 techniques nor even all 10 main categories. For instance, it is counterproductive to *signpost* what's coming (category 2), if the next item is intended as a surprise.

Normally, it's appropriate to apply one or two techniques for each of the 10 categories, as befits the story and the screenwriter's style. In any case, the word *chapter* is defined loosely as a *self-contained section*, which involves subjective judgement. One screenwriter's *section*, necessitating a *signpost* and a *conclusion*, may be another's *subsection*, which may only need a *link*.

An example whereby you might surprise the viewer (in a chemistry programme about the Periodic Table) is where the presenter releases a balloon filled with carbon dioxide, or a heavier gas, and it drops like a stone.

An example whereby you might delight the viewer, in a programme involving family life, is to show babies doing baby things, such as toddling then overbalancing onto their bottoms. Or, in a programme about animal behaviour, show baby animals playing.

In all of these cases, you are just setting the scene but doing it with a captivating shot (setting the scene is covered more fully in item 2a below).

1b. Fascinate, entertain/amuse, appetize, create suspense (in order to sustain attention)

FASCINATING THE LEARNER

In general, whatever the topic, producers look for the most interesting/fascinating examples.

For example, in a video about how we see rainbows, it would be fascinating to include a rare sight – a rainbow in the form of a full circle. (Aircraft pilots occasionally see such a complete circle below them.) Such a rare sight can be set up experimentally – a carefully controlled spray of water under special lighting conditions will demonstrate a rainbow that is in the form of a complete circle.

Another group of examples involves time-lapse recording: speeding up the motion of the tidal cycle, flowers growing, bacteria dividing. These may or may not be essential experiential objectives in any particular case, but such sights are invariably fascinating.

Note that *fascinate* also appears in dimension C of Table 5.2, being one of the possible educational objectives under the affective domain.

ENTERTAINING OR USING HUMOUR

Entertainment is certainly not inimical to learning, nor does it necessitate superficial coverage of the subject. Bringing out the intrinsic fascination of a subject is a powerful aid to learning, precisely because it is so entertaining. Some might argue that this is the only kind of entertainment that should be used – bringing out the intrinsic fascination of the topic (the real fascination, rather than just *dressing up* the topic). But perhaps we should not be too hard-nosed about this.

For example, everyone likes animations (almost without exception) even when they do not seem to add that much to the viewer's knowledge. So, if the budget will bear it (or if the animation can be done cheaply) perhaps you should include animation (even though it is not too useful cognitively) just to entertain and hence create a positive feeling towards the learning material and sustain attention. However, this is a tricky decision: see the caveat at the end of section 1.2 in Chapter 1.

Here's another example. A submissive gesture in rhesus monkeys is *looking away* from the aggressor. Another submissive gesture is a *quivering grimace*, which is extremely amusing. Having shown both gestures in a video, a production choice needs to be made later in the video as to which gesture to show when defining the term *subordinate* (using the phrase 'and the submissive animal is called "subordinate"'). A clear choice is the *quivering grimace* precisely because it is more entertaining than the *looking away* gesture.

Both entertainment and humour are pleasant and memorable, hence can be powerful for getting a message across and for the learning to endure. However, there are some dangers. One danger with humour is that it is notoriously difficult to do well. An important ingredient in humour is the pacing. This ingredient can be enhanced by creative editing. It can also be diminished by editors without a sense of rhythm. However, when the humour is delivered by a presenter, face-to-camera, no editing can compensate for inadequate acting ability. Presenters of educational video are rarely professional actors. Yet even professional actors will tell you that comedy is the most difficult genre to accomplish well.

There is another danger with both entertainment and humour – the technique could swamp the message! If humour is overdone, some viewers could be *entranced* to such an extent that they remember the humorous situation but fail to learn the message robustly. They might even learn the *wrong* message: for example, if the video satirizes the wrong way to do it, this might be so memorable that the subsequent correct way gets forgotten.

APPETIZING

The first video of a series could show intriguing extracts from future videos, creating an appetite for those videos. This necessitates producing the first video late, say after videos 2, 3, and 4. This requires production to be well in advance of delivery schedules, but is a useful strategy for the following reason. After videos 2, 3 and 4 have been completed, the full flavour of the course is more clearly fixed in the minds of the producers, who can therefore *launch* that flavour in the first video.

CREATING SUSPENSE

This encourages the learner out of a purely receptive mode into a more productive, mindful mode. For example, in a video giving advice to exam candidates, the following sentence of narration should ensure a suspenseful, attentive audience: 'This video follows four candidates through their exam preparation, revealing the revision techniques that resulted in the greatest success.' Creating suspense then relieving it is likely to embed the message more firmly in the viewer's mind.

A simple technique that works in some cases to create suspense is to start on a big close-up of a scene and gradually zoom out to reveal the whole scene. Suspense can also be created with the reverse technique – gradually zoom in to a big enough close-up so that previously indistinguishable details can now be seen clearly.

2. Signpost (tell the viewer what is coming)

2a Set the scene/introduce

The scene could be set by

- introducing the interviewee's expertise
- introducing the location (e.g. 'This factory makes …')
- establishing the theme of the story (or of the chapter), before going into more depth
- establishing the boundary of the situation (i.e. the programme will stay within this boundary)
- introduce some background information, upon which viewers can build the subsequent content

It may be that none of these techniques is essential in any particular video. For example, it may be obvious that viewers already possess the background knowledge upon which the subsequent content knowledge can be built (although that knowledge might still need to be *activated*, as recommended by Merrill (2002a).

Caution: sometimes a long introduction can be boring. An apocryphal senior producer in BBC Education would always shock his junior producers when he scrutinized their first script. He would immediately put a line through their first paragraph. His rationale was that the start should be punchy – it should hit viewers with a hook, not an introduction. In other words, his advice was, *Get to the interesting part straight away, by throwing away the beginning that you first thought of (or at least, postponing it).*

2b. Distant signpost

Tell the learner what is coming later, for example: 'In this programme we're going to investigate three ideas, inflation, the exchange rate, the interest rate.'

Whereas the previous item, 2a, told us some of the story, this item, 2b, and the rest of the signposts, 2c, 2d, 2e, only tell us *about* the story – they just *refer to* the story.

2c. Chapter heading

This tells the learner what immediately follows. For example, in a video about the brain, at the end of a section (chapter) describing the natural cavities in the brain (the ventricles), the narrator says,

> So that's the ventricles, now for the visual system.

The second half of the sentence is the chapter heading – it names the chapter (*the visual system*) and announces that the chapter is coming next (*now for*).

The intended effect is to activate the viewer's existing knowledge about the visual system (the viewer's mental schema for *visual system*). The viewer can then incorporate the information into that schema, thereby modifying it.

2d. Focus signpost: what to look out for

This directs the learner's attention to particular aspects of the next item. For example,

> As you watch the flight of the helicopter, concentrate on what happens when it tilts forward …

Another example:

> In the next clip, concentrate on the arms of the spinning skater

2e. Contextual signpost/educational rationale (why it is coming)

Whenever the above signposts are used (2a, b, c or d), the educational rationale (why the item is coming) is usually understood. But sometimes it *is* appropriate to add the rationale explicitly. For example:

> We are going to look at the sport of boxing because this illustrates well what we want to investigate – the variety of arguments that people put forward to justify the use of violence.

The question of how much signposting you include, or what kind, is a matter of judgement. Too much signposting can spoil the flow of the story. Signpost when it is really necessary, not just as a matter of course.

3. Facilitate attentive viewing (encourage and enable sustained concentration)

3a. Pose questions

- Most often, question, pause, answer (i.e. rhetorical questions). The pause could be of any length because it could include an intervening sequence that leads up to the answer. For example, in a video about dominance hierarchy the narrative runs as follows:

> You would expect the older daughter to remain dominant, but in adolescence the younger daughter becomes dominant. Why does this happen? [*Pause while dominance behaviour is observed and viewers reflect on the question posed.*] Well, the reason for this dominance resides in the past, when the daughter was a baby. [*Pause to observe mother defending baby.*] The mother defended the baby against undue attention by the older sisters. The older sisters therefore came to associate the mother's dominance with the baby.

- Special case: pose implicit visual questions by *partial animation* so that viewers have to imagine the *in-between* pictures.
- Explicit questions, with a visual device that informs viewers when the answer will be revealed. For example, the question might be 'What are the reflective symmetries of this object?' This would be repeated as a printed caption on screen, with a line of little boxes below. After a pause of 5 seconds, the boxes would disappear one by one over a further period of 5 seconds. The idea is to let the viewers know how long is being allowed for them to reflect on the question before the answer is revealed – the little boxes *count down* to the end of the reflection period. Various alternative 'count-down' techniques are possible, such as a continuous *wiping off the colour along a bar* rather than jumping off little boxes, or a rotating arrow on a clock-face.

Incidentally, when viewers consider the posed questions, they often need to activate and organize their existing knowledge and construct new knowledge. So posing questions also comes under category 4.

- A special case, *video cassette/disk stop–start questions, posed in supplementary print:* where the videos include captions every few minutes that ask the viewer to stop the tape and carry out an activity described in the supplementary notes. Examples have been given in the recorded video section in Chapter 4.

3b. Encourage prediction

- Inviting viewers to *guess what is coming next* is a good technique for keeping their minds active. For example, in a video about chemical elements, the teacher, holding two balloons, says, 'One balloon contains helium while the other contains carbon dioxide. What's going to happen when I release the balloons, what do you think?' and pauses before releasing the balloons.
- Also, *implicit questions*, so that viewers will be tempted to predict the answers, such as:
  a. identify/delineate the area of enquiry, e.g. 'we're going to investigate why, more and more these days, teenage boys lack self-esteem' (followed by a pause to encourage prediction)
  b. show the situation in such a way that viewers come to their own conclusions, before being told the answers, e.g. in a documentary about why some teenage boys turn to crime, show the debilitating home environments

Note that viewers necessarily base their predictions on their prior knowledge. Hence this knowledge gets *activated* (as recommended by Merrill, 2002a) whenever viewers accept the invitation to make predictions.

3c. Do not mesmerize (do not over-absorb)

Avoid the warm bath syndrome where students are so comfortably immersed in the story that their mental activity is submerged. This can be avoided by giving opportunities for viewers to stand back from the story.

This contrasts with the genre of pure drama, in which viewers should be totally immersed. Such immersion is not recommended for education, where the viewer needs to be guided to *stand aside* from the illustration and appraise its educational objectives. This guidance is the purpose of categories 2 (signposting), 9 (consolidation) and 10 (linking). Otherwise the experience could be totally passive, like wallowing mindlessly in a comforting warm bath.

A worse danger than *mesmeric entertainment* is for the viewer to perceive the *wrong* message through *mesmeric tunnel-vision* – i.e. not relating the local example to the global message.

In either case, the programme should ensure that the viewer *knows what to make of it*. Hence, the educational screenplay needs to make interventions, for example, to include signposting and consolidation, even if that spoils the flow of the story.

The extent to which it is acceptable to spoil the flow of the story is a matter of judgement. Compare the comment after section 2e above.

One type of video, used for example in teacher-training, is pure *actuality* (recording of actual, unscripted behaviour, such as video observation of classroom activity), without commentary on the sound-track. The commentary is supplied instead in a printed study guide, which students read before and after viewing the video. The study guide asks questions about the video-recorded classroom activity and suggests issues to reflect upon and compare with their own experiences.

If this type of *print-led* video is longer than about 3 minutes, it could easily induce mental lethargy, due to the absence of any narrative intervention that would guide viewers to *stand back and reflect*. The recommendation here would be to convert any 6-minute segment into two 3-minute segments.

4. Enable individual construction of knowledge

Cater in parallel for a range of viewers, enabling them to construct knowledge onto their individual cognitive frameworks. As noted earlier, constructivist theory asserts that knowledge is not passively received but actively built up by the learner, who selects information and organizes it in a way that is individually meaningful (weaving it into their existing knowledge), hence building a knowledge structure that is individually slanted, yet captures the essence of common knowledge.

Below are various techniques whereby viewers can be enabled to learn by constructing their individually slanted knowledge. The first five, 4a to 4e, encourage construction of knowledge by supplying opportunities, invitations and challenges for such construction. The last two, 4f and 4g, actually *support* the construction of knowledge by supplying various types of *scaffolding*.

4a. Words not duplicating pictures (i.e. not describing literally)

Words (commentary) should not be literal descriptions of the images. Conversely, pictures should not duplicate commentary words. That is, (occasionally) the connection between words and pictures should be more indirect than the reinforcement of item 8e, so that viewers have to make their own connections. More specifically, words and pictures should add meaning to each other, or one should generalize what the other is saying, or one should refine what the other is saying. When words and pictures parallel each other in such non-literal ways, the viewers are given a challenge to make their own connections, so a picture–word–*viewer* coalition is engendered. Thereby, the whole is rendered greater than the sum of its (word and picture) parts, with the viewer's help.

In addition to the purpose of encouraging viewer participation, the use of *parallel* words that express a general concept enables the picture to take the role of a specific illustration of the general concept. An example of this technique was given in the last chapter, in Table 5.11.

4b. Concretize (make tangible)/activate existing knowledge (then build on this)

Build onto viewers' existing knowledge by choosing examples and analogies that connect with their well-established cognitive structures – so that viewers can handle the ideas mentally. Perhaps a better word than *concrete* is *tangible*, in that *tangible* addresses not just the video item but also the learner's experience of it:

tangible = can be touched/felt/handled

Namely, the presentation should engage with the viewer's established mental framework:

- by use of simple, well internalized language (instead of abstract language)
- by visual representation of abstract concepts, e.g. by specially constructed 3D models
- by showing real-life events recorded on location
- by using analogies and metaphors that anchor easily with the student's existing knowledge.

Note that, engaging with viewers' existing knowledge necessarily *activates* that knowledge. This accords with constructivist learning theory – this activation is a necessary precursor for viewers to construct new knowledge on the foundations of their existing knowledge. Activation of prior knowledge is one of Merrill's (2002a) five *first principles of instruction* (described in the last chapter).

For example, in a mathematics video dealing with the addition rule for logarithms,

$$\log (y \times z) = \log (y) + \log (z),$$

use weighing scales and load the trays with cardboard cut-outs of particular areas under the graph of the function $1/x$. When these areas correspond to the two sides of the addition rule, the scales will balance. (This only applies to learners who know that $\log (x)$ is the area from 1 to x under the graph of $1/x$.)

Another example is from a biology/psychology video about differential sensitivity in different parts of the body. This displayed a specially built homunculus (a distorted model of a human figure), the size of whose body parts correspond to their sensitivity. For example, human lips are far more sensitive than the small of the back, so the homunculus would have enormous lips and a minuscule back.

In general, use *analogy*; that is, use a familiar/concrete idea to characterize a new/abstract idea.

One of the hallmarks of Cognitive Flexibility Theory (Spiro *et al.* 1995, as cited by Driscoll 2000: 387) is the use of multiple metaphors and analogies, in order to help students develop mental models of complex phenomena.

4c. Do not obscure the geography

- When recording a sequence in a new location, start the sequence with *establishing shots*, i.e. shots that establish the geography of the situation.
- Close-ups should not be too tight, otherwise they *blinker.*
- Occasionally develop shots instead of cutting: e.g. zoom and pan following a moving person.

All these techniques relax the producer's control of the field of view, giving students the choice of which parts of the scene to look at. They can feel free to think their own thoughts.

4d. Do not blinker, disclose the context (the conceptual geography)

- Have *old* in the same shot with *new* for comparison. For example, when one item in a mathematical equation is shown to change, retain the original unchanged equation in the same shot, for comparison. Similarly for comparison of initial versus later stages of a situation.
- Show the presenter plus the object he/she has been talking about (instead of a *medium close-up* of the presenter).
- When there is a continuous transition, like a chemical change, show the *initial state* in the same size of shot as the *final state*. Hence, show a close-up of the test-tube *from the start* of a chemical change (speeded up if necessary), rather than starting with a shot of presenter plus the test-tube during the initial part of the chemical change (the tube is too small to be seen clearly in this wide shot).
- Sometimes it is useful to provide a *map* through the programme: e.g. in the form of a flow-chart which gets updated as the programme develops. Such a flow-chart is helpful for a complex topic. It gives a wider view of the conceptual environment than items 2b, distant signpost, and 9d, chapter ending.
- If developing an argument line by line of text on screen (or box by box of a flow-chart), do *not* always obscure the next line of text just because the commentary has not yet reached that point. That is, unless the concepts are particularly difficult, show two lines (or three) from the start and highlight each as the commentary reaches it. This enables students to choose whether or not to read ahead, rather than being forcibly blinkered.
- 2a again: establish the situation (i.e. 2a is a subheading of 4d)

All of these techniques, by disclosing the context, give viewers the conceptual elbow-room to construct knowledge about the issues portrayed.

4e. Pause (in the commentary) for contemplation

Generally, do not blanket the shots with commentary. For example, if 90 per cent of the video's duration is covered with commentary, that is too much – it gives no slack for contemplation. There is no hard and fast rule, but 80 per cent coverage is usually reasonable (so in a 25 minute programme, the words of the commentary would take 20 minutes), although some programmes would need only 50 per cent word coverage.

The rationale is to provide viewers with opportunities for contemplation and reflection so that they can construct knowledge.

There are two main ways of reducing word density, that is, introducing pauses into the stream of narration.

WORDS LEADING PICTURES

That is, after some commentary, pause (showing the picture without further commentary). There are two versions of this technique:

a. Thinking-time/contemplation regarding the section that has just finished. Some ideas are more difficult than others and hence require an extra pause for thinking-time. Usually this would be at the end of an item/chapter, in which case there would already be a short pause in order to *signal a change of topic* (5c). But if the idea is difficult, an extra pause is necessary, e.g. 2 seconds thinking-time as well as 2 seconds to signal the change of topic.
b. Contemplation of some *actuality* (actual behaviour, e.g. classroom activity). It is sometimes appropriate to leave an even longer pause after the commentary (e.g. 30 sec to 2 minutes) during which viewers contemplate the pictures: a picture (or sequence) may tell its own story without commentary (or following a brief commentary introduction). In fact the main purpose of the video may be to provide a record of some *actuality*.

PICTURES LEADING WORDS

That is, show the pictures for a while before the commentary starts. This is sometimes appropriate in order to promote thoughtful observation: the viewer is forced to conjecture about the picture before receiving help from the commentary. Usually, this would occur when the story changes direction and this change is shown pictorially for some time before any comment is made. Again, the purpose of the video might be to observe and analyse some *actuality*.

4f. Invent visual metaphors

Visual metaphors for abstract processes (e.g. specially concocted physical models, animations) in effect suggest the teacher's imagery to students. Learners can choose to incorporate this imagery into their knowledge structures – thereby supplanting other, ineffectual mental processes, as suggested by Salomon (1983). Note however that the teacher's imagery should not be alien to the learner: the metaphor has to relate easily to the learner's existing knowledge.

Examples were given under item 1.3 of Chapter 1. For instance, the concept of iteration can be portrayed with an animation in which the outputs of a procedure (the procedure pictured as a black box) are fed back repeatedly as new inputs to the box to produce new outputs. Another example is the homunculus in section 4b above.

Generally, a visual metaphor that is easily understood by the learner (anchors easily to the learner's prior knowledge) relates the viewer's prior knowledge to the knowledge to be learned. Hence it *scaffolds* the viewer's construction of knowledge. Some more direct scaffolding techniques are given next.

4g. Scaffold learners' construction of knowledge

A fuller account of the following scaffolding ideas can be found in Van Merriënboer (2001), McLoughlin *et al.* (2000) and Merrill (2002a). As you develop your story,

- progress from the specific to the general (e.g. show animals competing for food, *then* explain competing for resources of all kinds)
- progress from the simple to the complex (e.g. show interactions between a pair of animals *then* within a larger group of animals)
- progress from the concrete to the abstract (e.g. show a worked example of a problem before explaining the theoretical principles *or* show the solution that needs to be worked towards)
- ask students to complete the solution of a half-solved problem
- decompose the problem into subproblems
- pose a sequence of successively more difficult problems

However, there are occasions when one should proceed in reverse order, from general to specific and from complex to simple, as follows.

Going from specific to general may be valid when the concepts are very unfamiliar, but we should avoid spoon-feeding. That is, whenever learners possess some nascent ideas about a concept, we should start with the general concept – the overarching 'big idea'. This can serve to activate the learners' prior 'half-knowledge', which will get elaborated later by the specific material

Going from simple to complex is also not always appropriate. Van Merriënboer (2001) cites ample evidence that 'completion tasks' are better for learning. For example, one could present a complex design of a project to students, who then have to complete, evaluate or extend the design. Students learn better from such completion tasks (in which they start from the complex) than when asked to carry out the design from scratch.

Finally, remember, as noted in 4f, a visual metaphor serves to scaffold viewer's construction of knowledge.

5. Sensitize (put viewers into a receptive mindset)

In the techniques 5a to 5f below, you'll find two types of sensitizing, direct and indirect. For example, a particular style of music might sensitise viewers directly by putting them into an appropriate mood. The indirect version is when viewers are *desensitized* from potential distractions. That is, to ensure viewers are sensitized to a particular item of knowledge in a video segment, you might need to ensure they are not distracted or side-tracked by some other item contained in that segment. They might also be distracted by their lingering thoughts about a previous item or because they feel uncomfortable with something – these distractions too need to be prevented.

5a. Seed

During an early item, include a phrase, shot, example, which seems to be part of the current story (although perhaps incidental or redundant) whereas the scriptwriter's hidden rationale is to facilitate appreciation of a later item (i.e. to *seed* the later item). It is usually very difficult to detect any *seeds* in a completed script, because they are surreptitious. That is, they are hidden inside the early item to seem a natural ingredient of the current story.

During the drafting and redrafting of a script, a seed is usually an *afterthought* introduced by *backtracking*. That is, if the scriptwriter decides that an item is difficult to understand, he/she backtracks through earlier items to find one into which a seed can be introduced (surreptitiously) in order to facilitate understanding of the later item.

For example, a compound idea that needs digressions for parts of it can be presented as a single idea, without digressions, if parts of it have been seeded earlier. Here is a particular example. In a video on problem-solving, one of the problems concerns an ordinary clock, with short hour-hand and long minute-hand. There are no numbers round the perimeter but there are 12 bold hour marks and light minute marks between them.

The problem posed is: if the clock is turned upside-down, is there any time of day for which the hands of the clock show a proper clock time (the hands being in a correct relative position to each other)? Without going into the solution, suffice to say that viewers could not solve the problem unless they are completely familiar with two ideas:

1 What are the relative positions of the hands for proper clock times. For example, if the long minute-hand is vertically upwards, the hour-hand should point exactly at one of the 12 hour-marks.

2 As the minute-hand moves round, it pushes the hour-hand at the correct speed (which happens to be 1/12 the speed of the minute hand).

These two ideas have to be understood clearly by viewers if they are to have any chance of solving the problem or even understanding the solution when it is explained to them.

Hence, in order to *seed* viewers' understanding of the solution, the first idea is introduced earlier in a simple problem. The second idea is also covered earlier when the quiz master manually pushes round the minute-hand and viewers see it is pushing the hour-hand at the correct speed. In addition (also earlier) an animation shows the hands going round (speeded up) from 9 o'clock round to 3 o'clock, again seeding the second idea.

Another case for seeding is where a shot contains a lot of irrelevant information that might divert viewers from the intended message. For example, in a programme about animal behaviour, suppose that a shot is to illustrate the fact that a social group of *gorillas* never contains more than one adult male. If this is the first time in the video that gorillas have been seen, viewers could easily get distracted by other features of the shot, such as the fascinating resemblance to humans or the antics of youngsters playing. Such distraction is less likely if viewers have become accustomed to shots of gorillas. Hence the producer/screenwriter could contrive to show gorillas several times previously, for instance to show an example of the *ape* species or to illustrate that primates live in social groups. The producer could have used *chimps* to illustrate both points, but the use of gorillas *seeds* the minds of the viewers, enabling easier appreciation of the later *single-male-group* shot of gorillas.

Strictly speaking, the latter example is not an example of *sensitizing* but rather of *desensitizing*. That is, the preliminary displays of gorillas were intended to *lower* the viewer's sensitivity to distracting aspects of gorilla behaviour. However, when sensitivity to distraction is lowered, this necessarily *heightens* viewers' sensitivity to the intended message in the later shot

In that example, it was just the *topic* of ape that was repeated. It is also possible to use *exact repetition* of a shot. This is normally used for a different purpose – for the second occurrence to *reinforce* the first (see 8a, repetition). However, it can be used instead so that the first occurrence *seeds* the second. This could happen when a shot is repeated but new commentary defines a different context. For example, the first occurrence of the shot could identify a resource, such as a favourite resting-place for a troop of monkeys. The shot could be repeated some time later in the video, with new commentary pointing out a different context, such as 'Conflicts are not resolved by fights. Instead, one of the competing animals defers to the other.' What is intended here is for the prior occurrence of the shot to *seed* the mind of the viewer – the viewer has been sensitized to the shot, having seen it before, so does not need to process all aspects of the shot. Hence the viewer can focus more easily on the new context (which is being described by the new narration).

5b. Appropriate style of music and its timely occurrence (by design)

In British educational TV, music has been conventionally used when there are long gaps in the commentary. Hence, as soon as British viewers hear music, they expect to be left to contemplate the pictures and make their own interpretation, with little or no verbal guidance. In this respect, music sensitizes by putting the viewer into a contemplative mood. However, the style of music should be appropriate to the subject-matter (there are many different kinds of contemplative mood).

Also the occurrence should be appropriate: music over a whole programme tends to tranquillize rather than sensitize.

CAVEAT

Conventions vary with time and place, and even with target audience. The above convention largely held during the last quarter of the twentieth century for formal adult educational TV. British Schools TV tended to have more background music, even during commentary.

5c. Signal change of topic or change of learning mode

A signal is an indication (or hint) that something new is coming, but without saying what it is (hence it is not the same as a chapter heading). Both types of signal – change of topic, change of mood – are to prepare the viewer for a transition.

SIGNALLING A NEW TOPIC

Suppose a presenter has been demonstrating some equipment, for example, chemicals in test-tubes, then a change of topic could be signalled by cutting from a close-up of the equipment to a shot of the presenter plus equipment, as the presenter tidies up the equipment for a few seconds. Or the presenter might turn and start walking to a new location.

A frequent signal for a change of topic is a pause at the end of a topic followed by a change of shot and immediate new commentary. It is not what the commentary says that indicates the change, it is the fact that the commentary is immediate. (This comes up again under item 6b, vary tempo to indicate syntax.)

SIGNALLING A NEW MOOD OR LEARNING MODE

A new mood can be signalled by music or by a smile, or by noises off.

This comes under item 10c. However, as well as serving the function of linking, such indication (communication) has a second function – it can guide the learning mode by identifying that the depth of treatment will not be deep. (When students know that prior knowledge is being assumed, they realize that the treatment will just be a recap.) Hence, such communication signals a new learning mode.

5d. Consistent style

Maintaining a particular style, such as the colour of captions, facilitates the intake of the information. This is because learners become accustomed (or desensitized) to the irrelevant information (the consistent colour) so can ignore it. Hence they are more sensitive to the *relevant* information.

For a series of videos, create a *series style* in various respects, such as a common opening title sequence, the same studio set design, the same font for all text superimpositions. A consistent style makes viewers feel at home with the familiar surroundings. They do *not* need to waste any processing on these surroundings, which leaves them more sensitive/receptive to the knowledge that you intended them to gain.

5e. Conform to video grammar (prevents distraction)

There are many conventions in video productions, established techniques that could be called the *grammar of video*. Some conventions are fundamental, in that viewers have limited processing capacities that should not be exceeded. Other conventions are a matter of current fashion, such as when to use music or how *busy* the screen should look. But even in this case, if viewers are accustomed to a restricted range of pacing, shot transitions, sound effects, etc., they would be disturbed if this *grammar* were violated. Hence they would be *less sensitive* to what they should be learning from the video. Here are some of the elements of video grammar.

- When does a cut or camera-movement work? Answer: when there is an obvious motive for it. For example, cut on action (pointing, looking, turning to walk). Or cut on a verbal cue (a person says 'he is still at the office' and we cut immediately to the office scene).
- Do not cut from a shot in which the camera is zooming or moving. Movement (especially of the whole picture) requires extra mental processing. Hence the viewer's mind cannot settle down until the movement stops and the picture remains static for a second or so.
- Zoom in for extra emphasis, otherwise cut. (Some producers dislike zooms whatever the circumstance.)

- Adhere to current conventions; e.g. mix to denote passage of time or change of location (although this convention is declining in the UK). Mix when overall brightness of the next shot is very different.
- When cutting between two people, keep them the same size on the screen (unless you have a good reason to change the size).
- If a person is speaking to someone off screen, do not show the speaker centre screen. Rather, frame him or her as in Figure 6.1, slightly off-centre, allowing *talking space* in front of their mouth.
- When cutting between two shots of the same person (e.g. cutting as the person turns to walk), ensure both size and angle of shot are different – otherwise the person will appear to *jump* to a different part of the screen, which looks like an editing error. Such *jump-cuts* are disturbing.
- The same disturbing effect occurs if sound is cut instead of mixed.
- When two people are having a conversation, facing each other, as in the middle of Figure 6.2, the line between them is called the *line of action* or the *optical barrier* (the line along which the people are looking at each other). If the camera is on one side of this line, looking at one of the people, then if you cut to a shot of the other person, from a camera placed on the other side of this line, both people will be seen looking in the same direction, rather than looking towards each other. This gives the inaccurate impression that the second person has turned his/her back on the first person as follows.

In Figure 6.2, the image given by each camera (1, 2, 3, 4) is shown in the four boxes. Each box shows what the camera sees when it is *zoomed out*. However, the camera can zoom in to see only one of the two people. This *single person* shot is shown inside the dotted line. And the rule is: *do not cut between cameras 1 and 3*. These are on opposite sides of the *line* so such a cut shows both speakers looking to the left, and it appears that the man has been talking to the back of the woman's head. Similarly don't cut between

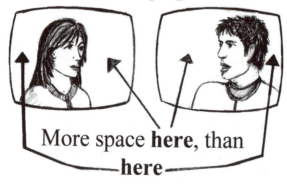

Figure 6.1   Allow *talking space*

Do not cross the *line of action*

Figure 6.2   Do not cross the line of action

cameras 2 and 4. In contrast, cutting between camera 1 and 2 is OK (both on the same side of the *line*). This cutting makes the speakers look as if they are facing each other, and so does cutting between cameras 3 and 4.

- A similar idea, and a more important one, is that you should maintain continuity of direction of movement between each shot and the next – by not crossing the *line of action*. This is also the name for the line along which activity is occurring, e.g. when one person kicks a ball towards another person. Crossing this line between one shot and the next (say between a wide shot and a close-up) causes a change in the direction of movement, e.g. *left* across the screen during the wide shot, then suddenly *right* across the screen after the cut to the close-up. If you really need to cross the line one resolution is to edit in an intervening *buffer* shot which is exactly *on* the line of action and/or edit in a lengthy *cut-away* shot.

Further points of video grammar can be found in Watts (1992).

5f. Reassure, build confidence

Students who lack confidence are less sensitive to what is being communicated. Giving reassurance or building the viewer's confidence are important for encouraging learners to persevere. For example, do not make light of intellectual difficulty by saying

> This equation is not too difficult. It's an example of a general idea. That is
> …

Better say

> This equation is rather complicated; you can study the details later at your leisure; for the time being I'm just interested in the general idea. That is …

Do indicate assumed external knowledge, e.g. 'you met an example of this last week in the audio-cassette when the social worker was interviewed', or 'this is not new, you've met something similar before, it's just another aspect of the dominance hierarchy that you studied weeks ago'. This indication also comes under items 5c and 10c. However, as well as guiding the learning mode (5c) and serving the function of linking (10c), such indication (communication) has a third function – it can reassure students who have not done the pre-work that:

- it has not been covered earlier in the programme when their concentration may have wavered
- it is not something they should have deduced from something covered earlier.

The reason why students might hold these misconceptions is that a presenter who is assuming prior student knowledge will present that section is in a less formal, *recapitulation* style (voiced in a *throw-away* tone). Many students would recognize from this style that the section is a recap of something covered earlier. So if they have *not* done the pre-work, they might imagine that the topic had been covered on the video itself and that they had missed it through inattention. They are also reassured that they can catch up with the pre-work after the programme.

Notice that the students who are reassured by the communication of external knowledge are those who have *not* done the pre-work. Such communication also helps students who *have* done the pre-work, but in a different way (see 10c).

Do also communicate source of *further* knowledge. This was covered under 5c because it guides the learning mode. But it also *reassures* because it stops viewers feeling frustrated, thinking they have missed details, or with their incomplete understanding.

An indirect but effective technique for being reassuring is to be informal and conversational. Some presenters find it difficult to be informal because they want to appear authoritative by using complex, technical language. As for being conversational, this is difficult if the presenter is reading from a script that sounds like the written word rather than the spoken word.

6. Elucidate (make the story clear/facilitate understanding)

6a. Specify logical status

What is the logical status of an item? Is it

- a proof
- a further piece of evidence
- an implication
- an illustration
- a summary
- an introduction
- a consequence
- a deduction
- a comparison
- a conjecture?

Elucidate the logical status with commentary or with a caption. For example, indicate

- a *consequence* with the words 'because of this' or 'as a result'
- a *comparison/contrast* with the words 'likewise' or 'in contrast'
- an *implication* with the word 'therefore'
- a *further piece of evidence* with the words 'in addition' or 'as well'

And so on.

6b. Vary tempo to indicate syntax

This item was covered in the last chapter in Tables 5.6 and 5.7, but an overview is given here for completeness. *Varying the tempo* refers to techniques of pacing the words and actions relative to the cuts between shots, so as to illuminate the story's syntax (*syntax* refers to questions like, 'is this a continuation of the last topic or is it a new topic?'). For example, the pacing term, *loose editing of an outgoing shot*, refers to a long pause after the commentary (or after the action) before the cut to a new shot. A *loose incoming shot* is one with a long pause between the cut and the start of the commentary or action. Conversely, *tight editing* involves short pauses.

Judicious variation of such pacing can illuminate the syntax, for example:

loose edit outgoing shot, tight edit incoming *implies* incoming shot deals with a new topic

The pause before the cut allows time for the *mental reverberations* of the last topic to die away before a new topic starts. The short pause after the cut ensures that any lingering thoughts about the last topic are quickly interrupted. Conversely,

> loose edit incoming *implies* incoming shot deals with the same topic as the outgoing shot

Table 6.4, like Table 5.7, gives all four permutations but also adds an exception in row 3 and a caveat to the above rule, in row 2. To illustrate the caveat, consider the two examples in Chapter 5 – the monkey story in Table 5.6 and the remediation version of the 'apocryphal' motorway services example. In both cases there was a tight/loose combination going into the final shot and this incoming shot had the same topic as the outgoing words – 'social behaviour' of the monkeys and 'public conveniences' in the services. However, for the latter, the topic of the outgoing *picture* (restaurants) was not the same, whereas the outgoing monkey picture did have the same topic (social behaviour).

> The question of whether a commentary pause is long enough depends not just on its duration: because the significant event is a pause in the viewer's mental processing. Hence a busy picture with rapid action makes a pause seem shorter to the viewer. In the same way, if there are meaningful sound effects during a pause, that pause seems shorter to the viewer.

Table 6.4   Loose vs. tight outgoing or incoming commentary

Outgoing words of commentary	Incoming words of commentary	Incoming topic same/new?
1. loose	tight	new topic (specified by the incoming commentary)
2. tight	loose	same as topic of outgoing words – and the loose incoming words allow time for viewers to contemplate the new shot in the context of the outgoing words. Note that these words may be *more than* tight – the final word may straddle the cut or even fall after it. Caveat: the topic may or may not be the same as the topic of the outgoing *picture*
3. loose	loose	same topic as outgoing picture. Exception: the incoming topic might be obviously different, indicated if the incoming picture is sufficiently informative that the topic has changed, e.g. cutting to a shot of the Eiffel Tower indicates that we will now look at the situation in Paris
4. tight	tight	topic is related to the outgoing words but the incoming words may modify the topic or elaborate on it

Note that the topic of the outgoing picture may not be the same as that of the outgoing words. This is implied in Table 6.4, in the second and fourth rows. When the outgoing words are tight, they introduce a new topic, illustrated by the pictures in the incoming shot. The rule is: if you want a piece of commentary to modify a topic or to introduce an entirely new topic (to be illustrated by the next shot), *cut immediately to the next shot.* Conversely, if you do not want a sentence to be related to the next shot, *put a lengthy pause before the cut.*

6c. Do not overload

Load is defined here as the *quantity* of separate items to be learned. Globally, avoiding excessive load means do not include too many teaching points, that is, do *not* cram the programme with too much information. Locally, it means do not include too many items of detail about an individual teaching point.

This issue concerns the *quantity* of items and is irrespective of whether the pace is too fast or too slow (*pace* is dealt with next).

If you have produced a draft screenplay and you then estimate that it is too long – e.g. 28 minutes long when you are restricted to 25 minutes – do not *condense* the presentation. Instead, choose to omit an item that is over 3 minutes long. This is often a difficult choice. For example, if there are five main items, a screenwriter is reluctant to omit any one of them. Usually it has taken considerable effort to weave all five into a coherent story.

6d. Restrict picture–word density (high pace of information)

- If there are some difficult concepts being presented, and the narration is supported on-screen by phrases of text, the text should not be shown all at once, but rather developed line by line, synchronizing with the narration. (However, this could irritate students if the concepts are not particularly difficult – see 4d.)
- Loosen up commentary over strong, meaningful visuals. For example, composite pictures necessitate attention-switching, hence require low-complexity commentary, with extra pauses. Another example is when you switch to a new presenter. This deserves and attracts a lot of the viewer's attention, especially if you superimpose the presenter's name. Hence, the new presenter should say something redundant, e.g. an acknowledgement of the previous presenter, 'Thanks Fred', or an acknowledgement of what has been said, 'So that's the case for experimental research.'
- Conversely, there are occasions when the viewer should not be distracted away from the commentary by a strong visual, e.g. when the commentary is providing study guidance that cannot be illustrated, such as a signpost, conclusion or link. For such commentary, choose either face-to-camera presenter or a general view/backdrop (sometimes called a *wallpaper shot*).

These last two points are exceptions to the general rule that words and pictures should reinforce each other (item 8e below). However, strong meaningful visuals do not need commentary to reinforce them and, conversely, verbal study guidance should not be diluted by visuals that have a different strong meaning.

6e. Moderate the intellectual depth/difficulty/complexity

Listeners find it easier to understand short sentences. One reason is that a long sentence can exceed the listener's memory span. Another reason is that long sentences normally contain conditional clauses, which are difficult to bear in mind. So you should convert every long sentence into two or more short ones.

For example, imagine you were speaking the latter four sentences. Listeners would understand you quite easily. But they would find it more difficult if you combined the four sentences into a single long sentence, as follows:

> If you have a very long sentence, especially if it contains conditional clauses (like this one), you should convert it into two or more short ones, because listeners will find that easier to understand, partly due to the fact that a long sentence can overload the listener's memory span and also because conditional clauses are difficult to bear in mind.

Notice that if you convert this long sentence back into the four earlier short ones, you are forced to repeat some of the words (*short, long* and *sentence*) so you are incidentally adding some user-friendly redundancy.

When you have new terminology to define, leave the definition until it is needed. You might be tempted to define such terms at the outset, during *signposting* what is coming. Resist the temptation – better find a way of signposting that does not require premature definitions

Optimal graphic design involves *clarity* (see item 6d) but it also involves *simplifying the concepts*. For example, in the first week of an undergraduate course on 'Biology, Brain and Behaviour', the designers originally intended to cover the complex relationships shown in Figure 6.3.

However, in the video introduction to the course, these relationships were simplified, as in Figure 6.4.

Students were familiar with the abbreviation Ψ to denote *psychology*. In any case the presenter verbalized all the items on the chart. He also expanded on them, for example saying 'social behaviour' when pointing to the word *social* (top) and saying 'subcellular events' when pointing to the word *subcellular* (bottom). He also pointed out which levels related to *behaviour* (third column of Figure 6.3) and which related to *brain*.

At the outset, the presenter explained the significance of the shading. The shaded and unshaded bands from top to bottom were shown as five different colours on the video. The bands indicate which discipline (left) relates to which phenomenon (right). For example, neuroanatomy (light coloured band) relates to

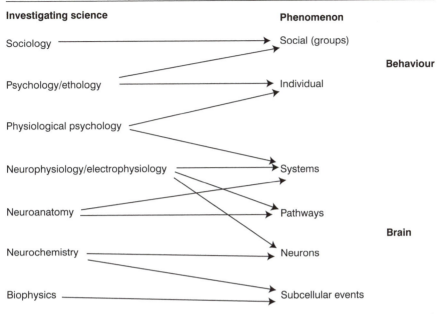

Figure 6.3 Levels of phenomena and their investigation in the brain and behavioural sciences

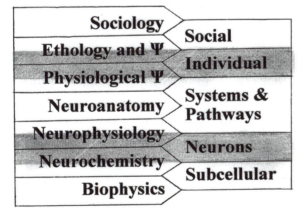

Figure 6.4 Simplification of the relationships, as shown on the video

systems and pathways (in the same light coloured band). Because of the zigzag arrangement, the coloured bands could be used to indicate when a discipline (left) relates to two phenomena (right) instead of one phenomenon. For example, neurophysiology relates to systems and pathways but also relates to neurons. Just below that, neurochemistry relates to both neurons and subcellular.

The simplifications, compared to Figure 6.3, are as follows.

- The discipline of electrophysiology has been omitted.
- Systems and pathways are combined in one band on the right, hence the discipline of physiological psychology is shown related both to systems and to pathways, instead of just to systems.
- The words 'behaviour' and 'brain' are omitted on the right.

Such simplifications can be justified on three counts:

- The spoken words in the programme can augment the simplified graphics and hence recover some of the complications (examples have been noted above).
- TV is not the appropriate medium to deal with minute details – because these require concentrated study at the individual student's own pace (better done by reading text).
- Even in the printed parts of the course, it is sometimes pedagogically preferable to present a simplified diagram or table, then to use footnotes or margin notes to add any necessary complications.

6f. Maximize (intellectual) clarity, eliminate ambiguity

When learners are *hanging on by their fingernails* the slightest intellectual ambiguity can knock them off the precipice.

Reappraise the screenplay for clear (unambiguous) exposition. You should draft and redraft your screenplay (picture–word composition) to ensure the clearest possible exposition. It is not unknown for a good educational screenplay to undergo eight drafts, each preceded by a script discussion by a team of three or more people. For example, clarity could require you to do the following.

- Ask yourself the question 'Is this the clearest example of the concept?'
- Design graphics to be clear (unambiguous), uncluttered, evocative. In general, look for ways in which graphic representation can clarify a topic – using flow-charts, concept maps, colour coding, shape coding, animation.
- Suppose it is decided to omit one of the five main items of the story in order to reduce the load (see 6c above). Considerable effort is usually needed to unweave the five items and to design new links making a coherent story out of the remaining four. If insufficient effort is devoted to this task, clarity will be compromised (and such insufficient effort in this situation is a real danger because of screenwriting fatigue – remember that excessive effort has already been expended in screenwriting five sections when only four were appropriate).

We have been dealing here with *intellectual* clarity. The next item deals with *sensory* clarity.

6g. Enhance legibility/audibility

When learners are **hanging on by their fingernails** the slightest visual or auditory ambiguity can knock them off the precipice.

- Direct the learner's visual attention to the appropriate part of screen or aspect of the picture – with commentary or superimposed highlights or a presenter pointing.
- A presenter pointing to a part of a diagram (either with finger or pointer) can sometimes be much clearer than *highlighting* that part using animation. This is because the viewer's eyes are told in advance in which direction to travel to reach the appropriate part of screen (because they follow the movement of the pointer). So the advice is, instead of highlighting an item on the screen, sometimes use a pointer that is always on screen and that moves towards the item being indicated. This could still be an animated pointer rather than hand-held. This is particularly helpful when the viewer is required to look at several parts in quick succession. (The directing of attention here is done during the shot, rather than before it, as is the case with technique 2c, focus.)
- Clarity of text on-screen must take priority over beauty – elegant fonts and colours can be less legible.
- Fill the frame: wasted space means wider shots and hence less legible shots. For example, compare Figure 6.3 above, which would have been illegible on-screen, with the video version in Figure 6.4.
- Because it is difficult to read at the same time as listening to narration, any text on screen should be *hyper-legible* – larger and less dense than would be acceptable in the absence of narration
- Parallax: if you move past an object, the nearer parts of the object pass through your field of view faster than the further parts, similarly if the object is moving past you or rotating. Using *parallax* is a powerful way of showing the realistic three-dimensionality of objects. To achieve parallax the camera or the object has to be moved. (For further details about depicting three dimensions, see 2.5 in Chapter 2.)
- The narration is audio not print, so write for the ear, not the eye, i.e. write *conversational* words, to be spoken and listened to, *not* to be read. The informality of conversational narration also helps to reassure students (as noted under 5f).

- When using words that have homophones (words that sound the same, but mean different things, e.g. *see, sea, c*), make sure their meaning is clear from the context.
- Avoid using words that are difficult to hear or to distinguish from other words, but if this is unavoidable (e.g. new technical terms), superimpose them in written form on the screen.

   Here are some words that are difficult to hear, because the last consonant of a word is the same as the first consonant of the next word. This happens twice in this phrase: 'The last task of the seventh theme' (which is difficult for the narrator to say too). Here are some words that are difficult to distinguish from other words: 'Right-indicate or signal'. They sound like: 'Write "indicator signal"'.

7. Texture the story

7a. Vary the format (to alleviate tedium, re-engage the learner)

Driscoll (2000: 327) notes 'No matter how interested someone is in the topic of a lecture, movie, demonstration, audio presentation, that interest will wane in the face of unending sameness.' Keller (1987) recommends for maintaining attention to an audiotape: 'the use of two or more narrators or varying the format (conversation or interview as opposed to narration)'. The same holds for video, which affords a much greater variety of formats. Some different formats for a video segment are:

- studio/location
- presenter in-vision/out-of-vision (narrating)
- documentary/exposition
- demonstration/dramatic enactment
- discussion/interview
- animation/caption-sequence/visual effects
- single presenter/two or more

A video should incorporate judicious switching between these formats from segment to segment, so as to sustain the viewers' interest. On each occasion when the format changes, say from one presenter to a new one, or from a presenter in-vision to an animation, there is a good chance that the learner will be re-engaged.

   This recommendation goes almost without saying. Such variation of formats is standard practice for the good video producer. In addition, the variety of presentational techniques would serve to maintain attraction – for example, camera moves and zooms, big close-ups, shot transitions, visual effects, specially constructed models. But don't overdo it. Variation of format or of presentational technique should seem natural, not just contrived for gaudy effect.

7b. Non-linear/non-sequential presentation (for digestibility)

A linear, sequential order of presentation would start at the *obvious beginning* and progress from cause to effect without detour, to the end. But this may subject the viewer to a long, monotonous, indigestible, single train of ideas. Instead, the story may flow more easily if you jump ahead (to see where we are heading) and then return to the postponed stages of the story.

Actually, non-linearity is already implicit in some of the study help items (e.g. 1b, create suspense, 8a, repetition). But 7b recommends non-linearity even during the main presentation of the subject-matter.

Of course, in multimedia, the learner may have a lot of further choice as to which order to receive the story.

7c. Vary gravity using lighter items

Rationale: avoid monotony and also avoid subjecting viewers to overlong concentration in an unvarying learning mode. In fact, this category means interspersing periods of heavy concentration with lighter items.

This technique is easy to forget when hard-pressed to meet a screenplay deadline following several revisions. However, it is well worth including in a checklist for your final revision. Otherwise, however good your story, if the learning mode is unvarying, you might lose viewers' attention – they cannot sustain heavy concentration for more than a few minutes at a time.

8. Reinforce

8a. Repetition (from a different angle)

Repetition for reinforcement can be repetition of words or of pictures. In either case, the repetition might be exact or, more usually, repetition of an idea from a different angle.

The following is an example where new words repeat an idea that was voiced earlier. Over a long-shot of animals in the wild, the first commentary says

> These animals are not easy to observe in the wild, so scientists have studied animals in captivity.

A few shots later, there is a closer shot of animals in captivity, and the idea is repeated with the commentary

We are now in an environment where observation is much easier.

This technique of *repetition from a different angle* is often referred to as *redundancy*.

A second reason for including redundancy is not to reinforce but rather to compensate for inattention. The point is, however hard you try to capture and maintain viewers' attention, their concentration may fade in and out during a video segment. Such lapses of concentration will occur at different times for different viewers. Hence, the need for occasional redundancy – repeat the ideas in different words, enlarge upon the idea.

In the above example, the words reiterated an idea. In the following example, it is the pictures that are repeated. Consider the shot described in Table 5.12 of the last chapter, in which a rhesus monkey (carrying her baby) walks over to her brother's shady resting place and he defers to her, giving up his place. It was noted that the shot was rather too fast, despite the carefully devised commentary, and that further clarification could have been achieved by repeating the shot but with new commentary:

> Watch that again. The smaller sister merely walks up and her brother gives up his seat to her.

Spiro *et al.* (1991), as cited by Driscoll (2000: 387), in their exposition of Cognitive Flexibility Theory, recommend that 'Revisiting the same material, at different times, in rearranged contexts, for different purposes, and from different conceptual perspectives, is essential for attaining the goals of advanced knowledge acquisition.'

Incidentally, repetition is usually for reinforcement, as in the above examples, but can have function 5a – that is, the first occurrence of an item could *seed* the second occurrence.

8b. Re-exemplify

Definition: give more than one specific example/instance of a general concept. Purpose: to reinforce depth and endurance of concept acquisition. However, there are actually several additional purposes, all working at the same time, depending on the ability and experience of the individual viewer.

For the high-ability viewer, or one whose previous knowledge makes the general concept easy, a single specific example might be sufficient for the concept to be understood. But *understanding* is not an all-or-nothing phenomenon. First, there are different depths of understanding. Secondly, understanding may fail to endure with time.

Hence, it does no harm to give a second example of the concept. This could *reinforce* understanding in both depth and endurance. Moreover, the high-ability viewers will not necessarily be bored with the second example; rather they could be pleased to have their understanding confirmed.

Simultaneously, the viewer with a lower ability to learn from video (or the viewer whose attention wandered temporarily) needs a second example to strengthen the *half-understood* concept. For a very difficult concept, a third example might be appropriate, especially for the lowest ability viewer.

Hence, the technique of re-exemplifying has an additional effect (on top of concept-acquisition). It also caters for a range of viewer abilities (one of the purposes of category 4 of Table 5.3).

8c. Compare/contrast (or counter-example)

When two objects or concepts or phenomena are compared for similarities between them, each concept is understood better through analogy with the second concept.

A similar effect can be achieved by doing the opposite – contrasting two concepts for their differences (or giving a direct counter-example to the first concept). This sharpens appreciation of the concept that is being contrasted: the viewer understands *what the concept is not*.

A PRODUCTION POINT

Suppose you are comparing concepts A and B, one after the other (e.g. comparing human faces and apes' faces to illustrate that apes are our closest relatives). If you show them only once each, then the comparison is not equitable – viewers' memories of A are fading by the time B has finished. So you need to show A, B, A, or better A, B, A, B.

8d. Denouement/dramatic climax

A dramatic climax reinforces by *inspiring* or *amazing* the viewers – leaving them with a feeling of satisfaction that something really worthwhile has been achieved. So it makes the chapter more memorable.

For example, at the end of a segment of an observational video on collaborative problem-solving, we see the delight on the face of the student who has just managed to consolidate the group's deliberations and thinks she knows how to solve the problem. (If the camera inadvertently misses the facial expression, it is worth stopping the group activity and asking the student to think back to that *eureka* moment and to re-enact it for the camera.)

In another instance, at the end of a video about *Dominance and Subordinacy* in a group of rhesus monkeys, the narrator asks: 'You may wonder what evolutionary advantage there could be for a subordinate animal in a relationship.' This is an intriguing question, because up to this point the video has always shown only the dominant animals winning resources without problems. After a pause to allow viewers to contemplate a repeat viewing of an animal being subordinate (e.g. allowing a dominant animal to steal its food), the narrator supplies the answer

> Based on a past history of encounters, a subordinate animal conserves energy and reduces the risk of injury by not contesting each object directly with a dominant animal.

The clues to this answer were apparent several times during the video, but according to the producer's appraisal of the target audience, many viewers would not have deduced the answer. Hence, these viewers finally see that subordinate (as well as dominant) animals gain from the dominance/subordinacy relationship – a satisfying (and unexpected) closure to the story. And even for viewers who could answer the question, it would be exciting, because they are unlikely to have considered the intriguing question before it was put by the narrator.

8e. Synergy between words and pictures

This was discussed with specific examples in the last chapter (Tables 5.12–5.13) but here are some additional points.

- Choose the shot that best amplifies rather than merely *accompanies* the words. For example, imagine a sequence in a foundry, with the commentary 'Safety is paramount when the heat is so fierce.' In this case, do not just show a wide shot of the foundry – rather, show a *close-up* of a *potentially dangerous activity*, such as a worker pouring white-hot molten metal.
- Conversely, choose words that amplify the shot, e.g. do not say 'this part of the object is' instead, say 'the top left part of the object is' or 'the pointed part ...' or 'the linking part ...'
- The duration of the shot and the wording of sentence should be composed carefully so that key words fall at the right place to create synergy. An example of this was given in the last chapter, Table 5.12, with the shot of the rhesus monkey carrying her child.
- Vary voice intonation, meaningfully.
- Sometimes it is helpful to reinforce narration with key words of screen text. Such uses of text can serve as visual reference points, which anchor attention and prevent the learner's mind from wandering. In addition, they can serve as visual mnemonics to avoid overloading auditory memory (the spoken words do not need to be retained in memory if they have been précis-ed by a key word or two of screen text).
- On some occasions, the words need to precede the pictures (to prepare the learners for the pictures). For example, Table 6.5 shows the storyboard for a video clip about ice-skating.

Table 6.5   Words preceding pictures

Pictures	Narration	Sequence
Skater, standing still	When a skater performs a pirouette, she can change the angular	1
She starts to pirouette, arms outstretched	speed of her spin by changing	2
Up to full speed now	the position of her arms,	3
She brings her arms in	either stretching them out, or	4
Arms go out	bringing them close to	5
Arms back in	her body [*pause I sec*]. In the first part of	6
Video clip freezes	this multimedia package, we are going to …	7

Notice that

1 the narration in sequence 1 refers to the action in sequence 2 (pirouette)
2 the narration in sequence 2 refers to the action in sequence 3 (change of speed)
3 the narration in sequence 3 refers to the action in sequence 4 (changing arm position)
4 the narration in sequence 4 refers to the action in sequence 5 (stretching arms out)
5 the narration in sequence 5 refers to the action in sequence 6 (bringing arms close)

Each time the viewers are warned of what is coming, so that they know what to look out for. To achieve this, the wording needs a lot of thought so that the phrases fall at the appropriate point. Even then, in this particular case, the narrator needed to deliver his first sentence in 11 seconds (up to the words '… close to her body'). This was rather faster than his normal speed but the screenwriter was unable to compose a shorter sentence while still meeting all the requirements. (So the speaker was asked to speak faster than usual, just for that sentence.)

Another example where words needed to precede the pictures was given in the last chapter, Tables 5.13–14, with the shot of the newts in the muddy water.

On other occasions, the pictures need to precede the words, for example, when the pictures are mathematical expressions that are difficult to listen to unless they can be seen. For example, in a mathematics video for students who are fairly new to algebra, consider the commentary 'minus b, plus or minus the square root of, b-squared minus four ac, all over two a'. This is impossible for most students to appreciate unless they can see the algebraic formula

$$\frac{-b \pm \sqrt{(b^2 - 4ac)}}{2a}$$

NOTE

Only eight examples have been discussed, but this item, creating synergy between words and pictures, is the biggest topic of the pedagogic screenwriting framework (Table 5.3).

9. Consolidate/conclude

9a. Recapitulate

Definition: list the topic headings covered recently. This jogs the learner's memory and encourages the learner to *rehearse* the topics. For example, following the first half of a video about the brain, the presenter says (over appropriate shots of parts of a model of the brain): 'We've looked at four parts of the brain, a part of the brain concerned with language, at the ventricles, at the visual system and at the sensory cortex.'

9b. Summarize key features/consolidate

Summarizing is more extensive than recapitulating – it extends back and elaborates on the chapter by giving a précis of the key features. For example, following the recapitulation quoted above, the presenter summarizes, by saying 'and in each case, as well as looking at their structure, we've looked at their function – what the parts of the brain actually do, the behaviour and the abilities and the sensations that they control'.

Consolidating is stronger still, implying *combine into one whole* as well as *solidify*. This idea is similar to one recommended by Wim Westera (1999), which he terms *integrating knowledge*, whereby when some new concepts have been introduced, it is useful to interrelate these concepts in an *integrator*. That is, conclude with a single sequence that brings together all the key features. For example, in a foreign-language video, the disparate elements of each sequence are consolidated in a final sequence when they are spoken in a single paragraph.

9c. Generalize

This goes outside the chapter. For example, a generalizing sentence from a programme about the brain is: 'This kind of topographic representation is typical of sensory systems in general and not just of the visual system.'

9d. Chapter ending

Name the chapter and say that it has finished (usually a single sentence). For example, in a video about the brain, at the end of a section (chapter) describing the natural cavities in the brain (the ventricles), the narrator says, 'So that's the ventricles, now for the visual system'. The first half of the sentence is the *chapter ending* – it names the chapter ('the ventricles') and announces that it has ended ('So that's').

Thereby the viewer *closes the book* on that chapter and knows which book has been closed (because it has been named). The topic has thus been labelled and *filed away* in the viewer's mind, and that mind is now cleared to receive the next topic.

All four types of *conclusion* in category 9 also do a second job – they reinforce, like all the items in category 8.

Educational TV vs. documentary TV

Category 9 is perhaps the category that most distinguishes *educational TV* from *documentary/informative TV*. This is because category 9 requires the viewer to stand back from the story and think about what should be learned from it. This characteristic is one of three main differences between educational and documentary TV. In the UK, there is a lot of overlap in production styles between the two. One justification is that viewers are accustomed to a professional standard for documentaries and might be disconcerted by amateurish production in educational TV. Moreover, where the styles do depart (and they do so in several respects), it could be argued that they depart too much. Indeed the two disciplines can learn a lot from each other: the specialist concerns of educational media design could inform and enhance general service non-fiction practice, and vice versa. Here are three major differences.

Study guidance

In educational video (or audio), more *guidance* tends to be given to the viewer about *what to make* of the material. This could be given in print or face-to-face prior to the screening. However, many research studies – e.g. by Bates (1987), Salomon (1983), Laurillard (1993) – have suggested that this guidance should be inside the video programme. The rationale is to empower the viewer to *stand back* from the situation in order to analyse it, rather than becoming too deeply immersed and mesmerized by the narrative. In contrast, the general service documentary producer would not want to interrupt the flow of the story by intervening with explicit viewer-guidance.

Preconceived objectives

In educational video, the *preconceived objectives* of the programme are *more clearly specified* before shooting. This may sound dangerous: if producers go out looking for a preconceived situation, there is a bias *to discover* it, whether or not it is there. However, the preconceived objectives for educational video are usually derived from a standard curriculum that has been gleaned from years of academic research and interpretation. In contrast, the *general service documentary* receives far less substantial research. The funds and the thinking-time are never sufficient for more than about a person-month of research. Moreover, the subject experts who are consulted during the research are firmly regarded as consultants rather than as co-authors. Such minimal research is likely to be less reliable than the academic literature. Hence the documentary producer might rethink preconceived objectives to accommodate unexpected findings, while the educational video producer feels justified in working to preconceived objectives derived from the literature. Nevertheless, educational producers should still take the term *documentary* seriously: if reality consistently *fails to* match academic preconceptions, then reality must be documented and false preconceptions re-evaluated. In any case, even for educational video, objectives should not be specified in precise detail from the outset. This is because the development of a coherent narrative might require some modifications to the objectives.

Academic cogency versus fascination

On grounds of academic cogency, the educational producer is more constrained about what to omit or include. For example, the general service documentary producer might feel free to omit fine caveats and exceptions to the rule, so as to avoid losing viewers' interest. The educational producer might feel bound to include such points, for completeness. Conversely, the educational producer might omit or underplay some fascinating, glamorous aspects of the situation if they are academically peripheral. The point is, the *most intriguing* illustration of a concept is the one that viewers would remember, but this may be to the exclusion of other illustrations that *better* illuminate the concept.

Conclusion

The educational producer might be accused of being pedantic and pedestrian, the general service producer of being superficial and gaudy. In both cases, the judgements are highly subjective. In both cases, the viewers do not know what they are missing. In both cases, producers are taking the attitude *we know what is best for you.* This attitude falls somewhere between being *patronizing* and being *sympathetic* to the viewer.

10. Link each chapter to the next one (and link to external knowledge)

A link is often a hybrid of 10a, content-link and 10b, story-link. A *pure* form of 10a is where the link is actually a cognitive objective – that is, the student is meant to learn the fact that one content-idea is linked to another. But even a pure *content-link* (10a) is likely to *help the story* (10b) at the same time.

The rationale for a *story-link* is to make the story *hang together*. The transition from one chapter to the next thereby seems *natural* or *logical*, rather than being a jump in the story for no obvious reason – and the student thereby feels comfortable with the transition (this therefore also falls under 5f, reassurance). Also, reception of the second item is easier if it is linked in the viewer's mind to the familiar first item (this therefore also falls into category 4 of Table 5.3, constructive learning).

The coherence of the educational story is of central importance. Coherence is a core purpose of structuring the material in the form of a story. It could be said that the very purpose of narrative is coherence. Thus, all the other main categories of the framework have a cohering purpose – the material is made to *cohere* or *stick together)* in viewers' minds.

10c. Indicate assumed external knowledge

Assumed external knowledge is knowledge that is external to the video but that the student is assumed to have learned. When it is indicated that such knowledge is being assumed, this accesses/activates the student's existing mental framework/schema, assuming the student has done the pre-work. Such activation is viewed by researchers from a wide variety of different philosophical perspective as an essential foundation for new knowledge. Merrill (2002a), a researcher with a somewhat *instructivist* perspective, takes this view, but so do many cognitive psychologists and constructivists (Driscoll, 2000).

For students who have not done the pre-work, the communication reassures (see 5f, above). Note that, because these two types of students are both helped (those who have done the pre-work and those who have not), this item caters for individual differences, as does the whole of category 4.

10d. Integrate with complementary learning

Compose the video to be an integral part of the current multiple media package. The effectiveness of video will be enhanced if it is designed to benefit from other recent learning experiences. For example, ensure that the terminology is consistent between all the media.

For print material that is directly tied to the video (broadcast notes for broadcast TV and video study guide for stop–start video), the necessity for integration goes without saying. Examples of such print materials were given earlier in this chapter and in Chapter 4.

Reclassification of the principles in the screenwriting framework in terms of their narrative stratagem

There is a reclassification of the principles in Table 5.3 that some previous students of screenwriting have found useful. We can characterize all the elements in terms of three archetypal narrative stratagems, represented at the three vertices of the triangle in Figure 6.5.

- Telling viewers about the story: explicit study guidance. For example, 9d, *chapter ending*, does this, as does 2d, *what to look out for*.
- ★ Surreptitious cognitive scaffolding: by creating an appropriate mental set with techniques that do not draw attention to themselves – they are virtually transparent. For example, 6b, *vary tempo to indicate syntax*, comes under this, as does the whole of category 7, *texture*.
- ◆ Telling the story: i.e. presenting the content. For example, 8a, *repetition* comes under this because a part of the story is told (again), although an element of surreptitious support is also involved, so principle 8a has to be positioned a little way from the vertex ◆ toward vertex ★)

Most of the other screenwriting principles fall under more than one of these three archetypes. For example, 10a, content link, comes fairly centrally along the bottom edge because linking includes content information (◆) while simultaneously (but surreptitiously) helping the viewers to take in the next chapter (★). Similarly 1b, create suspense, tells (some of) the story while simultaneously (but surreptitiously) motivating the viewer to attend expectantly.

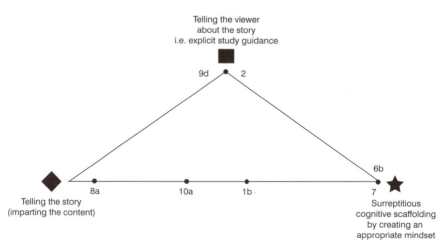

Figure 6.5 Alternative classification of elements of Table 5.2: narrative characterization (rather than pedagogic classification)

Activity

You might find it instructive to try and position all the principles of Table 5.3 in terms of the above three archetypes. The author's opinion on the appropriate placements is given in Appendix A1.1.

Conclusion

The proposed framework, Table 5.3, for screenwriting for video in educational multimedia, is offered as a basis for future debate among educational video producers and screenwriters concerning the essential elements of effective educational video design.

In the last few years, I've found that the framework has served as a reasonable foundation for analysis and constructive criticism of a wide variety of educational video programmes. As for the synthesis of programmes, that is never as easy as their analysis, but I believe the framework can help to build programmes as well as to take them apart.

The analysis has occurred mainly for stand-alone videos rather than for the video component of multimedia packages. In fact, the framework was originally developed for stand-alone videos and later modified for multimedia, although not drastically. For this reason alone, I've not the slightest doubt that the framework can be significantly bettered. I look forward to readers' reactions.

In any case, the framework/model is intended to be used flexibly, depending on producers' and screenwriters' individual styles and preferences, rather than being in any sense a prescriptive recipe. This would not be possible for a profession that is a complex mixture of craft, intuition, art and practical psychology.

For example, as mentioned earlier, no single chapter of a package should include all 46 subheadings and may not even include all 10 main headings. To give just one example, it may sometimes be counterproductive to signpost (category 2), in that the next item may be intended as a surprise, in which case viewers should not be told what is coming.

Indeed, every rule can be broken if there is a good reason. For example, a chapter ending (9d) is usually followed by a syntactic pause (which is varying the tempo, 6b) and then a heading for the new chapter (2c). An illustration of such a sequence, for a hypothetical package 'Mind and Body' might be the following narration in a video segment (ignoring pictures for simplicity).

- Chapter Ending – Pause – Chapter Heading
  'So that's dealt with the body. [*Pause*] Let's now consider the mind.'

However, depending on what comes before and after, and depending on the personal style of the screenwriter, here are three alternatives to the above sequence, all of which involve a *link* (10).

- Chapter Ending – Pause – Link – Chapter Heading
  'So that's dealt with the body. [*Pause*] But the body is controlled by the brain, which is the seat of the mind. So let's now consider the mind.'

- Chapter Ending – Pause – Chapter Heading – Link
  'So that's dealt with the body. [*Pause*] Let's now consider the mind – which controls the body – through the brain.'

- Pause – Link – Chapter Heading – Pause
  '[*Pause*] Now the body is controlled by the brain, which is the seat of the mind. So let's now consider the mind. [*Pause*]'

Note: in the latter case, where a pause has replaced the usual chapter ending, there is a danger of *steam-rolling* – that is, flattening the story, in the sense of obscuring the transition points. That is why a pause has been added at the end. This is unusual. Following a chapter heading, the viewer does not usually need a pause (i.e. wants to get on with the story). But in the above case, when the chapter ending is missing, the pause at the end allows the viewer to take a *mental breath*.

Concluding Reflective Activity: how do you use the framework in Table 5.3?

1 Analysis vs. synthesis. Using the framework to analyse existing video is certainly easier than using it to synthesize a new video. One way of synthesizing is to analyse early attempts and then revise them. What of the first attempt? You need to decide on the usage dimensions and the appropriate format (see principle 7a). Then write a half-page outline of content, then add a hook at the start. Next, look at the other nine categories. Are any included in your outline? Expand the outline, thinking about all ten categories. If this is difficult, expand the outline first and then modify it to include necessary items from the ten categories.

2 The 'messy' stages of screenplay development. For a long time (over many iterations) everything is up in the air and will not come together easily – bits of thoughts scattered about in one or more documents. This is inevitable if you are creative. Don't give up. You will be rewarded by the consolidation phase – that wonderful phase when you wake up *knowing* that you are about to put it all together. It may take another hour, or a day or even a week. But you *know* it's going to work, and you are looking forward to the *closure*. You are relishing the expectation of a great sense of achievement.

3 Abide by principles of professional integrity, such as those in Table 5.15.

Part IV

Picture–word synergy for audiovision and multimedia

Chapter 7

Principles of picture–word synergy for audiovision

➜ This chapter and the next deal with media other than video. However, the principles espoused are still audio-visual – they still concern picture–word composition, so they overlap with the philosophy of Chapter 5 and Chapter 6.

Audiovision is a low-tech medium: audio on cassette or CD guiding learners through visual materials that have been designed for that purpose (designed to be *talked through*). This medium had been employed successfully by the UK Open University since the 1970s, although interactive multimedia has superseded audiovision to an extent since 2000. Chapter 4 described learning tasks and teaching functions for which audiovision is particularly appropriate. Here is a summary of these functions:

    a. for topics/audiences where attention might wander with audio alone (visual points of reference anchor attention)
    b. when audio needs added visuals to avoid overloading auditory memory
    c. informal guidance through a *step-by-step process*
    d. talking students through practical procedures
    e. in situations that benefit from learners feeling that the teacher is looking over their shoulder, e.g. remedial tutorials
    f. the objects of study are visual resource materials, e.g. archaeological site plans, rock samples, supply and demand curves, transcripts of law court cases
    g. for detailed specification (in text) of student activities
    h. substitute for video when static pictures are sufficient
    i. substitute for video when the diagrams are too detailed to be legible on video
    j. also, audiovision might substitute for video for reasons of cost or staff expertise

The principles of picture–word synergy are set out in section 4 below. This section is preceded by some practical points, regarding graphics in section 1 and regarding the production process in sections 2 and 3.

1. Accompanying visual materials – typical examples

1.1   Existing course material, e.g. diagrams, text. The audio is in the form of a tutorial that manages the student's use of the learning materials.

1.2   Specially prepared visual materials, *customized for use with the tape* (recommended over option 1.1). A well-tried practice is to design the visuals in the form of a sequence of *frames* (printed boxes, on paper, containing equations, diagrams, etc.). The frames contain the key teaching points and the audio fleshes out these points.

1.3   Slides.

1.4   Home kit (e.g. plastic models, rock samples).

1.5   Customized computer-generated graphics (Koumi and Daniels 1994). As in the above cases, the audio component is decoupled from the sequence of the visuals – i.e. on a separate audio recording under the student's control, unlike multimedia packages (described in the next chapter) where the audio track is coupled to the development of the visuals (programmed to match the changes in the visuals).

In some cases, the materials can be *pure resource material* (e.g. rock samples), which the audio teaches about. Alternatively, they can incorporate their own teaching in the form of text, which the audio elaborates on (e.g. the rock samples could have labels that explain how they were formed). See item (f) above for more examples of resource materials.

2. How to prepare for the production

2.1   Consider/specify:

- the audiovision topic: i.e. choose those learning tasks in this week's syllabus that would benefit more from audiovision than from other available media. Conceivably these learning tasks could be scattered about during the week's work. However, this is worrisome for the student. Ideally, the week's syllabus should be organized in such a way that the audiovision learning constitutes a particular section of the week's work.

- the intended learning outcomes of the audiovision package. However, religious adherence to pre-specified objectives could constrain the development of a coherent pedagogic story. Many developers start with broad objectives and refine them once they flesh out the storyline and the content.

- learning context and complementary learning experiences – related knowledge studied recently (or to be studied soon) through other media. These experiences need to be borne in mind by designers, so that the student receives a coherent learning experience.

- target audience's age, commitment, previous knowledge gained outside the current course. These characteristics should affect the style and depth of the treatment.

2.2 Choose type of accompanying visual materials (e.g. which of those listed in section 1?)

2.3 Compose an outline (i.e. design the first draft of the visual materials). If accompanying materials are to be special audio-customized print, contained in *frames*, then the outline can be a draft of these frames.

2.4 Incorporate feedback from colleagues.
Circulate copies of your frames to your colleagues and make revisions based on their feedback. To make it easier for your busy colleagues to supply feedback and for you to incorporate it, the frames alone (before the audio is added) should constitute a full outline of the content. Pedagogic rationale for this policy is given in note 4.16.

2.5 Tape-record a first draft of the audio commentary.
Working from the draft of the frames, speak your first draft commentary straight into a tape recorder, *before writing it out as a script*. This ensures that your commentary sounds like the *spoken* word (*conversational* speech) rather than the *written* word.
Then listen to the tape and transcribe it. You can then work on the transcript to improve it. But resist reverting to a *print* style: read it out aloud again to make sure it is still comfortable to say and that it sounds conversational.
Another advantage of recording without a script is that you get all the way through at an early stage. Otherwise it is very easy to get stuck on the first section, repeatedly improving it while giving little attention to subsequent sections.

2.6 Write down the frame numbers in the margin once the script is transcribed. This helps future drafting and redrafting.

3. The production process

3.1 Schedule the recording of the final audio script, far enough ahead to be preceded by several script discussions.

3.2 Schedule the rehearsal before pm of recording day minus 1 – to allow time for final alterations before recording

3.3 Schedule script discussions (to discuss each draft of the audiovision package), spaced sufficiently apart to enable redrafting, circulation and reflection of each new draft.

3.4 Type the rehearsal script and the final script so that they are easy to read: 7 words per line, 1½-spacing; mark the pauses, e.g. (*pause 2 secs*); end the page at a paragraph ending (not in mid-paragraph, otherwise this might result in an unnatural pause between pages).

3.5   Rehearse. Recruit the aid of a colleague (preferably one who is not too familiar with the material) to take on the role of the student, i.e. look at the *frames* while hearing the speaker – there will be one or more occasions when the match between the commentary and the graphics can be improved by changing one or the other

3.6   Direct the recording, getting the best out of the speakers

- Place the script on a sloping lectern, angled at 45 degrees towards the speaker.
- Record only two pages at a time, both visible side by side in front of the speaker.
- Make drinking-water available.
- Recommend deep breathing for nervous speakers.
- Give frequent praise during the recording (self-confident speakers sound more natural).
- Change the wording if the speaker is having difficulty.
- As a final check, recruit a colleague to take on the role of the student again.

3.7   Edit. Mark up the script to facilitate editing. Block edit first, then fine edit. Block editing means put all the takes into the correct order, apart from small retakes. For example, you might record all the way through, making a few mistakes and retaking them as you go through. Then at the end you might decide to rerecord the first page now that the speaker has overcome the initial *nervous* performance. Block editing means put that rerecording of the first page at the front. Fine editing means tighten up pauses, cut out paper-shuffles, replace sentences with their retakes.

4. Design principles for audiovision

The principles are divided into several categories:

- Navigational guidance and student control
- Use of language
- Layout of frames
- Relationship of text to commentary
- The speaker should be like a personal tutor
- Visuals and words should reinforce each other
- Interactive elements
- Educational story-telling (judiciously balance *effective exposition* by the teacher, against *independent exploration* by the student)

Navigational guidance and student control

4.1 Specify in the printed materials which audio recording to play. Conversely, specify in an announcement at the start of the tape, which printed materials to look at. Also in both the announcement and the printed materials, identify any required pre-work, for example, say: 'before listening to this tape, you should have read ...'

4.2 Give each frame a number and quote the number to direct students' attention to that frame.

4.3 To help students find their place on the tape, the main speaker should mention frame numbers frequently. For example if the speaker has finished dealing with equation 1 in Frame 3, then instead of saying 'Now for equation 2' it is better to say 'Now for equation 2 in Frame 3'. Then, for example, if students are browsing through the frames, and they want to listen to the commentary relating to a particular frame, they can fast-spool the tape forward or backward and sample the tape until they hear that frame-number. This will be easier if frame numbers are mentioned frequently.

4.4 Give each frame a title so that students (and you) can refer to them easily – and to help students navigate when skimming through later.

Use of language

4.5 Listeners find it easier to understand short sentences. One reason is that a long sentence can exceed the listener's memory span. Another reason is that long sentences normally contain conditional clauses, which are difficult to bear in mind. So you should convert every long sentence into two or more short ones.

For example, imagine you were speaking the last four sentences. Listeners would understand you quite easily. But they would find it more difficult if you combined the four sentences into a single long sentence, as follows:

If you have a very long sentence, especially if it contains conditional clauses (like this one), you should convert it into two or more short ones, because listeners will find that easier to understand, partly due to the fact that a long sentence can overload the listener's memory span and also because conditional clauses are difficult to bear in mind.

Notice that, if you convert this long sentence back into the four earlier short ones, you are forced to repeat some of the words (*short*, *long* and *sentence*) so you are incidentally adding some user-friendly redundancy.

4.6 Avoid using words that are difficult to say or to hear or to distinguish from other words. As well as long sentences, it is difficult to say phrases in which the last consonant of a word is the same as the first consonant of the next word. This happens twice in the phrase: 'The last task of the seventh theme …' (And this is difficult to hear too.)

Here is an example of words that are difficult to distinguish from other words: 'Right-indicate or signal' sounds like 'Write "indicator signal"'. If you cannot avoid wording that is difficult to hear, make sure the meaning is clear from the context, and/or repeat difficult words in the text.

4.7   The narration is audio not print, so write for the ear, not the eye. That is, write *conversational* speech, to be spoken and listened to, *not* to be read). One way to achieve this has been described in item 2.5.

Layout of frames

4.8   The layout of frames should be easy for the eye to follow while listening. So you should design uncluttered, sparse layout. This is because students cannot easily process dense visual layout while listening to commentary. In particular, concerning text, a rule of thumb is to use only 25 per cent of normal print density, ordered from left to right and top to bottom, and appropriately spaced to lead the eye naturally through the frame.

4.9   Some writers use landscape layout for the frames, as shown in Figure 7.1. A landscape layout enables four frames per page (rather than two, which is suitable on a portrait layout). The four frames on the same page make it easier for students to switch attention between nearby frames (and it saves paper).

4.10   If a self-contained argument requires more than four frames, and if students would be required to look back and forth between these frames, you could try and cover the argument in eight frames and position them on facing pages, as in Figure 7.1.

Comment: advantage over multimedia packages

For an interactive multimedia package, such cross-referencing between eight frames' worth of information would not be possible – that much information would be illegible on a single screen. Hence audiovision is better suited than interactive multimedia for tasks that require comparison and analysis of large quantities of information.

Relationship of text to commentary

4.11   There are various essential items of text, such as mathematical equations and the labels on the axes of a graph. In addition, succinct items of explanatory text can serve as visual mnemonics to avoid overloading auditory memory: the spoken words do not need to be retained in memory if they have been précis-ed by a key word or two of screen text. Key words

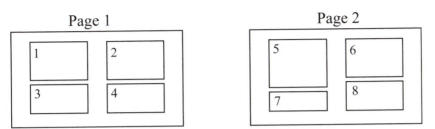

Figure 7.1 Two pages of frames in landscape format

can also serve as visual reference points that anchor attention and prevent the learner's mind from wandering. This type of visual material, as well as diagrams and equations, is what widens the scope of audio – it enables the teaching of more topics in more detail.

4.12 But you can have too much text. There are many audiovision packages in which the text duplicates the commentary (also many Power Point presentations). This is likely to have a negative effect. Literate students can read faster than you can speak and it is onerous to try to match their reading pace with that of the narration. Consequently, if students attend to both sources, there will be semantic interference.

In fact, the semantic interference might well be preceded by phonological interference – in Baddeley's conception of working memory, visual text is converted into a phonological code and processed in the same system as spoken text (Baddeley 1992). Moreover, Inhoff *et al.* (2004) report a preponderance of evidence that a visual word's phonological representation is determined before its meaning is known.

This interference can be largely avoided if the text is a judicious précis of the audio commentary, not a duplicate.

4.13 When the audio narration is précis-ed by text, students will search the text in an attempt to track what they are hearing. To facilitate this tracking, the text should *reproduce key words* of the narration rather than *paraphrasing* the narration. So if the text has 'basic ideas', the narration should include the same words, 'basic ideas', rather than paraphrasing them into (say) 'fundamental notions'.

4.14 Apart from the preceding *key word* recommendation, it is difficult to make hard and fast rules about how to phrase the text so that it anchors the audio commentary rather than interfering with its apprehension. However, formative evaluation during rehearsal and recording can help to make these judgements. Following the initial design, many ad hoc refinements can be made through adopting the role of the learner during rehearsal and recording of the audio commentary (3.5 and 3.6).

4.15   In the text, as well as *key words*, always include *new technical terms*, which you should also mention in the audio commentary, so that the learners hear the pronunciation.

4.16   Item 2.4 recommended that you should design frames to be a full outline of the topic, sufficient for your busy colleagues to grasp, without having to read through your audio script. If the frames are sufficient for your colleagues (subject-matter experts whose memories may need refreshing), they should also be sufficient for the students (aspiring experts) when they revise. And they can revise more quickly if they don't listen to the audio.

You can achieve such a full outline with an economic amount of text. This is because the text gains new meaning once students have listened to the audio commentary; so when they look at the frames later, students will recall much of the extra meaning that was supplied by the commentary.

4.17   It may sometimes not be possible to follow recommendation 4.8, that is, to make frames sparse enough to be followed during listening to the tape. This difficulty would arise if the topic needs detailed printed information at certain points. But this problem has a solution. If a frame is unavoidably complicated, just tell students to pause the tape and familiarize themselves with it before you comment on it.

But avoid such dense frames as far as possible. If you really need several such frames, then you have chosen the wrong medium.

4.18   There are two places where you can include dense text without worrying about clashing with the listening. This is at the front of the frames and at the end. That is, you can have a text introduction to the topic, to be read before listening to the audio, and a text summary, to be read immediately after listening to the audio. In this case, the visual elements of the whole package, including the introduction and the summary, would be what students could read in the future for revision, without needing to replay the audio.

4.19   A reasonable average for frequency of frames: 1 frame per 1½ minutes of audio.

4.20   A reasonable duration: 17 to 35 minutes audio, taking 1½ to 3 hours study time. (UK OU average is approximately, 30 minutes audio, taking 2½ hours study time.)

The main speaker should be like a personal tutor

4.21   For the announcement that tells students about pre-work and about which visuals to use (4.1), you could use a different speaker with a matter-of-fact, administrative tone. This frees the main narrator to be informal from the outset, taking the role of a personal tutor.

4.22   When recording, the speaker is probably *not* looking at the visuals/frames, but rather reading the script. But the *style* of the audio should be *as if* each listener has a personal tutor looking over his or her shoulder at the same visual.

4.23 The production may have been a team effort, but in order to be personal, the speaker needs to take sole credit as the individual author. That is, say 'I' rather than 'we'. Also, address the listener directly as 'you', not as 'some of you'. The *impersonal* words and phrases are crossed out in the following example:

~~We have~~ I have drawn an extra cloud in the diagram, in case ~~some of~~ you have not met this idea before …

4.24 To avoid being authoritarian you should *invite* students to carry out an activity, rather than *tell* them. Alternatively, use a *music jingle* as a signal to stop the tape. Some teachers feel that a jingle makes the package more authoritarian, while others feel it arouses students. Some teachers use a jingle as well as inviting students to stop.

The visuals and the audio should reinforce each other

4.25 Make teaching points about a visual when they are looking at it, and not in a wordy introduction while they are looking at the previous visual. The following sentence suffers from that problem:

I want to do three things – I want to give an overview of the stages in the argument; then I'll explain each stage in detail; and finally I'll explain how the stages relate: I've outlined these three things in Frame 6.

Instead, direct the students to look at frame 6 from the start, not at the end, as in:

In Frame 6, I've outlined the three things I want to do – I want to give an overview of the stages in the argument: then I'll explain each stage in detail; and finally I'll explain how the stages relate.

The reason why this ordering is preferable is that when the table appears from the outset, it gives students a visual reference on which to anchor the points being made in the narration.

Another example of when looking at images should precede listening to the corresponding narration is when the images are mathematical expressions that are difficult to listen to unless they can be seen. For example, in a mathematics lesson for students who are fairly new to algebra, consider the commentary 'minus b, plus or minus the square root of, b-squared minus four ac, all over two a'. This is impossible for most students to appreciate unless they are first told to look at the algebraic formula

$$\frac{-b \pm \sqrt{(b^2 - 4ac)}}{2a}$$

4.26   Give students enough time to digest the visuals. For example, include sufficient pause in the commentary for students' eyes to settle on a new frame before commenting on it.

4.27   When moving from one idea to the next, while still on the same frame, create a vertical *gap* in the spacing of the graphics and a *matching pause* in the audio commentary.

4.28   Give clear guidance about what to do and where to look. If the frames are well designed, the layout should lead the student's eyes naturally to each item. However, occasionally, you may need to direct their gaze by saying 'at the top of the frame …' or 'in equation 2 …'

4.29   Your audio content should minimize memory load. For example, avoid a long list of verbal instructions. If it is unavoidable, recap the list in print and number the items so that you can refer to them.

Interactive elements – how to refer to activities in advance

4.30   If you ask students to write one or two words on a diagram or to pick up an object, insert a 2 or 3 second pause. However, a longer activity (one that you judge to need 10 seconds) might require 5 seconds for some students and 20 seconds for others. So in this case, just advise students to stop the tape.

4.31   If the activity needs a lot of preparatory explanation on the tape, avoid any wording or pacing that might prompt them to stop the tape before you've finished preparing them. For example, do not say

In frame 8, there is a related question for you to try. [*Pause 2 seconds*] But before you do, I need to explain something … [Explanation.]

This might lead to premature stopping, during the 2 second pause. So instead, begin with a postponing phrase, like

In a moment I'm going to ask you to try the question in frame 8. But I need to explain something first … [Explanation.]

Interactive elements – after they have tackled the activity

4.32 The document that students use for revision will include their own annotations, made during the interspersed activities. Hence it is preferable that students should annotate the document rather than use a separate piece of paper. So leave space in the frame for students to write their answers.

4.33 When you include more than one activity during a *tape stop*, help students' memories by indicating in print when to restart the tape.

4.34 Comments or answers for the activities can be in print or on the audio, depending on which medium is more appropriate: do the students need a printed record?

4.35 Even if the comment or answer is in print, it is still worthwhile mentioning the activity on audio, after the tape-stop. This reminds students what they should have just done during a tape-stop. (You can never tell when they will restart the tape: it may be two days later.) For example, after a tape-stop jingle, do not merely say 'You should now be able to'. Instead say 'If you have calculated the values in Table 2.1, you should now be able to'.

4.36 Or you could go through the answers, talking about them, if you feel that verbal elaboration would help.

Interactive elements – number of tape-stops

4.37 Too frequent tape-stops could irritate students. As a general rule the interspersed audio narration should be substantial – more than three paragraphs.

4.38 You can overdo interactivity. Students will not be happy with activities if they do not perceive them as useful.

Educational story-telling

Judiciously balance *effective exposition* by the teacher, against *independent exploration* by the student. The efficacy (even the necessity) of narrative structure has been proposed by many writers, such as Gudmundsdottir (1995) and Gibson (1996). The guidelines below are adapted from the principles for pedagogic video design, in Table 5.3 of Chapter 5, which is further elaborated in Chapter 6.

4.39 Hook (capture and sustain attention): e.g. capture attention with the unexpected; sustain attention by creating suspense.

4.40 Signpost: clearly indicate where the story is going, what is happening next, why it is happening, what to look out for.

4.41 Facilitate concentration/activation

- Have short pauses for contemplation.
- Encourage prediction.

- Put the answers to problems on a separate page from the questions. Alternatively, you could ask students to be prepared with a piece of paper to mask the answers from themselves.

4.42   Encourage/enable constructive learning

- Spoken words should not be a literal duplication of the visuals (because you want to encourage students to make the picture–word connection for themselves).
- Concretize: that is, relate to (hence *activate*) students' previous knowledge.
- Disclose the context of your arguments, e.g. set the scene before going into details.
- Support/scaffold the learner's construction of knowledge. Here are three examples.

    Proceed from conrete to abstract and from simple to complex. However, going from simple to complex is not always appropriate. Van Merriënboer (2001) cites evidence that completion tasks on computer designs are better for learning than asking students to carry out the design from scratch.

    Concerning scaffolding of problem-solving, Merrill (2002a) and Van Merriënboer (2001) recommend several techniques, such as: show a worked example of a similar problem before asking students to solve a problem, or show a simple *half-way-there* problem before posing the full problem, or divide the problem into subproblems, or pose a sequence of successively more difficult problems.

    The type and extent of scaffolding depends on the ability of the learner. In any case, the scaffolding should be withdrawn little by little as learners progress. For more on scaffolding, see McLoughlin *et al.* (2000), Van Merriënboer (2001), or Merrill (2002a).

4.43   Elucidate: moderate the load, pace and depth, maximize clarity. Do not overload students with too many teaching points or too fast a pace, or too much intellectual depth. This depends on the level and prior knowledge of the students.

    For example, regarding depth, deal with the specific before the general, especially when the concepts are unfamiliar. However, avoid spoon-feeding. If you judge that the learners possess some nascent ideas about a concept, then starting with the general, overarching *big idea* might serve to activate the learners' prior *half-knowledge*, which will get elaborated later by the specific material to be learned.

    Regarding clarity, for example, design graphics to be clear (unambiguous), uncluttered, evocative. In general, look for ways in which graphic representation can clarify a topic – using flow-charts, concept maps, colour coding, shape coding.

4.44 Texture: insert occasional light items to vary the mood, vary the format, exploit the unique presentational characteristics of audio, i.e. tone of voice, sequence, pacing, phrasing, timbre, sounds of real-world.

4.45 Reinforce: give more than one example of a concept, use *comparison* and *contrast*, ensure *synergy* (as in 4.25 to 4.29) between visuals and audio.

4.46 Consolidation of learning could be achieved through students solving end-of-chapter problems and referring to model answers.

4.47 Link between sections and organize sections so that they connect naturally. Also, link with other components of the learning system, e.g. print, face-to-face activity

Conclusion: draft and redraft

4.48 Given all the above, it should be clear that you could not design a perfect picture–word package with your first draft – you need several draft designs and script discussions.

Chapter 8

Screenwriting principles for a multimedia package

Picture–word synergy for multimedia with audio commentary

Following a short summary of relevant literature, this chapter offers a framework of guidelines for designing multimedia packages. These guidelines overlap with those for audiovision in Chapter 7. However, there are many new points and elaborations due to the extra facility of interactivity and of audio being coupled synchronously to the visuals. In particular, these guidelines concentrate on techniques for achieving pedagogic synergy between audio commentary and visual elements. They also include proposals for pedagogically optimum production techniques and interactive features, together with techniques for salvaging narrative coherence. The framework derives from the author's experience of producing and appraising multimedia packages, mainly at the UK Open University.

Introduction

Van Merriënboer (2001) noted with regret that little is known about the optimal combination of audio, screen texts and illustrations in pictures or video. In fact there are some substantial papers at the macro-level, by educational technologists such as Laurillard and Taylor at the UK Open University. These do address some design techniques, which appear below, but mainly they discuss global questions, such as how learners might cope without a fixed linear narrative (Laurillard 1998; Laurillard *et al.* 2000) and how to describe multimedia learning systems using an analytical framework (Taylor *et al.* 1997). However, the literature appears to lack any *comprehensive* framework of micro-level design principles for optimal integration of visuals and audio. This is despite the many investigations into the use of audio commentary in multimedia presentations. Some of these investigations are summarized below, confirming mixed results in the comparison of screen text with audio commentary.

Following this summary, the major part of this chapter consists of a framework of design guidelines for multimedia packages. These guidelines are in the form of practicable design principles: for example, that 'there are occasions when the words should come first, in order to prepare the viewer for the pictures', such as

In the next animation, concentrate on the arms of the spinning skater. [*Animation starts with skater's arms held wide, then pulled in.*]

The design guidelines have not been subjected to scientific investigation and therefore do not appear in the literature. They are derived from multimedia package designs at the UK Open University and incorporate an abundance of practitioners' knowledge regarding optimal integration of audio commentary and graphics build-up. The pedigree of the guidelines warrants a degree of confidence in their efficacy. At the very least, they could generate fruitful hypotheses for future investigation.

The literature relating visuals and audio commentary

Tabbers *et al.* (2001) report several recent studies by Sweller, Mayer and others, in which multimedia presentations consisted of pictorial information and explanatory text. Many of these demonstrated the superiority of auditory text (spoken commentary) over visual, on-screen text. In various experiments learners in the audio condition spent less time in subsequent problem-solving, attained higher test scores and reported expending less mental effort. The investigators attributed these results to the so-called *modality effect* or *modality principle*. This presupposes *dual coding*, whereby auditory and visual inputs can be processed simultaneously in *working memory*, which thereby leaves extra capacity for the learning process.

In their own study, Tabbers *et al.* (2001) presented diagrams plus audio commentary to one group, but to a second group they replaced the audio commentary with identical visual text, on screen for the same duration. They found that the audio group achieved higher learning scores. However, when two other groups were allowed to spend as much time as they liked on the same materials, the superiority of the audio condition disappeared. The authors conjecture that the so-called modality effect of earlier studies might be due to lack of time rather than lack of memory resources. (Mind you, the students in the visual text condition needed to spend longer on task to achieve their comparable scores, so the audio condition could still claim superior efficiency.)

Others have found that addition of audio need not be beneficial to learning. Beccue *et al.* (2001) added an audio component to a multimedia package, without changing the visuals (graphics and animation). The audio was a conversational version of a printed lab manual that college students could read prior to studying the multimedia package. The improvement in scores between pre- and post-test was greater for the group with added audio than for the control group, but not significantly. Many students suggested that the audio imposed a slower pace than they were used to. The authors theorized that the pace set by the audio might be helpful for slow learners and detrimental to fast learners (resulting in an average improvement score that was not significantly better than that in the no-audio presentation).

Kalyuga (2000) observed a similar effect, finding that *novices* performed better with diagram-plus-audio than with diagram-only. However, the reverse was found for *experienced learners*. In another experiment, Kalyuga (2000) found that audio commentary did indeed result in better learning, but only when the identical visual text was absent. Specifically, a diagram was explained in three different ways: visual text, audio text, visual text presented simultaneously with identical audio text. The visual-plus-audio group achieved much lower scores than the audio-only.

Kalyuga's interpretation of this result was that working memory was overloaded by the necessity to relate corresponding elements of visual and auditory content, thus interfering with learning. He concluded that the elimination of a redundant visual source of information was beneficial.

However, this interpretation would predict that elimination of a redundant *audio* source would also be beneficial, that is, that the visual group would learn better than the visual-plus-audio group. In fact, the result was slightly in the opposite direction, which also meant that the audio-only group learned much better than the visual-only group. Hence a more convincing explanation is a *split attention* effect. In the visual-only condition, students had to split visual attention between the diagram and the visual text. This imposes a greater cognitive load than the audio-only condition, in which students had only one thing to look at (the diagram) while listening simultaneously to a spoken description.

Moreno and Mayer (2000) presented an animation accompanied by either audio text or visual text. They also found a strong split-attention effect, which they express as a Split-Attention Principle:

> Students learn better when the instructional material does not require them to split their attention between multiple sources of mutually referring information.

In their experiment, the information in visual text referred to the information in the animated diagrams and vice versa.

In a refinement of these experiments, Tabbers *et al.* (2000) compared two strategies for decreasing cognitive load of multimedia instructions: *preventing split-attention* (preventing visual search by adding visual cues) or *presenting text as audio* (replacing screen text with audio commentary). They found that students who received visual cues scored higher on reproduction tests. However, the modality effect was opposite to that expected, in that visual text resulted in higher scores than audio commentary.

The authors advanced some speculative reasons for this reversal of previous findings.

- Students reported expending significantly greater mental effort in the visual text condition. Whatever the reason for the greater effort (possibly that reading visual text is more learner-active than listening to audio text), it could have resulted in deeper processing and hence better learning.
- Students could choose to replay the audio text segments (and to reread the visual text). However, in both conditions, it is likely that students had partly understood the texts on first listening (or first reading). Hence, in the visual text condition, students who reread the text could skip any visual text that they had already understood, whereas in the audio condition, students who relistened would be forced to process some redundant auditory information.

These are reasonable conjectures for why learning was superior in the visual text condition. A third likely reason (which does not conflict with the two conjectures) was the complexity of the task. Students studied how to design a blueprint for training in complex skills, based on Van Merriënboer's Four Component Instructional Design model. The task is certainly complex. It necessitates self-paced, head-down, concentrated study of complicated diagrams and relationships (students were allowed an hour to work through the multimedia learning task). As argued by Koumi (1994a), such tasks cannot easily be supported by audio commentary, because this is a time-based (transient) medium. Instead, what's needed is a static (printed) set of guidelines that students can revisit repeatedly while they carry out intensive, self-paced study of the diagrams.

The above arguments may throw some light on the various conflicting results. However, there may be more fundamental reasons for the inconsistencies, as follows.

Hede (2002) points out that conflicting results are not surprising, considering the myriad of contingent factors that have been shown to moderate multimedia effects, including:

- nature of visual and audio input
- positive and negative modality effects (dual coding vs. interference)
- interactivity and cognitive engagement
- cognitive overload

An overlapping set of factors that would result in conflicting results derives from the pedagogic design of the package. The set includes

- navigational features and student control
- use of language
- layout of screen (e.g. use of sparse vs. dense screen-text)
- relationship of (sparse) text with conversational audio commentary
- synergy between visuals and commentary
- design of interactive features

- balance between structured narrative exposition and independent student exploration

These are some of the category headings for the design guidelines proposed later in this chapter. It will be argued that the micro-level (practicable) design principles in these categories are important for optimizing the pedagogic efficacy of a multimedia package. The aforementioned studies, in manipulating the format of a multimedia package, may have introduced debilitating distortions into a previously effective pedagogic design. If so, the inconsistent results might be artefacts of disparate qualities of pedagogic design.

This point can be elaborated as follows. During the design of an audio-visual package, decisions are often made to modify or omit a segment of narration and/or a visual element. A good media producer, faced with the removal of some visuals, would try to compensate by rescripting the audio component – and would redraft the visuals if denied some of the audio. In contrast the aforementioned studies impose restrictions on the visual elements and/or the audio elements, without controlling for the pedagogic disruption, namely the consequent disharmony between visual text and diagrams or between visuals and audio. In fact, the experimenters could not easily control for these distortions, because to date there are no published micro-level design guidelines that focus on harmony/synergy. This chapter aims to provide a framework of such guidelines.

The provenance of the design framework below

UK Open University multimedia packages are typically produced over several script conferences by a team of experienced teachers who know their target audience well. For such a team, permitted sufficient thinking-time, the ensuing learning material is based upon several lifetimes of teaching experience.

Successive script conferences build creative momentum in which the critical analysis becomes progressively deeper. Effectively, the team is carrying out a whole series of developmental evaluations, as *thought experiments*, each member of the team repeatedly taking on the role of a hypothetical student. In addition, many of these design teams include an educational technologist, who contributes research experience and knowledge of current learning theories. Over time, the team will have developed a consensus design model, even if it is rather vague and intuitive.

This chapter seeks to pull together these tacit design models and make them explicit, in the form of the framework below. No doubt the framework owes a debt to learning theories that have permeated the collective psyche of audio-visual practitioners. In addition, the framework has been successively refined through the author's appraisal and co-authorship of UK Open University multimedia packages and those of other institutions. Critical comments regarding this first published attempt will be welcomed.

The design framework

A multimedia package might include video clips containing their own commentary. The screenwriting principles for designing video commentary have been addressed in Chapters 5 and 6. However, when the rest of the multimedia package also contains an audio commentary, there are further screenwriting principles to consider. These principles/guidelines appear in section 4 below. This section is preceded by some practical points, regarding the visuals in section 1 and regarding the development process in sections 2 and 3. These preliminary sections are essential complements to the guideline section.

1. The visuals

The visuals can be equations, printed text (both often built up line by line from top to bottom of the screen), diagrams, animations, video. Usually, the screen would be divided into sections, for example, video on the left, text on the right.

In all cases, the visuals could be *pure resource material*, which the audio teaches about, or can *incorporate their own teaching*, in the form of visual text, which the audio elaborates on. Or, there could be a mixture, that is, some of the visuals on the screen could be resource material and other visuals could be teaching about the resource material.

Some examples of pure resource materials:

- in a mathematical modelling package – slow motion video recording of a vibrating string, showing a clear (not blurred) image of the shape of the string
- in an economics package – diagrams of archetypal supply and demand curves
- in a geology package – photographs (or video) of rock strata
- in a package about evolution – photographs and descriptions of the species and subspecies of finches in the Galapogos islands, as described by Taylor *et al.* (1997)
- in a package on the relationship between Homer's poems and archaeological data on Ancient Greece – the text of Homer's poems and archaeological site plans, as described by Laurillard (1998)

In all these cases, the audio could do all the teaching about the visual resource material. More likely, there would be some screen text accompanying the visuals, giving an outline explanation, and the audio would elaborate on the outline.

So far, only the expository part of the package has been alluded to. In addition, the interactive elements also involve visuals. Some of the text would be in the form of interactive dialogue boxes whereby students carry out activities, inputting their own text in response to questions.

2. How to prepare for the production

2.1   Consider/specify:

- the topic: that is, the subtopic or learning task in this week's syllabus that would benefit more from a multimedia package than from other available media.
- the intended learning outcomes of the multimedia package, in one or more domains: cognitive, experiential, affective. These specifications need to be reappraised and refined as the content is developed: it is only when the details of the pedagogic storyline are developed that detailed objectives can be finalized. This point was argued in Chapter 5.
- complementary learning experiences – related knowledge studied recently (or to be studied soon) through other media. These experiences need to be borne in mind when designing the multimedia package, so that the student receives a coherent learning experience.
- target audience characteristics, e.g. age, commitment, previous knowledge gained outside the current course. These characteristics should affect the style and depth of the treatment.

2.2   Decide on software and delivery platform

Which programming environment should be used (e.g. Director™, Toolbook™, Boxmind-Enlighten)? Should the package be delivered on a CD-ROM, via the web, or both? Should there be links to commercial software such as spreadsheets or mathematical packages? These are complex technical questions. For an informative discussion, see Taylor *et al.* (1997).

2.3   Decide on type of visual materials

Is video needed? Should the graphics be in the form of 2D diagrams that are built up in stages or should there be full 3D animation?

2.4   Compose an outline, on paper, of the multimedia *screens.* A screen consists of a sequence of visuals/graphics that develops autonomously over time (without needing the learner's intervention). For example, a title might appear at the top, followed one second later by an equation on the left-hand side of the screen. This might then be followed, after a sentence of audio commentary, by a second equation, followed two seconds later by a phrase of printed text on the right-hand side of the screen. The next screen of graphics starts when the student has elected to move on, e.g. by pressing *NEXT*.

2.5   Incorporate feedback from colleagues. Circulate copies of your (numbered) screen designs to your colleagues and make revisions based on their feedback. To facilitate useful feedback from busy colleagues, the screens alone (before the audio is added) should constitute a full outline of the content. Further rationale for this policy is argued in guideline 4.21.

2.6   Tape-record a first draft of the audio commentary. Working from the draft of the screen graphics, speak your first draft commentary straight into a tape recorder *before* writing it out as a script. This ensures that your commentary sounds like the *spoken* word (*conversational speech*) rather than the *written* word.

    Listen to the tape and transcribe it. You can then work on the transcript to improve it. When you work on the transcript, resist reverting to a *print* style: read it out aloud again to make sure it is still comfortable to say. (This second draft will be recorded as a guide track – as explained in 3.4.)

    Another advantage of recording without a script is that you get all the way through at an early stage. Otherwise it is very easy to get stuck on the first section, improving it over and over while giving little attention to subsequent sections. You could end up with draft 5 of section 1, draft 4 of section 2, and so on, down to draft 1 of section 5. In that case, when later sections are redrafted, you would be forced to return to earlier sections and modify them again, in order to integrate them with the improved later sections. Hence you end up with at least one extra redrafting. During all this time, you do not have a good overview of the whole package.

2.7   On the audio script, note the screen numbers in the margin. This will help you navigate through your draft script as you modify it during your design of script and screens.

3. The production

3.1   Schedule the recording of the final audio script far enough ahead to be preceded by several script discussions.

3.2   Schedule the rehearsal before p.m. of recording day minus 1 – to allow time for final alterations before recording

3.3   Schedule script discussions and materials development, with meetings spaced sufficiently apart to enable redrafting and dissemination to the development team for their reflection on each new draft.

3.4   After the screens are programmed, so that a first draft can be viewed, the speaker should record the second draft of the audio commentary (i.e. the improvement of the first transcription, as explained in 2.6). This should be done in sections, each corresponding to a particular screen, using the computer's microphone to record audio files and lay them onto the audio line. This is only a guide-track – the final audio-track will be recorded and laid later.

3.5   Programme the graphics build-up so that visuals to appear at particular points on the audio line, for example, between particular words.

3.6   Finalize the screens (this will require several iterations, invariably introducing unforeseen programming problems).

3.7   Print out the screens (omitting the interim build-up stages – just showing what each screen looks like finally).

3.8   Type the rehearsal script and the final script so that they are easy to read: 7 words per line, 1½-line spacing, mark the pauses, e.g. (*pause 2 secs*), end the page at a paragraph ending (not in mid-paragraph), so as to avoid unnatural pauses between pages, label the script to correspond to individual screens and hence to end up with individual audio files.

3.9   Rehearse the speaker

As a producer/director (if you are not also the speaker), take on the role of the student, that is, look at a printout of the screens while hearing the speaker. There will be one or more occasions when the harmony between the commentary and the graphics can be improved by changing one or the other. If you are the speaker, recruit the aid of a colleague to take the student's role, preferably a colleague who has not seen the material.

3.10   Direct the recording of the final sound-track, getting the best out of the speakers, for example:

- Place the script on a sloping lectern, angled at 45 degrees towards the speaker.
- Record only two pages at a time, both visible side by side in front of the speaker.
- Make drinking-water available.
- Recommend deep breathing to calm the nerves.
- Give frequent praise during the recording (self-confident speakers sound more natural).
- Change the wording if the speaker is having difficulty.
- As a final check, take on the role of the student again, or recruit a colleague to take the role – there will usually be suggestions for some final changes.

3.11   Edit. Mark up the script clearly and comprehensively to facilitate editing. While busily recording, it is easy to skimp on describing exactly what needs to be edited. *Block edit first, then fine edit.* Block editing means put all the takes into the correct order, apart from small retakes. For example, you might record all the way through, making a few mistakes and retaking them as you go through. Then at the end you might decide to rerecord the first page now that the speaker has overcome the initial *nervous* performance. Block editing means put that rerecording of the first page at the front. Fine editing means tighten up pauses, cut out paper-shuffles, replace sentences with their retakes.

3.12   Digitize the edited sound recording into individual files, one for each screen, and copy to a digital storage device.

3.13   Lay onto the multimedia package audio-line.

3.14   Adjust the picture build-up so that it is geared to the new (final) sound-track (until this stage, the pictures were geared to the guide-track, which has now been replaced).

4. Pedagogic guidelines for screen/audio design for multimedia

The guidelines are divided into several categories:

- Navigational guidance and student control
- Use of language
- Layout and build-up of the screen
- Do not lead by the nose
- Relationship of screen text to audio commentary
- Speaker should be like a personal tutor
- Visuals and commentary should reinforce each other
- Interactive elements
- Keeping students reassured
- Educational narrative
- How can narrative coherence be salvaged?

Navigational guidance and student control

4.1   If the multimedia package is on CD-ROM, specify in the printed materials which CD-ROM to play. Conversely, specify in a screen-text announcement at the start of the CD-ROM which part of the course goes with the CD-ROM. Also in the announcement, identify, more specifically, any required pre-work, for example, write: 'Before playing this CD-ROM, you should have read …'

4.2   Give each section a title that remains at the top of the screen while the rest of the screen develops.

4.3   Start with a *contents page* from which learners can access the different sections (normally in whatever order they wish). The contents page should record where students have been, by ticking or highlighting the title of each section that has been accessed.

4.4   An *audio-bar* at the top of each screen should move to indicate how far the audio file for that screen has progressed. The speed of the audio-bar is a useful cue for students (the bar for a 20 second audio file would move twice as fast as that for a 40 second audio file).

4.5   Note from 3.12 that each audio file corresponds to a screen. That is, the graphics build-up of the screen finishes approximately at the end of the audio file. To progress further, students would need to click on *NEXT*. Hence students have a visual indication (the audio bar) of when the graphics build-up is about to finish.

Occasionally, this indication would be rather inaccurate, when the graphics build-up finishes well before the audio file. For example, the narration might supply a 30 second summary of the finalized screen. Conversely, there will be rare occasions when the narration finishes in advance of the graphics build-up. For example, the final sentence might be, *Let's see that again, in slow motion*, after which an animation might repeat in slow motion, taking 30 seconds.

Despite these exceptions, the audio-bar enables students to predict approximately when a screen will finish. Hence unlike self-standing video (with scenes of unpredictable duration), the multimedia package is effectively subdivided into short segments (screens) with the pause at the end of each being determined by when the student chooses to click *NEXT*.

4.6 As noted by Taylor *et al.* (1997), when students are revisiting a screen, they do not always want to listen to the audio-track. This can also be true of experienced students visiting for the first time, as discussed by Beccue *et al.* (2001) and Kalyuga (2000). It could also be true of busy colleagues who are formatively evaluating your design. User choice of whether to hear the commentary can be achieved by including a *skip* button (next to the *audio-bar*), with which learners can jump to the end of the current audio file. This would also skip past the graphics build-up, jumping straight to the full-screen graphics.

Use of language

4.7 Listeners find it easier to understand short sentences. One reason is that a long sentence can exceed the listener's memory span. Another reason is that long sentences normally contain conditional clauses, which are difficult to bear in mind. So you should convert every long sentence into two or more short ones.

For example, imagine you were speaking the four sentences in the paragraph immediately above. Listeners would understand you quite easily. But they would find it more difficult if you combined the four sentences into a single long sentence, as follows:

If you have a very long sentence, especially if it contains conditional clauses (like this one), you should convert it into two or more short ones, because listeners will find that easier to understand, partly due to the fact that a long sentence can overload the listener's memory span and also because conditional clauses are difficult to bear in mind.

Notice that if you convert this long sentence back into the four earlier short ones, you are forced to repeat some of the words (e.g. *short*, *long* and *sentence*) so you are incidentally adding some user-friendly redundancy.

4.8 Avoid using words that are difficult to say or to hear or to distinguish from other words. The long sentence in the previous item is difficult to say, as are cases when the last consonant of a word is the same as the first consonant of the next word. This happens twice in the phrase: 'The last task of the seventh theme ...' (And this is difficult to hear too.) Here is an example of words that are difficult to distinguish from other words: 'Right-indicate or signal' sounds like 'Write "indicator signal"'. If you cannot avoid wording that is difficult to hear, make sure the meaning is clear from the context, and/or repeat difficult words in the screen text.

4.9 The narration is audio not print, so write for the ear, not the eye. That is, write *conversational speech*, to be spoken and listened to, *not* to be read. One way to achieve this has been described in section 2.6, but here it is again.

- Draft out the screens.
- Then, working from this draft of the screen graphics, speak your first draft commentary, in a conversational style, straight into a tape recorder. Do this *before* writing out the commentary as a script.
- Listen to the tape and transcribe it, then work on the transcript to improve it. When you work on the transcript, resist reverting to a *print* style: read it out aloud again to make sure it is still conversational and comfortable to say.

Layout and build-up of the screen

4.10 Maintain a consistent layout between the different types of visuals. For example, text on the left, video window on the right, equations or diagrams below the corresponding visual.

4.11 The layout of screens should be easy for the eye to follow while listening. So you should design uncluttered, sparse layout. This is because students cannot easily process dense visual layout while listening to commentary. In particular, concerning visual text, a rule of thumb is to use only 25 per cent of normal print density, ordered from left to right and top to bottom, and appropriately spaced to lead the eye naturally through the screen.

These considerations are even more important if the text is in the form of mathematical equations.

Note that the 25 per cent figure is just a rough starting value. More specific pedagogic determinants of screen text density are discussed later.

4.12 Even when the text is sparse, the standard technique is to *develop* a screen of graphics line by line.

Do not lead by the nose

4.13 Piecemeal development of a screen can be overdone, to the extent that learners feel *blinkered*. For example, it may sometimes feel natural for two or three lines to appear together rather than one at a time. That is, do *not* always obscure the next sentence of screen text just because the spoken commentary has not yet reached that point. So, unless it would confuse students or spoil a surprise, let students choose whether or not to read ahead.

4.14   Students should be free to skip to any section/chapter of the package, in any order they wish. Such total freedom of random access gives students the flexibility to construct knowledge to their own recipes.

Admittedly, students who depart from the recommended order might thereby lose the narrative. However, the contents page (or map) tells them the teacher's intended structure. More comprehensive strategies for preserving the narrative are described in 4.51.

Relationship of screen text to audio commentary

4.15   There are various essential items of screen text, such as mathematical equations and the labels on the axes of a graph. In addition, some explanation of content could be supplied as screen text.

The first question that arises is why include explanatory screen text at all? Could the audio commentary not suffice? The answer is that *succinct* items of screen text can serve as visual reference points, which anchor attention and prevent the learner's mind from wandering. In addition, they can serve as visual mnemonics to avoid overloading auditory memory – the spoken words do not need to be retained in memory if they have been précis-ed by a key word or two of screen text.

4.16   But you can have too much text. Kalyuga (2000) reports that many multimedia packages with audio commentary present identical visual text simultaneously. At best this seems unnecessary. More likely, there will be a negative effect. Literate students can read faster than you can speak and it is onerous to try to match their reading pace with that of the narration. Consequently, if students attend to both sources, the asynchronous processing would result in semantic interference. That is, as Hede (2002) puts it, information 'from one source (will) disrupt semantic processing of information from the other source'.

In fact, the semantic interference might well be preceded by phonological interference – in Baddeley's conception of working memory, visual text is converted into a phonological code and processed in the same system as spoken text (Baddeley 1992). Moreover, Inhoff *et al.* (2004) report a preponderance of evidence that a visual word's phonological representation is determined before its meaning is known.

Possibly the phonological interference would be more severe than the semantic, because there might be two types of phonological interference. One type is the asynchronous processing resulting from the visual text arriving in working memory later than the audio text. In addition, there might be a *split attention* effect. This would occur because students would attempt to match the two phonological streams and hence would divide attention between them.

These interference effects can be largely avoided if the screen text is a judicious précis of the audio commentary, not a duplicate.

Often more important than the semantic and phonological interference is the splitting of visual attention. Reading the text takes up time that could be spent studying the diagram. If the diagram is changing, some of the changes could be missed. For example, a critical type of change that should not be missed is when part of a diagram is highlighted as it is mentioned by the narration. If this highlighting is missed, students will not be clear which part of the diagram is being described.

4.17   When the audio narration is précis-ed by on-screen text, students will search the text in an attempt to track what they are hearing. If there is more than one line of text (as recommended in 4.13) this tracking could be difficult, which would disrupt students' understanding. Hence the on-screen text should *reproduce key words* of the narration, and the narrator should speak these key words verbatim rather than paraphrasing them. For example, if the text is 'Basic ideas' a suitable narration might be,

First, let's consider the basic ideas – the ideas that define the subject.

The narrator's tone of voice can help students' tracking by *stressing* the key words, *basic* and *ideas.*

In contrast, it would not be suitable for the narration to paraphrase the text by replacing the word *basic* with the word *fundamental* and the word *ideas* with the word *notions.* So it would not be suitable to say

First, let's consider the fundamental notions of the subject – the notions that define the subject.

Of course every rule has exceptions. Some paraphrasing is occasionally useful as a way of adding extra meaning. For example, if the narration says

The Help menu guides students on how to use the software.

the screen text could read

User friendly

4.18   Apart from the preceding *key word* recommendation, it is difficult to make hard and fast rules about how to phrase the screen text so that it helps rather than hinders the learning process – so that it anchors the audio commentary rather than interfering with its apprehension. There are many variables involved. One is the complexity of the non-verbal visual information (e.g. diagrams), which could interfere with processing of visual text. But even if the visuals are fairly simple, another factor is the complexity of the learning task itself. A very complex task would require deep concentration. To facilitate this concentration, the on-screen text would need to be more than usually sparse.

Formative evaluation during rehearsal and recording can help to make these judgements. Following the initial design, many ad hoc refinements can be made through adopting the role of the learner during rehearsal and recording of the audio commentary (see 3.9 and 3.10). In this role, if you find that some audio and screen text are conflicting rather than harmonizing, then you can change the audio or the screen text or both.

Occasionally, even this practice can be unsuccessful because the material does not lend itself to a time-based presentation (see 4.22).

4.19   In the screen text, as well as *key words*, always include *new technical terms* (which you should always mention in the audio commentary, so that the learners hear the pronunciation).

4.20   It is useful to include a transcript of the audio commentary that students can access for each screen by clicking on a *SCRIPT* button (the transcript appears as a *drop down*). Then, for example, if students are revising by skimming/browsing through the screens, they may want quick access to the commentary relating to a particular screen. It is much quicker to read a transcript than to listen to a spoken commentary. In any case the transcript is essential for deaf students.

Admittedly, the spoken text is coupled synchronously to the sequential development of the screen graphics, whereas the printed transcript appears all at once. However, the students who are revising the material are fairly familiar with it, so they should not be too disadvantaged by the temporal decoupling of text and pictures.

4.21   Hearing students would not need to access the above transcript if the screens alone were sufficient for revision purposes. Making the screens adequate for revision is a good idea, for the following reason. A good strategy was advocated in section 2.5: *design screens to be a full outline of the topic*, sufficient for your busy colleagues to grasp (and thereby supply you with formative evaluation) without having to listen through the audio commentary. These colleagues are subject-matter experts whose memories may need refreshing, so if the screens are sufficient for them, they should also be sufficient for the students (aspiring experts) when they revise. In fact, as suggested by item 4.6, students who are revisiting a screen might even find it tiresome to be forced into listening to the whole narration again, just because a crucial piece of information is missing from the screen text.

You might object that the amount of screen text advocated above leaves nothing for the audio commentary to do. Well, you do not need to go into a lot of detail in the screens: remember that the text gains new meaning for the students once they have listened to the commentary, hence when looking at the screens later, students will recall much of the extra meaning. (And they have access to the transcript if they get stuck.)

4.22 It may sometimes not be possible to make screens sparse enough to be followed during listening to the audio: the topic may need detailed printed information at certain points, or complex diagrams or both. But this problem has a solution. If a screen is unavoidably complicated, just tell students to familiarize themselves with it before you comment on it – and have a *CONTINUE* button for them to click, just below the screen text.

But avoid such dense screens as far as possible. If you really need several such screens, then you have chosen the wrong medium. Some learning tasks are not well-served with a time-based medium, but rather need learner-paced reflection (as enabled by the print medium).

4.23 The last item relates to the finding by Tabbers *et al.* (2000), mentioned earlier, that learners studying a complex task through a multimedia package performed better when the audio commentary was replaced by printed text and students could study the text and diagrams for as much time as they liked. Notice that, in this condition, the medium is no longer *multimedia* but rather *print*. This is the preferred medium when the learning task is complex and requires self-paced, concentrated reflection. Taken together with the previous item, the conclusion is that audio commentary can be too difficult to follow and integrate with the visuals, if either the visuals or the learning task are complex enough to require self-paced study.

4.24 There are two places where you can include dense screen text without worrying about clashing with the listening. This is at the front of the screens and at the end. That is, you can have a screen text introduction to the topic, to be read before listening to the audio that accompanies the first graphics screen. And you can have a screen text summary, to be read immediately after listening to the final audio commentary.

Speaker should be like a personal tutor

4.25 When recording, the speaker is not looking at the screen or even a copy of the screen, but rather reading the script. However the *style* of the audio should be *as if* each listener has a personal tutor looking over his or her shoulder at the same screen. The sensation that student and speaker are looking at the same thing is enhanced when the on-screen text *reproduces key words* from the narration (as recommended in 4.17).

4.26 The production may have been a team effort, but in order to be personal, the speaker should take sole credit as the individual author. That is, say 'I' rather than 'we'. Also, address the listener directly as 'you', not as 'some of you'. The *impersonal* words and phrases are crossed out in the following example:

~~We have~~ I have drawn an extra cloud in the diagram, in case ~~some of~~ you have not met this idea before …

4.27   To avoid being authoritarian, when telling students to carry out an activity, phrase it as an *invitation* rather than an order.

Visuals and commentary should reinforce each other

4.28   Indicate clearly where to look on the screen. This often requires a visual cue such as highlighting a part of a diagram when it is mentioned (or flashing the part on and off). Alternatively, or in addition, it may be prudent for the narrator to orient the learner's gaze by saying, 'at the top of the screen' or 'underneath the video window' or 'after the peak of the graph', etc.

4.29   Highlighting an item when it is mentioned (as above) is an example of the images synchronizing with the corresponding words. Such synchronization is appropriate in many situations. However, there are many other situations in which the words should precede or follow the corresponding visuals, as follows.

4.30   Make teaching points about a visual when students are looking at it, and not in a wordy introduction before the image appears. For example, the following sentence is premature:

I want to do three things – I want to give an overview of the stages in the argument; then I'll explain each stage in detail; and finally I'll explain how the stages relate: I've outlined these three things in the chart [*chart appears*].

Instead, it is natural to show the chart at the *start* of the words (not the end):

[*Chart appears*] Here, I've outlined the three things I want to do – I want to give an overview of the stages in the argument: then I'll explain each stage in detail; and finally I'll explain how the stages relate.

The reason why this sequencing is preferable (the image preceding the words) is that, when the chart appears from the outset, it gives students a visual reference on which to anchor the points being made in the narration.

Another example of when the pictures should lead the narration is if the pictures are mathematical expressions that are difficult to listen to unless they can be seen. For example, in a mathematics package for students who are fairly new to algebra, consider the commentary 'minus b, plus or minus the square root of, b-squared minus four ac, all over two a'. This is impossible for most students to appreciate unless they can see the algebraic formula

$$\frac{-b \pm \sqrt{(b^2 - 4ac)}}{2a}$$

4.31 In contrast, there are occasions when the narration should come first, in order to prepare the viewer for the pictures, such as:

In the next video clip, concentrate on how the ice-skater positions her arms so as to speed up her spin [*Clip starts with skater's arms held wide, then pulled in*].

4.32 When moving from one idea to the next while still on the same screen, create a vertical *gap* in the spacing of the screen graphics and a *matching pause* in the spoken commentary.

4.33 Give students enough time to perceive the visuals. For example, give time for their eyes to settle on a new screen before commenting about it. A notorious error is to position the words at the beginning of the audio file rather than preceding the words with a pause, say for two seconds. However, there is no hard and fast rule. Sometimes, it is appropriate to start the words immediately, sometimes to pause two seconds, sometimes after a lengthy build-up of graphics.

Interactive elements

4.34 Whenever students carry out an activity, there should be a facility for them to keep a record of their endeavour inside the package, rather than on a scrap of paper. For example, they could type into a *notepad*, on screen, as exemplified in the Homer package described by Laurillard (1998). With these embellishments, the resulting narrative has been *co-authored* by the package and the student.

4.35 The package should provide appropriate *scaffolding* for student activities. For example, if a student types an incorrect answer into a dialogue box, there should be an option to get one or more hints then try again, and eventually to be told the correct answer. If there is no *correct* answer (as in open questions), the package should still offer feedback, in the form of a model answer. Laurillard (1998) recommends withholding the model answer until the student has made a sizeable attempt. Admittedly students could cheat here by typing a few *nonsense* sentences, which the package would interpret as *sizeable* and hence grant access to the model answers.

However, the conditional blocking is likely to encourage students to make a reasonable attempt.

Further scaffolding techniques are described in item 4.46.

4.36 Whenever students are to carry out an activity, there would normally be a *NEXT* button at the end of the final activity dialogue box. When students click on *NEXT* in order for the package to continue, it is common for the dialogue box to disappear, hence erasing any record of the activity. However, the result of that activity (e.g. a number that the student has typed) may be needed as reference for the next segment of the package. In that case it is a good idea to keep the number on screen, in the same location on the screen as the student typed it. That is, the rest of the dialogue box disappears but the typed number remains.

4.37 After an activity, the subsequent audio commentary would commonly not refer to the activity. However, it may sometimes be a good idea to refer to it. For example, the commentary might say 'the value of the average is what we need to use in the next exercise'. This makes the package more personal, giving the feeling that there is a tutor standing behind the student's shoulder.

4.38 Too frequent interactive dialogue boxes could irritate students. As a general rule the interspersed presentation should be substantial – involving more than three paragraphs of audio narration.

4.39 You can overdo interactivity. Students will not be happy with activities if they do *not* perceive them as useful.

Keeping students reassured

4.40 Do not make light of the intellectual difficulty. For example, don't say: 'This equation is not too difficult. It's an example of a general idea. That is … ' Better say: 'This equation is rather complicated; you can study the details later at your leisure; for the time being I'm just interested in the general idea. That is … '

4.41 Students' self-confidence will increase (which will help their later accomplishments) through experiencing success – not at trivial activities, but rather at challenging tasks. Driscoll (2000: 329) suggests that the teacher (in our case the multimedia package) should give just enough assistance to perform tasks students are not quite capable of performing on their own. This might be done by offering stronger and stronger hints, so as to accommodate a range of student abilities.

4.42 Whenever you are assuming some prior knowledge (e.g. from last week's studies), you will be speaking more quickly, in a shorthand style. Students will recognize that this style indicates a recap; they might therefore fear that they have inadvertently missed something you just said. They need to be reassured that it was last week that they should have met that topic.

That is, for reassurance, you often need to communicate what you've assumed about students' prior knowledge.

Educational narrative

Judiciously balance *effective exposition* by the teacher against *independent exploration* by the student. The efficacy (even the necessity) of narrative structure has been proposed by many writers, such as Gudmundsdottir (1995), Gibson (1996), Laurillard (1998) and Laurillard *et al.* (2000). How can a narrative structure be organized when the package allows the learner considerable (if not total) freedom of random access? This question will be tackled in the next section, after *narrative structure* is defined, in terms of the guidelines below. (The guidelines are adapted from the principles for pedagogic video design, in Table 5.3 of Chapter 5, which is further elaborated in Chapter 6.)

4.43 Hook (capture and sustain attention): for example, capture attention with the unexpected; sustain attention by creating suspense.

4.44 Signpost: for example, clearly indicate where the story is going, what is happening next, why it is happening, what to look out for.

4.45 Facilitate concentration: for example, short pauses for contemplation, encourage prediction.

4.46 Encourage/enable constructive learning, for example:

- Spoken words should not be a literal duplication of the visuals (because you want to encourage students to make the picture–word connection for themselves).
- Concretize: i.e. relate to (hence *activate*) students' previous knowledge.
- Disclose the context of your arguments, e.g. set the scene before going into details.
- Support/scaffold the learner's construction of knowledge. For example, proceed from concrete to abstract and from simple to complex. Another technique concerns scaffolding of problem-solving, Merrill (2002a) and Van Merriënboer (2001) recommend several techniques, such as: show a worked example of a similar problem before asking students to solve a problem, or show a simple *half-way-there* problem before posing the full problem, or divide the problem into subproblems, or pose a sequence of successively more difficult problems.

COMMENT

As noted in Chapter 6, going from simple to complex is also not always appropriate. Van Merriënboer (2001) cites ample evidence that *completion tasks* are better for learning. For example, one could present a complex design of a project to students, who then have to complete, evaluate or extend the design. Students learn better from such completion tasks (in which they start from the complex) than when they are asked to carry out the design from scratch.

The type and extent of scaffolding depends on the ability of the learner in relation to the material; some target audiences need little or no scaffolding and in any case the scaffolding should be withdrawn little by little as learners progress. For more on scaffolding see McLoughlin *et al.* (2000), van Merriënboer (2001) or Merrill (2002a).

4.47   Elucidate: moderate the load, pace and depth, maximize clarity. Do not overload students with too many teaching points or too fast a pace, or too much intellectual depth. The appropriate load, pace and depth depends on the level and prior knowledge of the students (e.g. regarding depth, deal with the specific before the general, especially for children).

Regarding clarity, for example, when you have new terminology to define, leave the definition until it is needed. You might be tempted to define such terms at the outset, when *signposting* what is coming. Resist the temptation – it is better to find a way of signposting that does not require premature definitions.

4.48   Texture: for example, insert occasional light items, vary the format whenever it seems natural to vary the mood, exploit the unique characteristics of audio, that is, tone of voice, sequence, pacing, phrasing, timbre, real-world sounds.

4.49   Reinforce: give more than one example of a concept, use *comparison* and *contrast*, ensure *synergy* (as in 4.28 to 4.33) between visuals and commentary.

4.50   Consolidation of learning could be achieved through students solving end-of-chapter problems and referring to model answers.

4.51   How can narrative coherence be salvaged?

Item 4.14 recommended that the package should allow learners total freedom of random access. In that case, the narrative coherence would disappear. Nevertheless, the above narrative structuring principles would help those learners who do follow the recommended order. For the more adventurous learners who stray from the recommended order, there are various techniques whereby the narrative can be preserved, for example, the contents page (or map) tells students the teacher's intended structure. More comprehensive strategies for preserving the narrative are discussed by Laurillard *et al.* (2000). They recommend a series of design features that afford learners the opportunity to maintain a narrative line, including:

- a clear statement of an overall goal – to support generation of a task-related plan
- continual reminders of the goal – to support keeping to the plan
- interactive activities – to provide adaptive feedback on actions; to motivate repeat actions to improve performance
- an editable Notepad – to enable students to articulate their conceptions
- a model answer – as feedback on their conceptions; to motivate reflection on their conceptions

COMMENTS

Concerning the statement of the goal and reminders of the goal, these can become more specific as learners progress through the package and become more able to understand the language and what is expected of them. Such *progressive disclosure* was recommended in Chapter 5. Concerning the Notepad, this can convert the narrative into a collaboration between student and package designer.

A final strategy for preserving narrative structure would be to move away from total learner autonomy by restricting random access. One way to do this would be to discourage students from progressing from chapter to chapter until they make a sizeable attempt at the end-of-chapter consolidation activity (similar to the advice by Laurillard (1998), quoted in item 4.35, to conditionally block access to model answers).

4.52   Conclusion. Given all the above, it should be clear that you cannot design a perfect picture–word package with your first draft: you need several draft designs and script discussions. In fact, you will need more than you expect because the programming modifications that are required to implement each draft will rarely produce precisely what you envisaged.

Recommendations for future research and design development

Two types of research papers were outlined at the beginning of this chapter. One type reported on experimental studies of individual audio and visual variables. The other type, by UK Open University writers, consisted of summative studies that dealt primarily with macro-level design issues. How do these two sources relate to the above framework of micro-level design guidelines?

The micro-level guidelines in relation to summative, macro-level studies

The guidelines could add flesh to the further development of the overarching issues espoused in the macro-level papers by Laurillard, Taylor and others. In return, such issues need to be borne in mind for future development of design guidelines.

The micro-level guidelines in relation to experimental studies

The guidelines derive from practitioners. They are more detailed than the levels of investigation carried out in the aforementioned experimental studies. This discordance is natural. The variables that can be investigated using a scientifically acceptable experimental study are simpler than the complex integration of design principles that must be used by practitioners.

On the other hand, these design principles are intuitive and have not been studied scientifically. The framework of design guidelines is offered as a fledgling design theory for researchers to investigate the practitioners' intuitions. It would be heartening if this chapter could start an iterative process whereby researchers and practitioners collaborate to improve the design of multimedia packages.

Currently, it appears that there is no widespread collaboration between practitioners and researchers. Instead, the aforementioned experimental studies build on theoretical interpretations of previous experiments, such as those compiled by Moreno and Mayer (2000). Based on these results and on various learning theories, the latter authors propose a cognitive theory of multimedia learning that comprises six principles of instructional design:

- split-attention
- modality
- redundancy
- spatial contiguity
- temporal contiguity
- coherence

These six principles exemplify the mismatch between the research literature and the concerns of practitioners.

The split-attention principle was discussed earlier (visual attention detrimentally split between screen text and corresponding diagrams). The principle is intuitively reasonable. Note however that it leads to the either/or recommendation that audio commentary is always superior to screen text. So there is no conception of a judicious combination of the two, as recommended in items 4.15 to 4.24 – namely that screen text should be a judicious précis of the narration, serving as visual mnemonic and an anchor for the narration. This leaves open the danger of splitting visual attention, but with sparse screen text, the effect should not be too detrimental.

The modality principle asserts that

> Students learn better when the verbal information is presented auditorily as speech than visually as on-screen text both for concurrent and sequential presentations.

It was noted earlier that Tabbers *et al.* (2000) reported a counterexample in the case of a complex task that required self-paced reflection of the on-screen text.

Furthermore, note the surprising *sequential* condition, in addition to the usual *concurrent* presentation of explanatory text. Moreno and Mayer actually tested the effect of presenting the whole text *before* the whole animation and also *after* the whole animation (and found that audio text was superior in both conditions, as well as when presented concurrently).

The purpose was to determine whether the superiority of audio text was a memory-capacity effect (screen text and diagrams overloading visual working memory) rather than a split-attention effect (insufficient attention paid, in the concurrent presentation, to either or both visual components – screen text and diagrams). They concluded that a memory-capacity effect was at least a contributing factor. Tabbers in his Ph.D. thesis (2002), convincingly contests this explanation, arguing that the split-attention effect alone is sufficient to explain the superiority of audio text. That is, audio text prevents split attention between verbal and pictorial information.

In a later paper, Mayer and Moreno (2003) appear to use the terms *modality effect* and *split attention effect* interchangeably (pp. 45, 46), concluding that

> the use of narrated animation represents a method for off-loading (or reassigning) some of the processing demands from the visual (processing) channel to the verbal channel.

Putting aside these theoretical controversies, the above extreme manipulation of the variables might possibly help to build a learning theory, but is of little use to the practitioner. Of what use is it to know *for sequential presentation* that the auditory condition is superior to the visual? If an animation needs to be complemented by audio commentary (true in most cases), there is no point in delaying the commentary rather than synchronizing it. No multimedia designer would contemplate such a design because it would severely limit any *synergy* between commentary and diagrams.

This leads to a serious point. Creating synergy between diagrams and synchronized audio commentary is not a trivial endeavour. A bad designer could accidentally fabricate a package in which the composition and pacing of the audio commentary actually clashed with the concurrent diagrams, hence *interfering* with learning. With such a disharmonious design, the dissonance might be reduced by separating the diagrams from the commentary – presenting diagrams and commentary sequentially rather than concurrently. The sequential package would still fail, but not quite as badly. Much better to accept the challenge of creating synergy in a concurrent presentation. Techniques for achieving such synergy are described in items 4.28 to 4.33.

The spatial contiguity principle asserts that

> Students learn better when on-screen text and visual materials are physically integrated rather than separated.

This is not surprising, but the mistake of spatially separating text from diagrams is quite common, so the principle is worth stating.

In another sense, the principle is rendered redundant by another finding from the experiment that supported it. It was also found that replacing the on-screen text by audio narration produced even better learning. The authors interpreted this as reconfirming the modality principle – although Tabbers (2002) would presumably argue that a simpler explanation is that visual attention still gets split even when text and diagram are contiguous. In either case, the spatial contiguity principle would be rendered useless, since the recommendation would have to be that on-screen text should be deleted altogether, in favour of audio narration.

However, the authors used text that duplicated the audio rather than being a judicious précis. It was argued above that key words of the audio narration should be presented as on-screen text, thereby *reinforcing* and *anchoring* the narration. In such a design, the contiguity principle still has currency – there should be facilitative positioning of text and diagrams.

The temporal contiguity principle asserts that

> Students learn better when verbal and visual materials are temporally synchronized rather than separated in time.

However, this principle is a macro-level guideline that cannot help the practising multimedia designer. In fact, the authors and others have demonstrated that the principle does not hold unless the temporal separation is considerable (e.g. when a large chunk of animation is preceded by the whole narration). Compare this principle with the micro-level guidelines, 4.28 to 4.33 above, which exemplify the fine judgements of pacing and sequence made by the intuitive designer who *gets inside the head of the learner*.

Again, consider the redundancy principle, which asserts that

> Students learn better from animation and narration than from animation, narration, and text if the visual information is presented simultaneously to the verbal information.

Once again, this principle assumes that the text is identical, word for word, with the narration. This approach was rejected a priori by UK OU designers, who surmised that simultaneous reading and listening would be uncomfortable (item 4.16 elucidates this rationale). Instead, the concern of OU designers is the subtle issue of how succinct the text should be in order to anchor the narration but not interfere with it (see 4.15 to 4.18).

As an aside, in contrast to the above deleterious effect of *redundancy*, there are many respects in which this book has recommended redundancy as being beneficial to learning, as a method of reinforcement or as compensating for cognitive overload or inattention. For example, one technique for moderating intellectual difficulty (principle 6e of Table 5.3) is to convert a long sentence into several shorter sentences. This necessitates repeating several words, which adds some user-friendly redundancy. Then again, principle 8a of Table 5.3 recommends *repetition from a different angle*.

The coherence principle asserts that

> Students learn better when extraneous material is excluded rather than included in multimedia explanations.

This principle was supported in an experiment by Moreno and Mayer (2000) in which learning was significantly worse when music was added to an animation with narration. This effect relates to one with a more evocative name, the *seductive-augmentation effect* – defined by Thalheimer (2004) as a negative effect on *learning base material* when the presentation is augmented by interesting but inessential text, sounds or visuals (the augmentation *seduces* the learner's attention/processing away from the essential items). Thalheimer reviewed 24 research comparisons, 16 of which showed that adding interesting items hurt learning, 7 showed no difference and 1 showed a learning increment.

Intuitively we feel that making the presentation interesting is a good idea, because it engages the learner. But how does this fit with the above results? Here are two possibilities.

In the UK Open University, producers would typically spend hours choosing music that was appropriate to the mood of the story. Typically, even after sifting through printed descriptions of music tracks and discarding many choices, at least 80 per cent of the music tracks chosen for consideration were found to *jar* with the storyline. In any case, music was normally only played when there was a deliberate pause in the commentary, designed to allow viewers to reflect on the pictures. It is clear that the above experimenters did not follow these provisos, so it is not surprising that their music interfered with learning.

A second interpretation of the results is speculative but intriguing. All 16 experiments showing a significant negative effect involved very short learning tasks, average 4 minutes. An interesting conjecture by Thalheimer is that for longer tasks, in which attention might flag, adding interesting elements to sustain attention might have a positive effect *on balance*. That is, if the seductive augmentations do indeed cause a learning decrement (say 20 per cent), this may be the price we have to pay to keep learners attentive for longer periods. If seductive augmentations really do distract, the negative effect may be more than compensated by their *sustained-attention* effect.

To conclude, all six principles recommended by Moreno and Mayer (2000) are pitched at a macro-level that may be suitable for theory-building but that only skims the surface of the detailed design concerns of the practitioner.

A diligent search of the literature has failed to uncover any more practicable design principles. Admittedly, the six principles could serve as a useful backdrop for the practitioner. However, value is more likely to be obtained in the reverse direction. Namely, before we try to derive design principles based on macro-level learning theories, and refine them through experimental studies, we would be better advised to start from experienced teachers' intuitive, micro-level design guidelines, and progress in the opposite direction, namely

micro-level design principles, as espoused above (a fledgling design theory) → experimental studies → refined theory/design principles → …

Each of the proposed design principles could generate questions to be investigated.

- Regarding guideline 4.18, how should the screen text be phrased, in relation to the audio commentary, so that it anchors the commentary rather than interfering with it?
- Regarding guideline 4.21, just *how sparse* should the screen text be? Should the screens by themselves (without the audio) be just barely comprehensible to a really top expert in the subject-matter, or should they constitute a more substantial outline of the content?

Note that these questions concern the nature of the visual text rather than whether it is present or absent. This illustrates the philosophical conflict between the experimental studies and the design guidelines in this chapter. The guidelines aim to integrate narration and visuals (diagrams and visual text) in order to achieve optimum synergy between these two constituents. In contrast, the aforementioned experimental studies manipulate the two constituents separately, thereby compromising their synergy. As argued near the beginning of the chapter, a good media designer would rescript the narration if denied harmonious visuals and would redraft the visuals if denied harmonious narration. The above experimental studies could not countenance any such reconstruction of audio-visual synergy because this would have defeated their manipulation of the separate constituents!

Collaboration between researchers and practitioners would have a much increased chance of being productive if the investigations compared different ways of *integrating* narration and visuals – different composite designs aimed at optimum audio-visual synergy – rather than trying to unpick the two constituents and manipulate them separately.

Appendixes

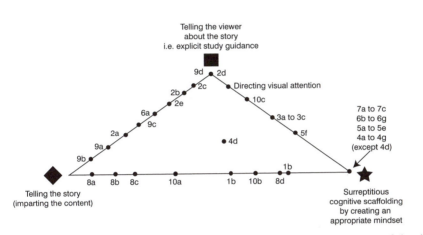

Figure A1.1 Alternative classification of the principles of Table 5.3, in terms of the three *narrative archetypes* of Figure 6.5. (Note. Principle 6g, Enhance legibility/audibility, refers to a variety of techniques, most of which fall into the surreptitious category (bottom right), as indicated. However, those techniques under 6g for directing visual attention, such as highlighting portions of the screen, are largely explicit study guidance, hence these techniques are positioned near the top of the triangle, as shown.)

Table A2.1 Revised Bloom's Taxonomy (Anderson and Krathwohl (eds) 2001)

	A. Factual knowledge a. terminology b. details	B. Conceptual knowledge a. classifications b. principles c. theories	C. Procedural knowledge a. skills or algorithms b. techniques/method c. criteria for using procedures	D. Meta-cognitive knowledge a. strategic b. cognitive task (customize processing according to task) c. self-knowledge
Simple to complex processing below but e.g. 2.7 is more complex than 3.1				
1. Remember 1.1. Recognition 1.2. Recalling				
2. Understand (grasp/construct meaning) 2.1 Interpreting 2.2 Exemplifying 2.3 Classifying 2.4 Summarizing 2.5 Inferring 2.6 Comparing 2.7 Explaining				
3. Apply 3.1 Executing 3.2 Implementing				
4. Analyze 4.1 Differentiating 4.2 Organizing 4.3 Attributing				

5.   Evaluate
5.1   Checking
5.2   Critiquing

6.   Create
6.1   Generate
6.2   Plan (design)
6.3   Produce

Notes

These writers use a flipped version, with vertical Knowledge axis and horizontal Processes
Further elaboration can be found in LookSmart's FindArticles > Theory into Practice 2002 http://www.findarticles.com/m0NQM/4_41/issue.jhtml
In particular see the two articles: Rote versus meaningful learning (1) by Richard E. Mayer and
A revision of Bloom's Taxonomy: an overview. (Benjamin S. Bloom, University of Chicago) by David R. Krathwohl

References

Anderson, L.W. and Krathwohl, D.R. (eds) (2001) *A Taxonomy for Learning, Teaching, and Assessing: A Revision of Bloom's Taxonomy of Educational Objectives*, New York: Longman.

Anderson, T., Rourke, L., Garrison, D.R. and Archer, W. (2001) 'Assessing teaching presence in a computer conferencing context', *Journal of Asynchronous Learning Networks*, 5(2). Online: <http://www.aln.org/publications/jaln/v5n2/v5n2_anderson.asp> (accessed Sept. 2005).

Andrusyszyn, M.A. and Davie, L. (1997) 'Facilitating reflection through interactive journal writing in an online graduate course: a qualitative study', *Journal of Distance Education*, 12(1/2). Online: <http://cade.athabascau.ca/vol12.1/andrusyszyndavie.html> (accessed Oct. 2005).

Baddeley, A.D. (1992) 'Working memory', *Science*, 255: 556–9.

Baggeley, J. (1980) *Psychology of the TV Image*, Westmead: Gower.

Bates, A.W. (1981) 'Towards a better research framework for evaluating the effectiveness of educational media', *British Journal of Educational Technology*, 12(3): 215–33.

—— (1984) *Broadcasting in Education*, London: Constable.

—— (1987) *Educational Television*, units 25/26 of the OU Course EH207, Milton Keynes: Open University Press.

—— (1988) 'Television, learning and distance education', *Journal of Educational Television*, 14(3): 213–55.

—— and Poole, G. (2003) *Effective Teaching with Technology in Higher Education*, San Francisco: Jossey-Bass.

Beccue, B., Vila, J. and Whitley, L.K. (2001) 'The effects of adding audio instructions to a multimedia computer based training environment', *Journal of Educational Multimedia and Hypermedia*, 10(1): 47–67. Online: <http://www.aace.org/dl/files/JEMH/jemh-10-01-47.pdf> (accessed April 2005).

Brown, J.S., Collins, A. and Duguid, P. (1989) 'Situated cognition and the culture of learning', *Educational Researcher*, 18(1): 32–42. Online: <http://www.exploratorium.edu/IFI/resources/museumeducation/situated.html> (accessed Jan. 2005)

Bruner, J.S. (1977) *The Process of Education*, Cambridge, MA: Harvard UP.

—— (1999) 'Folk pedagogies', in Jenny Leach and Bob Moon (eds) *Learners and Pedagogy*, London: Paul Chapman Publishing.

Bullen, M. (1998) 'Participation and critical thinking in online university distance education', *Journal of Distance Education*, 13(2): 1–32.

Burt, G. (1997) 'The media selection decision: implications of student feedback on a first generation multimedia', *Educational Media International* 34(2): 66–74.

Cash, J.R., Behrmann, M.B., Stadt, R.W. and Daniels, H.M. (1997), 'Effectiveness of cognitive apprenticeship instructional methods in college automotive technology classrooms', *Journal of Industrial Teacher Education*, 34(2). Online: <http://scholar. lib.vt.edu/ejournals/JITE/v34n2/Cash.html> (accessed July 2005).

Cennamo, K.S. (1993) 'Learning from video: factors influencing learners' preconceptions and invested mental effort', *Educational Technology Research and Development*, 41(3): 33–45. Online: <http://www.usq.edu.au/material/unit/resource/cennamo/learning.htm> (accessed Sept. 2005).

Clark, R.E. (1983) 'Reconsidering research on learning from media', *Review of Educational Research*, 53(4): 445–59.

—— (1994) 'Media will never influence learning', *Educational Technology Research and Development*, 42(2): 21–9.

Crooks, B. and Kirkwood, A. (1988) 'Video-cassettes by design in Open University courses', *Open Learning*, 3(3): 13–17.

De Koning, K., Bredeweg, B., Breuker, J. and Wielinga, B. (2000) 'Model-based reasoning about learner behaviour', *Artificial Intelligence*, 117(2): 173–229.

DeLuca, S.M. (1991) *Instructional Video*, Boston, MA: Focal Press.

Driscoll, M.P. (2000) *Psychology of Learning for Instruction*, Boston, MA: Allyn & Bacon.

Eustace, G. (1990) *Writing for Corporate Video*, Boston, MA: Focal Press.

Gibson, S. (1996) 'Is all coherence gone? The role of narrative in web design', *Interpersonal Computing and Technology*, 4(2): 7–26. Online: <http://www.helsinki.fi/science/ optek/1996/n2/gibson.txt> (accessed April 2005).

Greenfield, P.M. (1984) *Mind and Media* (especially chs 5 and 9), Cambridge, MA, and London: Harvard Universitry Press and Fontana.

Gudmundsdottir, S. (1995) 'The narrative nature of pedagogical content knowledge', in H. McEwan and K. Egan (eds) *Narrative in Teaching, Learning and Research*, pp. 24–38. New York: Teachers College. Online: <http://www.sv.ntnu.no/ped/sigrun/publikasjoner/ PCKNARR.html> (accessed April 2005)

Gunawardena, C., Lowe, C.A. and Anderson, T. (1997) 'Analysis of a global online debate and the development of an interaction analysis model for examining social construction of knowledge in computer conferencing', *Journal of Educational Computing Research*, 17(4): 397–431.

Hawkridge, D. (1993) 'Challenging educational technology', unpublished manuscript.

Hede, A. (2002) 'An integrated model of multimedia effects on learning', *Journal of Educational Multimedia and Hypermedia*, 11(2): 177–91. Online: <http://www.aace. org/dl/files/JEMH/JEMH112177.pdf> (accessed Sept. 2005).

Henri, F. and Rigault, C. (1996) 'Collaborative distance education and computer conferencing', in T. Liao (ed.), *Advanced Educational Technology: Research Issues and Future Potential*, pp. 45–76, Berlin: Springer-Verlag.

Hoijer, B. (1990) 'Learning from television viewers' reception of informative television discourse', in C. Tidhar (ed.), *ETV Broadcasting Research in the Nineties: Readings from the Tel Aviv Research Seminar 1990*, pp. 161–75, Tel Aviv: Israel Educational TV Special Research Publication.

Inhoff, A.W., Connine, C., Eiter, B., Radach, R. and Heller, D. (2004) 'Phonological representation of words in working memory during sentence reading', *Psychonomic*

Bulletin and Review, 11: 320–5. Online: <http://psychology.binghamton.edu/Faculty/ Inhoff_Connine_Radach_PBR.pdf,> (accessed Dec. 2004).

Kanuka, H. and Anderson, T. (1998) 'Online social interchange, discord, and knowledge construction', *Journal of Distance Education*, 13(1): 57–74.

Keller, J.M. (1987) 'Strategies for stimulating the motivation to learn', *Performance and Instruction* 26(8): 1–7.

Kemp, J.E. (1985) *The Instructional Design Process*, ch. 9. New York: Harper & Row.

Kalyuga, S. (2000) 'When using sound with a text or picture is not beneficial for learning', *Australian Journal of Educational Technology*, 16(2): 161–72. Online: <http://www. ascilite.org.au/ajet/ajet16/kalyuga.html> (accessed Sept. 2005).

Koumi, J. (1991) 'Narrative screenwriting for educational TV', *Journal of Educational Television*, 17(3): 131–48.

—— (1994a) 'Media comparison and deployment: a practitioner's view', *British Journal of Educational Technology*, 25(1): 41–57.

—— (1994b) 'Efficiency with low-tech: audio-vision (audio cassette, guiding learners through visual materials)', *Aspects of Educational and Training Technology*, vol. 27, pp. 226–9, New Jersey: Kogan Page.

—— and Daniels, J. (1994) 'Case study: audio-guided learning with computer graphics', *Education and Training Technology International*, 31(2): 143–55. Online: <http://www. usq.edu.au/material/unit/resource/kuomi/koumi2.htm> (accessed March 2005).

—— and Hung, P. (1995) 'Video programme production at two Open Universities: a comparison between the UK and Taiwan, R.O.C.', *Proceedings of the IX AAOU Annual Conference in Taipei*, pp. 139–47, Taipei: National Open University of Taiwan.

Kozma, R.B. (1991) 'Learning with media', *Review of Educational Research*, 61(2): 179–211.

—— (1994) 'Will media influence learning? Reframing the debate', *Educational Technology Research and Development*, 42(2): 7–19.

Krathwohl, D.R. (2002) 'A revision of Bloom's Taxonomy: an overview', *Theory into Practice*. Online: <http://www.findarticles.com/m0NQM/4_41/issue.jhtml> (accessed Sept. 2005).

Laurillard, D. (1991) 'Mediating the message: television programme design and students' understanding', *Instructional Science*, 20: 3–23.

—— (1993) *Rethinking University Teaching: A Framework for the Effective Use of Educational Technology*, London: Routledge.

—— (1998) 'Multimedia and the learner's experience of narrative', *Computers and Education*, 31(2): 229–42.

—— Stratford, M., Luckin, R., Plowman, L. and Taylor, J. (2000) 'Affordances for learning in a non-linear narrative medium', *Journal of Interactive Media in Education*, 2000(2). Online: <http://www-jime.open.ac.uk/00/2/laurillard-00-2-paper.html> (accessed Oct. 2005).

Lin, C.A. and Cresswell, K.W. (1989), 'Effects of televised lecture presentation styles on student learning', *Journal of Educational Television*, 15(1): 37–52.

McCormick, R. and Paechter, C. (eds) (1999) *Learning and Knowledge*, London: Paul Chapman Publishing.

McLoughlin, C., Winnips, J.C. and Oliver, R. (2000) 'Supporting constructivist learning through learner support on-line', paper accepted for EDMEDIA 2000. Online: <http:// users.edte.utwente.nl/winnips/papers/support.html> (accessed Jan. 2004).

Macmillan, C.J.B. and Garrison, J.W. (1994), 'Process-product research on teaching: ten years later', *Educational Theory on the Web*, 44(4). Online: <http://www.ed.uiuc.edu/EPS/Educational-Theory/Contents/44_4_Garrison.asp> (accessed Jan. 2004).

Mayer, R.E. (2002), 'Rote versus meaningful learning (1)', *Theory into Practice*. Online: <http://www.findarticles.com/m0NQM/4_41/issue.jhtml> (accessed Sept. 2005).

—— and Moreno, R. (2003) 'Nine ways to reduce cognitive load in multimedia learning', *Educational Psychologist*, 38(1): 43–52.

Merrill, M.D. (2002a) 'First principles of instruction', *Educational Technology Research and Development*, 50(3): 43–59. Online: <http://www.id2.usu.edu/Papers/5FirstPrinciples.PDF> (accessed Jan. 2005).

—— (2002b) 'A pebble-in-the-pond model for instructional design', *Performance Improvement*, 41(7). Online: <http://www.ispi.org/pdf/Merrill.pdf> (accessed Jan. 2004).

Moreno, R. and Mayer, R.E. (2000) 'A learner-centered approach to multimedia explanations: deriving instructional design principles from cognitive theory', *Interactive Multimedia Electronic Journal of Computer-Enhanced Learning*, 2(2). Online: <http://imej.wfu.edu/articles/2000/2/05/index.asp> (accessed Dec. 2004).

Murray, T. (1999) 'Authoring intelligent tutoring systems: an analysis of the state of the art', *International Journal of Artificial Intelligence in Education*, 10: 98–129.

Ohlsson, S. (1991) 'System hacking meets learning theory: reflections on the goals and standards of research in artificial intelligence and education', *Journal of Artificial Intelligence in Education*, 2(3): 5–18.

Parer, M.S., Young, C. and McMillan, R. (1993) *Video in Distance Education*, Gippsland: Monash University.

Pratt, D.D. (1997) *Five Perspectives on Teaching in Higher Education*, Malabar, FL: Krieger Publishing.

Raiser, R.A. and Dick, W. (1996) *Instructional Planning: A Guide for Teachers*, Boston, MA: Allyn & Bacon.

Romiszowski, A.J. (1988) *The Selection and Use of Instructional Media*, London: Kogan Page.

Rowntree, D. (1990) *Teaching through Self Instruction*, London: Kogan Page.

Salomon, G. (1983) 'Using television as a unique teaching resource for OU courses', Milton Keynes: Open University (mimeo).

Sherry, L. (1996) 'Issues in distance learning', *International Journal of Educational Telecommunications*, 1(4): 337–65. Online: <http://carbon.cudenver.edu/~lsherry/pubs/issues.html> (accessed Sept. 2005).

Spencer, K. (1991) 'Modes, media and methods: the search for educational effectiveness', *British Journal of Educational Technology*, 22(1): 12–22.

Stacey, E. (1999) 'Collaborative learning in an online environment', *Journal of Distance Education*, 14(2): 14–33.

Steen, J.V. (2002) 'Young readers, the fifth world survey of Newspapers in Education Programmes'. Online: <http://www.wan-press.org/downloads/files/nie/reaching.pdf> (accessed Sept. 2005).

Stratford, M. (1998) 'Innovations in large scale supported distance teaching', ch. 16 in M. Eisenstadt and T. Vincent (eds) *The Knowledge Web*, London: Kogan Page.

Tabbers H.K. (2002) 'The modality of text in multimedia instructions', doctoral thesis, Open University of the Netherlands. Online: <http://www.ou.nl/otecresearch/publications/

Huib/doctoral%20dissertation%20Huib%20Tabbers%20-%20web%20version.pdf> (accessed May 2005).

—— Martens, R.L. and Van Merriënboer, J.J.G (2000) 'Multimedia instructions and cognitive load theory: split attention and modality effects', paper presented at the AECT 2000 in Long Beach, CA. Online: <http://www.ou.nl/otecresearch/publications/ Huib/AECT2000%20Huib%20Tabbers.pdf> (accessed Sept. 2005).

—— (2001) 'The modality effect in multimedia instructions', annual conference of the Cognitive Science Society, 2001. Online: <http://www.hcrc.ed.ac.uk/cogsci2001/pdf-files/1024.pdf> (accessed Sept. 2005).

Tagg, A. and Dickinson, J. (1995) 'Tutor messaging and its effectiveness in encouraging student participation on computer conferences', *Journal of Distance Education*, 10(2): 33–55.

Taylor, J., Sumner, T. and Law, A. (1997) 'Talking about multimedia: a layered design framework', *Journal of Educational Media*, 23(2/3): 215–41.

Thalheimer, W. (2004) 'Bells, whistles, neon and purple prose: when interesting words, sounds, and visuals hurt learning and performance – a review of the seductive-augmentation research'. Online: <http://www.work-learning.com/Seductive_ Augmentations.htm> (accessed Nov. 2004).

Van Merriënboer, J.J.G. (2001) 'Instructional design for competency-based learning', *Interactive Educational Multimedia* 3: 12–26. Online: <http://www.ub.es/multimedia/ iem/down/c3/Competency-based_Learning.pdf> (accessed Jan. 2005).

Vygotsky, L.S. (1962) *Thought and Language*, Cambridge, MA: MIT Press.

—— (1978) *Mind in Society*, Cambridge, MA: Harvard University Press.

Watts, H. (1992) *Directing on Camera*, London: Aavo Media.

Westera, W. (1999) 'A didactic framework for audiovisual design', *Journal of Educational Media*, 24(2): 87–102.

Index